TOMORROW JERUSALEM

The Story of Nat Turner

and the

Southampton Slave Insurrection

By Bill Bryant

Copyright © 2000, 2001 by Bill Bryant
All rights reserved.
No part of this book may be reproduced, stored in a retrieval system, or transmitted by any means, electronic, mechanical, photocopying, recording, or otherwise, without written permission from the author.

ISBN: 0 75961 149 1

This book is printed on acid free paper.

*This work is dedicated
to the good people
of Southampton County,
and everywhere else,
together!*

Table of Contents

INTRODUCTION	vii
Prelude	1
A Circumstance	23
The Revelation	63
The Rising	97
The Search	165
The Aftermath	243
"That Thicket"	257

INTRODUCTION

In August of 1831, in the peaceful countryside southwest of the Nottoway River and the town of Jerusalem in Southampton County, Virginia, the forces of history powerfully converged — and the future of humanity changed.

There, where it seemed least likely to happen, the slaves rose up.

The rising was brutal but brief.

So was the immediate reaction.

But the consequences were vast and enduring.

It was the beginning of the end of slavery in the United States.

Yet the Southampton Slave Insurrection — one of the most influential events in American history — remains obscure.

And its leader — one of the most influential people in American history — is a unique mystery.

May the obscurity and the mystery begin to end here and now.

*

This is the story of Nat Turner.

But it is not his story alone.

This is also the story of the other people of Southampton, white and black, who shared his time and place — most of them ordinary God-fearing, Jesus-loving sons and daughters of Virginia, and of Africa, hard-working folks living very modest lives, with limited horizons.

It so happened that their Southampton was a fertile seedbed for the continuing American Revolution — a place unique, where the pressures and contradictions, combined with the presence of Nat Turner, made an eruption of the slaves inevitable.

Remarkably, nine other people who shared Nat's time and place would help to make the future different — five of them in critical roles during the final years of the slavery crisis.

All of the people in this story once lived and breathed, laughed and cried, and knew the meanings of family and community.

Their story belongs to all of us.

May their tragedy enlighten us.

United States 1831

x

Virginia 1831

Southampton 1831

Jerusalem

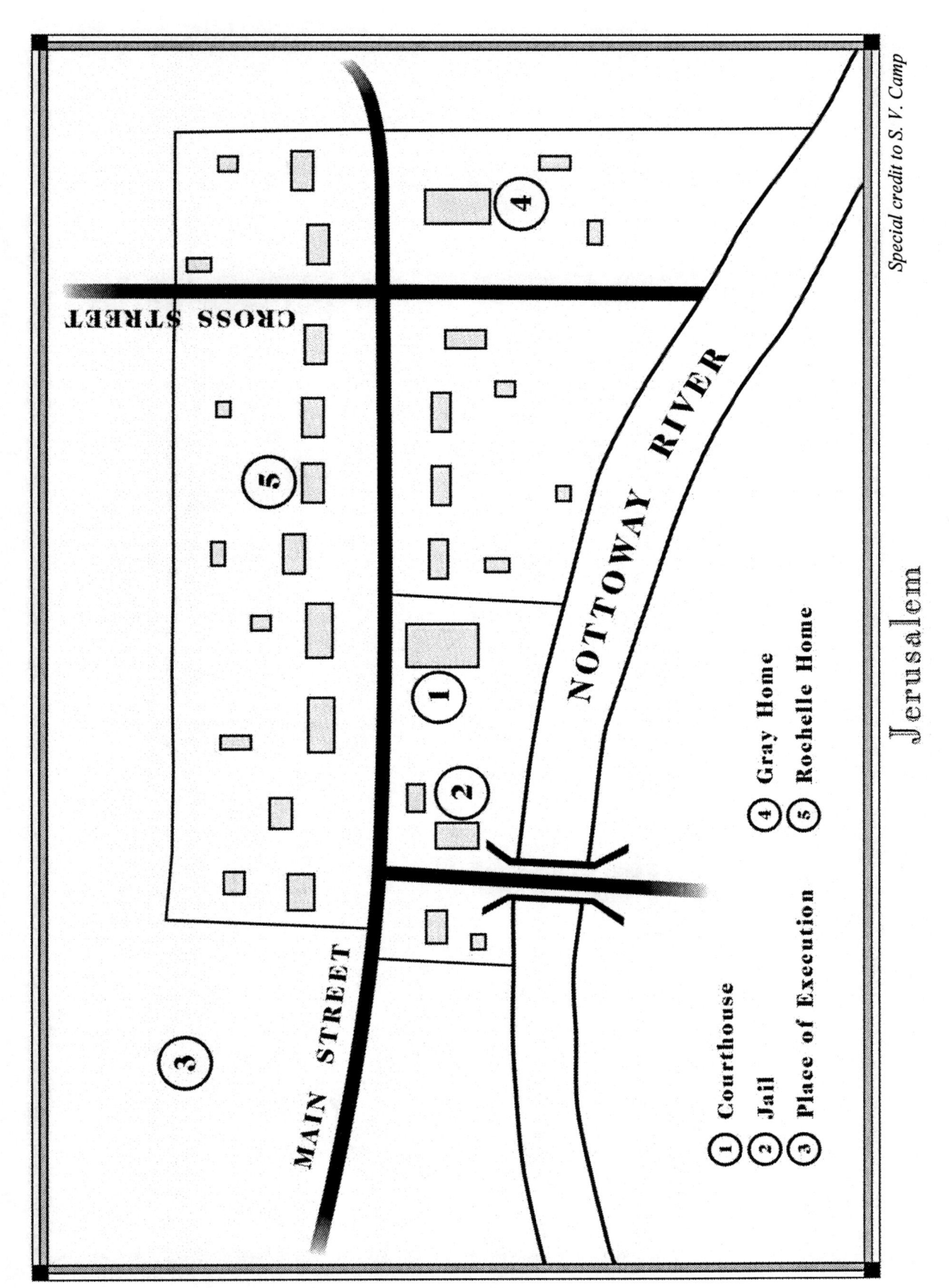

1. Courthouse
2. Jail
3. Place of Execution
4. Gray Home
5. Rochelle Home

MAIN STREET
CROSS STREET
NOTTOWAY RIVER

Special credit to S. V. Camp

Nat Turner

Tomorrow Jerusalem: The Story of Nat Turner and the Southampton Slave Insurrection

Prelude

Bill Bryant

*Tomorrow Jerusalem: The Story of Nat Turner
and the Southampton Slave Insurrection*

Early January 1831
JOSEPH TRAVIS Place

    Yesterday evening, in firelight, he had visited with his wife and young son and infant daughter in their cabin on a nearby farm. He could not spend enough time with them.
    All night, in starlight, he had meditated at his secret place within the swampland around Cabin Pond. He could not spend too much time there.
    Now, in the gentle chill of the predawn darkness, slowly he turned off the roadway onto the lane leading home.
    The first faint suggestion of the Sun along the eastern treeline shocked the old rooster, again, declaring his discovery of the new day from atop the chicken coop on the far side of the outbuildings clustered near the main house.
    A lamplight appeared in the window of the upstairs bedroom shared by Joseph Travis and his wife Sally and their infant son, little Joe. Still asleep in the bedroom across the hall were the teenaged Putnam Moore, Sally's son by her late first husband, and Joel Westbrook, Joseph's apprentice carriage-maker.
    In the cabins, the people were awakening.

*

    Now walking more briskly along the lane, he is visible only as a shadow of himself among shadows – a man of slightly less than average height, but of solid and sturdy build, a man of broad shoulders.
    The unseen features of his face are distinctly African – the nose large and flat, the eyes large and deep set, the hair under his floppy hat short and tightly curled, his beard confined to a wispy mustache and a tuft of hair on the top of his chin.
    His face is without expression, his impression plain and ordinary.
    The color of his skin is light – olive, really, more his mother's than his father's color.
    Nat Turner is home to do a few chores and assign others (for he is the overseer at this place), then to eat, then to go into town ... into Jerusalem.

* * *

    By the time Nat arrived at the main house, Sally was already serving breakfast – coffee, of course, with scrambled eggs and bacon and sausage, and fresh hot biscuits with Caribbean molasses. There would be ham, leftover fried chicken and cornbread in the basket Sally was already preparing, for the trip.
    Seated at the dining table were Joseph, the master, and Hark, the uncommonly powerful slave who helped with the heavier work of the farm and the brandy still and the carriage-making shop.
    Amid murmured good mornings, Nat sat at the table with the other men, soon joined by Sally.
    And quietly they ate together, careful not to disturb the sleepers upstairs.

Bill Bryant

The food was good, as always.

*

In due time, Joseph and Hark and Nat emerged from the house into the silent soft gray dawn of the farmyard. The teenaged boy Moses and the younger boy Samuel were waiting with two horses, at the wagon.

Hark hitched the horses to the wagon, then climbed onto the seatboard alongside Joseph, who took the reins.

Nat climbed onto the back and settled down against the back of the seat, making himself comfortable among some empty burlap bags.

As the wagon moved slowly away from the house, into the lane, Sally came outside, with little Joe in her arms, to wave goodbye.

Nat smiled, raised his hand, and waved.

Next to his mother Nancy and his wife Cherry, only Sally ever came close to understanding Nat, really. And whatever, during their lifelong friendship, she simply could not understand, she always graciously accepted. More than once, she had risked herself on his behalf, and he appreciated it.

Next to Nancy and Cherry, Sally was Nat's best friend.

The man at the reins was a good person, too, an able craftsman, a master more than kind — and a loving companion for Sally, who deserved the best.

Nat reached into his coat pocket and brought forth his Bible, just to hold.

* * *

Past the lane leading to the simple dwelling of Sally's brother athiel the wagon moved, past the place of the widow Harris, past Newsom farm, turning from their own road onto another, and tually another, and another. The horses needed little guidance or ragement to follow the serpentine paths coiling this way and that h the heavily forested countryside, past the winter-barren along the edges of the swamps where one could hide — or be forever.

ing in and abruptly out of sleep as the wagon's wheels felt d rutted ground, his dreaming and his imagining flowing to envision the future he alone could see, Nat was unmindful ssing countryside.

it well enough.

its woodlands and swamplands and fields, its lanes and races and paths and private ways, literally like the back — some parts better than others, of course, but the whole ough indeed.

ly below the Nottoway River.

several masters had always given him considerable where he wanted to go — just so long as his chores got e — and he had always taken full advantage of the

ce becoming Nat the Preacher.

Preaching Place, a clearing in the woods, for the blacks of his own neighborhood. But his ministry,

Tomorrow Jerusalem: The Story of Nat Turner and the Southampton Slave Insurrection

such as it was, such as it could be, embraced the whole of Southampton County.

Thus, he walked, or rode one of the master's mules, extensively, visiting farms whose owners either welcomed or tolerated his attention to the spiritual well being of their slaves, conducting prayer and praise meetings near certain white churches on certain special Sundays.

Thus, he got to know a lot of folks, white and black, free and slave.

Thus, he himself became known by many — his limited fame and infamy in local lore assured through at least the next few generations by what had happened a few years ago, with Etheldred Brantley, when a public debate had led to a very public spectacle, which made him proud every time he thought of it, every day.

Only 30 years old, Nat had done rather well for himself, so far, all things considered, for a slave.

* * *

As the wagon moved from the southwestern area of the county northeasterly toward its center, the warming sunshine increasingly blessed the new morning of Southampton's vastness of more than 600 square miles, touching neighbors in all directions.

To the north: Sussex County and Surry County.

To the west: Greensville County.

To the east, across the Blackwater River: Isle of Wight County and Nansemond County.

To the south, in North Carolina: Northampton County and Hertford County — with whose people the Southamptonians were closely linked, by commerce and kinfolk, perhaps more closely linked than with their neighbors in Virginia.

The lazily flowing Nottoway River, meandering from northwest to southeast, delicately sliced Southampton into upper and lower sections. Lower Southampton, more recently settled, was about as close as one could get to what remained of the frontier in the Tidewater of Virginia. Below the Nottoway, the people were fewer, the farms smaller, the distances between places greater than above the Nottoway.

Most travelers crossed the river at the bridge at Jerusalem, or over the Cypress Bridge downstream, or on the ferry further downstream at Monroe, where the river widened.

Nat had seen only one map of the county — his own, a crude approximation with few details, but adequate to his purpose.

* * *

Southampton's fertile uplands produced an abundance of cotton and tobacco, rice and corn and other food crops, including hay for the animals.

The bottomlands were good for keeping pigs and grazing cattle, sheep, oxen, mules and horses — work horses most of them, but also some bred for the hunt, or for racing. The latter was re-emerging as

Bill Bryant

a popular gambling sport, not without severe critics among the more righteous people of Southampton.

Many farmers also cultivated apple and peach orchards, and operated stills for the manufacture of cider and brandy – especially the apple brandy whose fine reputation extended far beyond the county, making it a major cash-earning export. The popular thirst for brandy, too, displeased the righteous.

The county's plentiful loblolly pines provided lumber, shingles, turpentine and barrel staves for domestic use, plus lumber and tar for naval construction.

*

In season, wildflowers rampaged along the roadsides and around the edges of the fields and throughout the meadows, and the woodlands were sprinkled delightfully with the white and pink blossoms of the dogwood trees.

Houses and cabins, most of plain design and simple construction, were made more pleasing to the eyes by colorful patches of lovingly tended flowers – also more pleasing to the nose, amid the strongly competing odors of the privies and pastures, sties and stables.

Almost every farm raised its own chickens, guinea hens, turkeys, pigs and cattle, and knew what to do with them, right down to the bone.

Dogs, mostly just pets but some also meant for hunting or guarding, barked seldom, sometimes to greet the master, sometimes for no apparent good reason.

Cats, who had no masters, only servants, meowed always with a purpose, and likewise purred, in pleasure and to please.

*

Wild animal life abounded.

The Nottoway and the Blackwater, and the Meherrin along the North Carolina border, teemed with fish, and with great snapping turtles and quickly slithering water moccasins, hovering dragonflies and jitterbugs skittering across the water's surface.

The forests and swamps were alive with deer, squirrels, rabbits, beavers and possums, roving wildcats and bears, turkeys and box turtles and snakes – green snakes and black snakes and brown snakes and copperheads and rattlers – not to mention the flies and mosquitoes and gnats and moths, the ticks and fleas and chiggers, bees and wasps, fireflies and butterflies, cicadas and crickets relentlessly communicating through the night, bullfrogs deeply calling from within the swamps.

Songbirds sang, crows cawed, owls hooted, woodpeckers pecked, hummingbirds flitted hither and yon between sudden stops among the garden flowers and honeysuckle vines. Eagles grandly soared, usually alone. Ducks noisily flew together in disorderly formation, geese neatly spelled the letter V.

Sometimes, you could hear a distant huge onrushing wind, faint at first but steadily increasing until there it was – an awesome overarching, surging flight of blackbirds, a solid dark mass of

*Tomorrow Jerusalem: The Story of Nat Turner
and the Southampton Slave Insurrection*

frantic wings — thousands upon thousands of them, seemingly millions of them — enough of them to eclipse the Sun, almost, sometimes.

To see one buzzard circling high in the sky could make a chill run down your spine. To see a dozen of them grounded in a cotton field, around some lifeless feast, could make you shudder to think.

Spiders spun intricate webs to catch their victims.

*

Only one historical event of note had ever disturbed the peace and quiet of Southampton.

It happened during the War for Independence, almost 50 years ago, when the people of the county were performing an important role in supplying food to the American armies.

And that is precisely why, in July of 1781, en route to Yorktown, the justly feared and widely hated Banastre Tarleton and 700 British cavalrymen attacked and destroyed the thriving little port of South Quay, on the Blackwater.

Because of that act, and because of other misdeeds perpetrated by the British during the War of 1812 (particularly their urging the slaves to insurrection), the British were not well liked by most of the white people of Southampton; indeed, the British were hated, and still feared, by many. This opinion was not shared by some of the black people.

The wars had created honored veterans — the dead, the wounded, the unscathed but haunted. Very few of the warriors of the Revolution were still alive, to be honored on the 4th of July. And the men who went away to fight in the later fracas usually had better things to do than sittin' around tellin' war stories.

There were no local heroes of note, or heroines — which, folks reasoned, was just as well, really, considering the crises from which heroes, and heroines, must emerge.

* * *

Nat was reading his Bible when the wagon turned onto the main road heading northerly toward Jerusalem.

The Bible, Nat's very own for many years, was small, compact, easy to carry in his pocket, easy to hold in his hands, always with him — always.

The printing inside the book was so tiny and delicate that only someone with excellent eyesight could hope to read it, written in language so elegant and complex that only someone with considerable intelligence could hope to understand it.

No one could, or did, deny Nat's great intelligence.

No one could, or did, deny his intimate familiarity with the Bible.

But there was some difference of opinion, especially among the whites, as to whether or not he fully understood the real meaning of the scriptures. After all, he was not a trained and ordained preacher, but just an exhorter. One could not, should not, expect too much from a slave.

Still, one had to admit, in this very religious place Nat Turner was a very religious man.

Bill Bryant

And if one had been paying close enough attention to his "preaching" during the past several years, one would know that the emphasis of his message had been shifting, gradually, from the New Testament to the Old Testament. But, of course, no one had noticed the shift – at least, none of the whites. Why should anyone pay such close attention to the exhortations of a slave?

Here and there in his Bible, in the margins, in pencil he had marked certain special passages ... with a simple cross.

*

Besides the Bible, there were various other reliable sources of useful facts and wisdom. (Not to mention gossip, and rumor.)

The books available to most folks were very few, and very limited in their range of interests, with a practical preference for agriculture, history, nature, the law and moral philosophy. (Not to mention children's schoolbooks, and almanacs.)

One could learn from listening carefully to the casual conversations at the religious, social and political gatherings. People who could write wrote letters to people in other places, and generally trusted the postal service. News always traveled well in these ways. (Not to mention the often hushed grapevine, and the field-hollerin'.)

The nearest newspapers were the Constitutional Whig and the Enquirer, both in Richmond, and the American Beacon, in Norfolk. All published, in addition to local items, excerpts from the newspapers in Lynchburg, Petersburg, Fredericksburg and Alexandria, and from the newspapers in Philadelphia and New York, and elsewhere, foreign as well as domestic. The news ranged from foreign wars and revolutions to the tediously detailed lengthy transactions of the Congress of the United States and the General Assembly of Virginia – as much of it as needed to fit the nonadvertising space available. (Not to mention the news which could not be reported, lest it agitate certain readers.)

The newspapers were dominated by advertisements of commerce and culture, of tempting yet limited appeal to readers in Southampton, so far away from the places of commerce and culture. But if you lived in or near one of the big cities, or could visit, the world was in the newspapers – new books, dancing slippers, the best bacon from Smithfield, the best sugar and molasses from Saint Croix and New Orleans, family medicines, umbrellas, combs, Paris fashions, seeds, whiskey, coal, cigars, horses, land, slaves – grocers, doctors, dentists, painting exhibitions, theatre and circus performances, schools, horse races, steeds standing at stud – the comings and goings of merchant ships and steamboats, with connections up and down the Atlantic coastline and even across the ocean to Europe. (Not to mention Africa.)

Nat, like most other men and women who could read, read every newspaper he could get his hands on – not every word, of course, because not every word was worth reading, but enough, at least, to glimpse distantly the world of the white people beyond Southampton.

* * *

*Tomorrow Jerusalem: The Story of Nat Turner
and the Southampton Slave Insurrection*

Nat was immersed in his Bible when the wagon passed the intersection with the Barrow Road, so called because of the exceptional man who had vigorously led the clearing of the new way through the countryside, opening much new land to settlement and farming.

John Thomas Barrow — Captain Barrow to the men of the Southampton militia — had finished his greatest work only a few years ago, but then had gone broke and lost his place, along his road, and now had to rent land elsewhere.

But Barrow was a proud man. He would survive his current adversity, somehow, and would never stop trying to prosper.

*

It was a place where and a time when the purposeful but usually unhurried pace of life was wedded to necessity — the routines of labor and the opportunities for leisure governed not by personal wishes but by the imperatives of the seasons, of planting and growing and harvesting and marketing.

Only the wealthy could live otherwise, and even for them there were the hardships, risks and dangers common to all.

As a rule, from early spring to midsummer and from late September to Christmas the people — almost all of the people — worked, hard, much harder than at other times, with brief holidays at Christmas, at Easter and on the 4th of July.

The exception to the rule was August, a month of rest for all, the month of jubilee for the blacks — a month when, in the words of one observer, it was impossible to describe the ease, happiness and sense of security felt by all.

August — a time for visiting family and friends, packing provisions and attending religious camp meetings and special church services ... a good time for fishing, and hunting (with your master's gun if you were a slave) ... a time for boxing, wrestling and horse races — an' dog-fightin' an' cock-fightin', condemned by some citizens as ignorant and barbaric ... a happy time for social gatherings and entertainments, sometimes with singing often accompanied by fiddles or banjos, whistles or mouth harps, tambourines or drums ... a time for abundant good food and, for some, abundant strong drink — not only the ciders and brandies with their various local and regional reputations, but also the common pokeberry wines and persimmon beers ... a thirsty time.

August ... the hottest month of the year.

*

It was a place where and a time when the expectations of life were more or less the same as anywhere else. Everywhere, people struggled. That's just the way it was.

And here, now, one could reasonably expect to live all of one's days in more peace and obscurity than almost anywhere elsewhere.

Or so it always seemed.

Bill Bryant

* * *

Nat was deep into the familiar story of Ezekiel when the wagon passed the intersection with the Indian Town Road, so called because it led to Simmons Town, four miles upstream from Jerusalem.

The small farms and humble dwellings of Simmons Town were home to the several dozen Indians – mostly Nottoways, mixed with survivors of the shattered tribes of the Meherrin, Susquehanna, Nansemond and Wyanoke – enduring from the time this region was known as Warrasqueake. That was before the Europeans, and soon thereafter the Africans, began arriving at the island named Jamestown, up on the great river of the Powhatans.

The Indian "problem" was not much of a problem here. Poverty, mostly.

*

Now, of course, this was a place of Europeans and Africans.

In 1830, according to national census figures not widely known even among the more educated whites, the population of Southampton (give or take a few) numbered 16,074, including 6,573 whites, 7,756 slaves and 1,745 free blacks – the latter an uncommonly large number compared to other counties in the Tidewater, a product of earlier evangelical appeals to Christian owners to free their slaves.

Even to the casual observer, unacquainted with the official reckoning, there seemed to be a clear majority of blacks.

Particularly below the Nottoway, relatively few of the white folks' farms required more than a couple of dozen slaves, including not only men and women, but also boys and girls too young to be counted fully as workers.

Several places had more than 50 slaves, but most had fewer than six.

A third of the farms, of the poorer whites and of certain other whites who opposed slavery in practice as well as in principle, had none.

*

The population of Southampton was young.

A variety of childhood illnesses, epidemic diseases and untreatable injuries claimed the lives of half of the white children and half of the black children by the age of six – placing an even greater value on the priceless lives of the very young.

The history of every family included many sadly brief chapters.

A galaxy of physical aches and pains and ailments and accidents, worsened by plain ignorance, continually thinned the older population. One learned, early on, to live with pain, to accept disability, to cope with mortality.

From childbirth to the final days, much of the best doctoring and nursing available was done by black folks, especially the older women.

Tomorrow Jerusalem: The Story of Nat Turner and the Southampton Slave Insurrection

*

Because the population was young, it was in some ways inexperienced, lacking the knowledge and insights and wisdom and judgement which tend to improve with advancing age.

The men particularly were apt to act too quickly, too rashly, too dangerously at times.

The strong unspoken rules of courtesy and civility which generally governed Virginia society also helped to control the individual passions of the moment.

*

Almost all of the people lived in the isolated independence of their home-places and immediate neighborhoods, sharing, often intimately, the labor and the gladness and the grieving.

The sense of community was important as a matter of survival, as well as of prosperity and progress, in the common struggle. You made a point of getting to know your neighbor as well as circumstances allowed, because you never knew when your neighbor, or you, might really need help. Usually, of course, there was more to like than dislike about another person, and the liking often as not led to good friendship, trust, affection — yes, even love sometimes. And in an emergency, the disliking could easily be ignored, for the sake of community.

Family was at the center of the real world of the people, and "family" often meant all of the people at the home-place.

True, the sharing and the caring tended to decrease as the white folks got older and became more prosperous, widening the practical distance between master and slave, even between childhood best friends.

True, too, some masters were stricter, harsher than others. Some were just cranky or tolerably mean-spirited. And some were downright cruel, only too happy to exercise their power, only too happy to use the whip.

The more severe the master's attitude, of course, the deeper the hidden resentment of the blacks — and the greater the open sympathy among some whites, who viewed the ill treatment of slaves as a misuse of property or an abuse of humanity or an evil, as damnable as slavery.

Some masters, and some slaves, earned widespread reputations, for badness, or for goodness.

And reputations were important.

*

Southampton itself had a reputation, beyond its famed brandy.

It was known as a place where, as a rule, slavery was mild, so compellingly close and understanding were so many of the whites and blacks, of sheer necessity if for no other reason ... and there were other reasons, of course.

And it was known as a place where, in fact, an unusually large number of the whites were in sympathy with the idea of emancipation —

Bill Bryant

presumably gradual emancipation, naturally with compensation to the owners, ideally with transportation of the blacks back to Africa, their homeland.

Already, in cooperation with the American Colonization Society, the county had arranged for 70 local free blacks to make the voyage. (Oddly, it seemed to some whites, some blacks resisted the notion of going "back" to Africa, thinking they were home already.)

The idea of emancipation, with or without compensation or transportation, had been firmly planted in Southampton several decades ago by the Methodist and Baptist preachers and traveling revivalists, and by the Quakers, many of whom (an unusually large number) lived in the county. The Methodists and Baptists had since moved toward an accommodation with slavery, and toward silence on the issue - but not the Quakers, who remained constantly outspoken and rigidly uncompromising with regard to human bondage.

More than once, the deeper doubts about slavery had risen to confront the religious conscience of the people of Southampton, and doubtless would again.

* * *

Staring at the road behind the wagon, Nat noted the gate to the long lane leading through woodlands and past great fields to the place of James Parker, a successful planter, a magistrate, a man of importance in the community.

Sprawled in the back of a commonplace work wagon, seemingly in the middle of nowhere, Nat knew he, too, was important.

He knew it because even as a sickly child he had been told he was special, told he was meant to be great, and told repeatedly.

And he knew it because as a man, as a slave and as a preacher, he had been convinced by the experiences of life and the reasoning of his own mind that he understood the meaning of greatness, for a preacher, a slave, a man.

And he knew it because the Spirit had told him so.

He could be very serious and somewhat distant in his specialness, particularly among the black folks, many of whom shared his general opinion of himself.

He could be very cheerful and friendly, particularly at home, where his story-telling and toy-making endeared him to the local children, white and black.

He had a reputation - several reputations.

*

Anyone, white or black, could become only so well known in such a place, at such a time.

The prominent Jeremiah Cobb, for example, a prospering planter and breeder of fast horses and chief among the county's magistrates, was known to far more whites than blacks.

The notable James and Peggy Ben, husband and wife and black and free and quite gifted at doctoring, were known to far more blacks than whites.

*Tomorrow Jerusalem: The Story of Nat Turner
and the Southampton Slave Insurrection*

In this society, many whites and many blacks knew Nat Turner, and many more knew of him.

White as well as black people who did know him (or thought they did) tended to like, respect and trust him. He was "notorious" for his virtues.

He never drank.

He never cursed.

He never stole.

He never carried money of his own.

And his Bible — that ultimate symbol of goodness — was always with him.

His obvious intelligence and exemplary personal conduct and occasional sense of mystery attracted people to him, even if he did keep them at some distance.

For many of the same qualities which supposedly commended him, a few white people disliked and even feared him — stubbornly remembering the infrequent times when Nat's conduct had not been, in their opinion, so exemplary and innocent, for a slave. His smartness and his self-assurance directly challenged their conception of what a slave should be.

Most folks who knew him would have agreed that he was at the very least very different — one might even say strange, sometimes — but tolerably so, in an unmenacing way ... harmless enough. Every community must claim its fair share of eccentric personalities — "characters" — and learn to tolerate them, live with them, knit them into the fabric of society; or try to.

*

He had an opinion about slavery.

He believed that the slaves should be free, and someday would be.

He was fortunate, blessed really, to be born the property of a good man, who gave to the slave boy the same advantages he gave to his own children; then likewise lucky to be owned by other good men. He enjoyed liberties and privileges rare for a slave. But he was still a slave — owned now not by Joseph Travis, nor by Sally, but by Sally's son Putnam ... He was the property of a boy.

He was fortunate, too, to have a wife and children. But he could not live with them.

And he was fortunate to live in a community where slavery was — for most — mild, lenient, relaxed. One did not have to face, daily, the ugliest realities of human bondage. But he, for one, did not have to see the whip ripping into flesh, to know that somewhere it was happening. And every time he thought of it — or of any of the other injustices inspired by the idea of one human being owning another human being — he seethed.

Fortunate or not, like any other slave he had turned the other cheek so often that his neck hurt. And the hurting never went away.

So, yes, he had an opinion about slavery, and many of the people closest to him, white as well as black, were aware of it. Privately, they knew how he really felt about slavery. Or thought they did.

He had even said it publicly: The slaves should be free, and someday would be.

Bill Bryant

* * *

Approaching noon, nearing the bridge over the river into town, Nat spotted the riders the instant they appeared on the road behind him.

There were two of them, young white men, riding hard, racing their horses, rapidly coming nearer, nearer - both horsemen reaching the bridge mere seconds ahead of the wagon.

Nat braced for the expected jerking of the wagon to the right as the master and his horses simultaneously reacted to the violent surge of noise and motion alongside them.

Across the narrow bridge the riders thundered.

It made Joseph Travis angry. "One o' these days, those fools'll get somebody killed!"

It made Hark angry, too. "Young folks be mighty reckless at times!"

"Dangerous!"

"Yassuh!"

"Got all the self-control of a chicken runnin' 'round with its head cut off!" Travis fumed as the wagon began rumbling over the planking of the bridge.

"Ol' chicken still got better sense!"

"You right about that!"

"Yassuh!"

"I tell you, Hark, this horse-racin' trouble has gotten a lot worse since the Jockey Club started up again - I swear, all some people in Southampton can think about nowadays is breedin' fast horses an' gamblin' at the races ... I do not approve o' the sportin' life - certainly not the way some o' these young men live it!"

"Yassuh!"

"Can't say as I approve o' lots o' things I see an' hear these days - Too many people spendin' too much time at the races an' not enough time at church - An' too many people drinkin' too much brandy ... I do not approve o' the hard drinkin'!"

"Yassuh!"

Travis tilted his head toward the back of the wagon. "Nat - You 'wake?"

"Yassuh, massuh," Nat said as he stretched his arms and legs in anticipation of the end of the journey. "Wide awake an' sober, Joseph!"

The master laughed.

JERUSALEM

The wagon moved from the end of the bridge up the slight embankment to the Main Street (the only other roadway in town being the Cross Street which angled into Main just downstream from the bridge.)

Main Street beyond the town limits led eastward, past the Methodist and the Baptist meeting houses, through sparsely populated countryside, toward the port of Norfolk, a good day's ride away - and led northwestward, through sparsely populated countryside, toward Petersburg and then Richmond, the capital city of Virginia, an even longer ride than to the coast.

Jerusalem, the only town of any size or consequence in Southampton, had been created by the General Assembly in 1791 on 10 acres of land along the Nottoway - created partly because the county courthouse was

*Tomorrow Jerusalem: The Story of Nat Turner
and the Southampton Slave Insurrection*

already here, partly to provide a central marketing place, to improve Southampton's economy.

The town's 25 dwellings accommodated four general mercantile stores, two inns (at one of which the stage-coaches to elsewhere paused), two taverns (into one of which even now the dismounted reckless riders were swaggering), a saddler's shop, a carriage-maker's shop, the offices of two resident doctors and three resident lawyers – plus the Masonic hall and, of course, the courthouse and the jail, near the bridge.

Jerusalem's population of approximately 175 increased significantly on days when court was in session and on market Saturdays, and on certain very special occasions, like the 4th of July.

Travis parked the wagon in front of the courthouse.

The most important building in the county, the courthouse was a substantial wooden structure with a courtroom in the front and the clerk of court's office and the sheriff's office in the rear, all well heated by stoves on cold winter days and well ventilated by large windows on hot summer days.

The nearby jail was a comparably substantial wooden structure of two floors with one front door (and a massive lock). On each floor were two cells 16 feet square, unheated, with only a few small windows to circulate the air, a little.

The public pillory and whipping post, once nearby, had been abolished by the law and dismantled, and were now a fading bad memory.

The hanging tree, not far away in a field on the northern edge of town, was so rarely employed it was almost forgotten.

Except for the noise of several boys rolling barrel hoops, the Main Street was quiet. A carriage was leaving town, heading east. A dozen or so people moved among the storefront displays of washboards and frying pans, barrels and lumber, poultry and fresh game, and various other mercantile wares.

Turning toward the bridge, escorted by two white men with shotguns, a coffle of chained slaves, five men and two women and a boy, headed southward. To a slave in Southampton, the sight was unnervingly familiar, a punishing reminder that the roads through the county were a major route to the Carolinas and the Deep South for slaves sold off the farms and great plantations of the Tidewater.

The master and the two slaves now stood in the middle of the street. "Nat," Travis said, "soon as you finish your own business, get me that bolt o' cloth at Trezevant's – an' don' forget to buy an almanac."

"Which one?"

"Don' matter. They're all pretty much the same – Sun's gonna rise an' set at the same time no matter which one you buy! Hark, you take care o' the horses, then fetch the seedbags – an' make sure you get the right money in change . . . I'm goin' to the carriage-maker's, then to the clerk's office. I should be done in two, maybe two an' a half hours – Now, y'all don' take forever, you hear me? You know how I hate travelin' in the dark!"

"Moon be full tonight, or almost full," Nat noted, "an' high in the sky – early on, at least."

Travis smiled. "Y'all get goin' – an' try to stay out o' trouble!"

* * *

Bill Bryant

For some reason, the simple clang of metal hoops colliding made the boys in the street howl with laughter.

It did seem that the two older boys, the teenaged George Henry Thomas and Simon Blunt, were laughing more at than with their younger playmates, James Henry Rochelle and Billy Mahone and Anthony Gardner.

George Henry (James Henry's cousin) and Simon were in town from the southside of the Nottoway, George Henry with his recently widowed mother and his two older sisters, Simon with his father, the well respected Doctor Simon Blunt.

James Henry's father was Southampton's clerk of court, the family living in one of the town's finest homes, and his uncle was the county's sheriff, whose extensive acreage south of the river reflected the prominence and the wealth of the Rochelles of Southampton.

Billy, the youngest and by far the smallest of the boys, was a sandy-haired freckle-faced four-year-old, a runt even among boys his own age but quite scrappy and quite smart. His father, the distinguished Colonel Fielding Mahone, was the proprietor of a store downriver at the town of Monroe, but having an ever harder time supporting his family. The little town seemed to be growing littler.

Anthony was black, and free. He and his parents were in town today for the last time, ready to begin a trip to Norfolk, with other Southampton free blacks, to board a ship, to Africa – their impending departure being the main reason Nat was in town today, to say goodbye.

* * *

Nat located Anthony's parents in a field near the Cross Street, among other blacks gathering there either to make the trip or to say farewell.

Assuming his proper poise of dignity and purpose, Nat joined them, and was welcomed.

Nat shared the bittersweet feelings of the occasion – a certain deep regret, of course, at seeing friends go away, surely never to be seen or even heard from again – but an even deeper happiness, of course, at their opportunity to make a new and wholly unfettered life for themselves in a new land, an old land, the land of their ancestors.

The early efforts of the American Colonization Society had enabled only a few of Southampton's free blacks to make the voyage "home" in recent years. But the trickle promised to become a steady flow likely to include some of the county's better brick-makers, blacksmiths, coopers, carpenters, shoe-makers and doctors of animals. Even the human healers James and Peggy Ben were expressing some interest in the idea of going, someday.

Nat understood the interest, but did not share it. He knew where he was meant to be. Here was his homeplace, here his ministry, here his destiny. He belonged to Southampton.

Here, as a rule (to which there were inevitable exceptions), slavery probably was "better" than in most other places. If one had to be a slave, there were far worse places to be, despite the howevers confronting even the most privileged of servants.

Here, as a rule (to which there could be no exceptions), the ability and the talent of free blacks were hedged in all directions, and the only ways narrowly open were difficult, the maybes of freedom always limited.

Tomorrow Jerusalem: The Story of Nat Turner and the Southampton Slave Insurrection

The inescapable howevers of even the most gentle form of slavery were as many as the elusive maybes of so-called freedom. But at least in Africa, in the dream of young Anthony's parents and the others, the maybes would have a better prospect of success. It was a dream worth prayin' for.

Therefore, for more than an hour, Nat visited among them.

And when he said his last goodbye and turned to go, he did not look back.

* * *

At the postal counter toward the front of Trezevant's store, postmaster and storekeeper Thomas Trezevant was conversing with several other white men when Nat entered.

"Gentlemen," Nat said, nodding.

"Nat," Trezevant said, nodding.

Nat proceeded to the back counter, to wait his turn behind Doctor Simon Blunt and his overseer Shadrach Futrell.

Briefly interrupted, the conversation continued among Trezevant and the other gentlemen - Levi Waller, an enterprising man whose property at an intersection on the Barrow Road included a variety of mercantile interests, plus a schoolhouse; William Crocker, the teacher at Waller's school; and a teacher at another southside school, John "Choctaw" Williams, so nicknamed because the features of his face looked Indian and his long dark hair flowed in waves down his back in the Indian style.

"There," Trezevant said, when Nat was out of hearing range, "is one smart nigra - too smart, some people might say. Reads, writes, reckons numbers - an' he knows this county better'n anybody at this counter, I'd be willin' to wager."

None of the others, all of whom had some acquaintance with Nat, would take the bet.

"Jus' goes to show," Waller said, "no harm comes from teachin' some of 'em how to read an' write an' do simple numbers. Makes better servants an' workers of 'em, if you treat 'em right ... like Joseph Travis does."

"I've heard it said," said Williams, "no man in the county is more humane an' fatherly to his people than Travis . . . You know, if we ever get around to startin' a school for some o' the blacks, Nat might make a good teacher."

Like a 4th of July firework, the far-fetched idea of such a school sparkled and sputtered, and died quickly enough to avert any serious discussion of it. In the current political climate of Virginia, the men agreed, the idea itself was almost criminal.

Besides, the gentlemen wholeheartedly agreed, the task of instructing more than a few white children better was enough of a challenge for the present and for the foreseeable future - doable, with much constant effort.

Since the Board of School Commissioners was created in 1818, the number of county-supported schools had increased to 19. All were small, most serving only a dozen or so pupils, mostly boys, usually through only the elementary grades, with a basic curriculum of reading, writing, reckoning, world geography and history, mostly American. It was a modest effort, still, but a vigorous beginning.

Some of the older boys could attend the Millfield Academy, near town. Some of the older girls could go to the Female Academy, down in Drewryville. For a few gifted and financially able young men, there was the College of William and Mary up in Williamsburg, or Mister Jefferson's new University of Virginia way over in Charlottesville – or maybe the University of Pennsylvania, particularly to study medicine, or distant Harvard College. Someday, maybe, some truly outstanding local boy might even obtain an appointment to the Military Academy at West Point, in New York. Teachers, too, could dream, couldn't they?

"In the meantime," Crocker ventured to say, "I'd be happy if jus' half o' our Southampton boys could know how to read the Declaration o' Independence, an' the Constitution."

"An' know how to use Mister Webster's dictionary," Williams added.

"An'," Trezevant said half-jokingly, with a frowning glance at the recently arrived mail-pouch, "be able to tell what's true an' what ain' true in the newspapers!"

The other men fully appreciated the humor, as well as the seriousness, of the remark.

"Like I was sayin' earlier," said Waller, stretching like he was considering getting ready to go, "I do think it would be a good idea for all o' the teachers in the county to get together every now an' then. A lot could be learned at that sort o' meetin'."

"Can't get together often enough," said Crocker, "in my opinion."

"Agreed," said Williams.

"An' in my opinion," said Trezevant, "you could say the same o' the militia! Ever since those damned politicians up in Richmond took away the good guns an' cut back on the drill time, our boys're not fit to fight the Nottoways, much less the British! 'Bout the only time the militia even pretends to be halfway fit is on the 4th o' July!"

Doctor Blunt and his overseer, their business at the back counter done, now approached the postal counter, Blunt moving oh so slowly and deliberately, oh so tenderly, in obvious great discomfort.

"Doctor," Trezevant said, trying to be cheerful, "you takin' real good care o' yourself?"

Blunt grunted, unwilling to be cheered, or unable. "I always take 'real good' care o' all my patients," he grumpily responded, then, unwilling to pause for any pleasantries, or unable: "Good day, gentlemen!"

Blunt was not only a respected physician, but also a prospering farmer, with more than 80 slaves – "servants," he preferred to call them – "my people," whom he treated well enough, all things considered. Especially when one of the black people was ill, the white man was there.

"Poor ol' fellow," Trezevant said, when Blunt was finally out the door. "Gout sure has slowed him down ... What was I – Oh yes, the militia! – An' what, pray tell, would we do if the slaves rose up?"

"It'll never happen," Williams calmly replied, as Waller and Crocker nodded. "Not around here."

"Well," Trezevant persisted, playing the Devil's advocate, "jus' you remember what the Governor said not long ago 'bout the 'spirit o' dissatisfaction an' insubordination' among the Tidewater slaves – It was in the newspapers!"

"Some o' the slaves, maybe, a few," Williams confidently reckoned. "But not around here!"

Waller was not quite so sure. "No way o' tellin' how far the tentacles o' the abolitionist agitators are reachin' – It's gotten so

Tomorrow Jerusalem: The Story of Nat Turner and the Southampton Slave Insurrection

I distrust every travelin' mercantile trader who comes by my place — An' you know, they found one o' those damnable David Walker pamphlets in a free black man's house near Richmond — An' it's a real incendiary piece o' writin', so I hear."

"You hear correctly — It is!" Trezevant declared, helpless to resist the impulse — compulsion, really — to share something which some might say ought not to be shared, even among gentlemen. "I know — I have seen it!"

"Where?" Waller was quickest to ask.

"Postmaster friend o' mine over in Sussex purchased a copy durin' a recent visit to Philadelphia — bought it at a public place, for only 25 cents ... He showed it to me."

Crocker leaned forward. "Is it as bad as they say it is?"

"Worse," Trezevant answered. "That scoundrel Walker comes right out an' tells the slaves to rise up — Says one good black man can kill six white men — Says the slaves o' Virginia could hold their own against any army on the continent!"

"Nonsense!" Waller declared with a deeply offended laugh. "There'll be one mighty blizzard in Hell that day!"

"He says," said Trezevant, "God will give 'em a Hannibal!"

Abruptly, the conversation died as Nat approached, a large bolt of fine red cloth cradled in his arms (and an almanac for 1831 tucked into his coat pocket alongside his Bible).

"Gentlemen," Nat said, nodding.

"Nat," Trezevant said, nodding.

At the front of the store, Nat opened the door, then casually leaned over to inspect an item in the display window.

The gentlemen resumed their conversation, in hushed tones.

"Thomas," Waller said, "what else does he say?"

"A lot more o' the same — You'll never guess how he ends it."

"How?" Crocker asked.

Nat stepped outside and slowly closed the door behind him.

"'All men are created equal ... '"

*

"' ... endowed by their Creator with certain inalienable rights,'" Nat said to himself, standing in the street, "'that among these are life, liberty an' the pursuit of happiness,'" he concluded — suddenly stepping aside to make way for the onrushing James Strange French, a man much too busy today to do more than nod indifferently as he quickly passed by.

As others often did, Nat stared at the man, wondering about him, about his seeming sense of great purpose — which, of course, was precisely the effect the man intended to cause. Nor was he merely playing the part of some minor actor.

James Strange French was in fact a man usually deep in thought, with truly weighty matters on his mind, a man who even in a small town always walked briskly, always as though he had somewhere important to go, to do something important.

Occasionally, French traveled. Recently, he had made yet another trip to the area of the Natural Bridge, a journey of almost a week in winter weather, to visit with kinfolk, supposedly.

A man of patrician manners. The sort of man who had cringed and cursed at the very thought of the plebeian Andrew Jackson taking up

Bill Bryant

residence at the White House in Washington City, such a man was James Strange French – a man increasingly preoccupied, with a steadily expanding air of self-importance, like someone entrusted with a delicious yet gravely serious secret.

(Indeed, completely unbeknownst to any of his friends and acquaintances here in Southampton County, French did possess a delicious yet gravely serious secret. Together with certain other like-minded men meeting from time to time at a very private place near the Natural Bridge, he was engaged in a very secret conspiracy to remove the current occupant of the White House and thereby alter the course of American history. James Strange French entertained an ambitious vision of the near future, and of his place in it – But it was a secret, for now, and absolutely had to be kept a secret, you understand. The vision had enemies.)

As others sometimes did, Nat could only wonder about who the lawyer James Strange French was, behind the posturing. Not that it mattered, really, to the slave. But it was challenging to wonder.

In no hurry, Nat started walking toward the clerk's office, careful to sidestep the fresh pile of horse droppings French hadn't noticed.

* * *

In the clerk's office, Joseph Travis and Thomas Gray were concluding their business with James Rochelle, Travis settling a tax matter, Gray finishing some paperwork relating to his recent purchase of the seven-gabled house and inn.

Rochelle was struggling for the words with which to encourage the somber Gray without seeming to pity or patronize him. "You'll see better times, Thomas – I'm sure you can make a go of it bein' a lawyer, an' runnin' the inn."

"I'm sure gonna try," Gray said, with weak conviction, opening the door. "I don' see how things can get much worse ... Thanks again, for your assistance."

"You are most welcome," Rochelle said with a smile which, as soon as Gray was gone, dissolved into a frown.

"Lawyer now, is he?" Travis asked.

"Since the 20th o' December," the clerk of court specified, "an' not enough business to support another lawyer – But I do wish the best for him. As much as I may disapprove o' some o' his opinions, I mus' say I have never seen a man have such a run o' bad luck, though I suspect he's responsible for some o' his misfortune, to be honest with you ... Still, you got to have some pity for the man – some Christian compassion."

"Amen to that," Travis said.

* * *

Thomas Gray did not want anyone's pity.

He merely wanted a reasonable opportunity to reverse the steeply declining fortunes of recent years, when his "luck" had been worse than bad. It had been terrible. And, he had enough common sense and now enough knowledge of the law to know, the situation could get even worse.

Tomorrow Jerusalem: The Story of Nat Turner and the Southampton Slave Insurrection

Having variously and briefly served as a county overseer of the poor, as a commissioner for the Indian land and as a justice of the peace, Gray had studied the lawbooks ably enough to be certified as a lawyer. Now, he hoped, the income from his legal practice and from the inn and from his acreage in the countryside would be adequate to keep him out of the poorhouse – or, worse, out of the jail, a place where a person like James Rochelle, doing his duty, could put a person like Thomas Gray, who could not pay his considerable debts.

In 1829, Gray had owned some 800 acres of farmland and 21 slaves. But now, he owned only some 300 acres and just one slave. To make matters worse, so much worse, his dear wife recently had died – which meant, in the very worst scenario, that his beloved infant daughter Ellen could be taken from him and made a ward of the county.

He could not ask his father for financial help, because he knew his father would deny it to him. The older Thomas Gray strongly disagreed with some of the younger Thomas Gray's opinions – particularly with reference to slavery, which the son in principle opposed, too outspokenly, too publicly, too often, for the father's liking.

The younger Gray openly believed that a man might have to own slaves, to make a living, but that didn't mean it was the right thing to do.

The older Gray privately reasoned that even if a man had certain doubts about slavery, he had a civic as well as a family duty to be judicious in the expression of those doubts, lest he contribute to the untimely agitation of the issue.

Thus, there was little contact between the two men, and little prospect of an improvement in their strained relationship. One was as principled as the other – and as stubborn.

When, sometimes, the son drowned his sorrows in brandy, the people closest to him were understanding.

He did not want anyone's pity. But he got a lot of it, almost too much of it for a proud man to endure.

* * *

Thomas Gray's mind was wandering among the usual depressing thoughts when, in the middle of the otherwise empty street, he very nearly collided with a preoccupied Nat Turner.

"Sorry, Mistuh Gray – Thomas!" Nat declared, with a sudden smile.

"Oh ... Nat, hello – That's all right. I should watch where I'm goin'."

"So should I, suh ... No harm done!"

Momentarily, the two men of similar age stood face to face, in the uncrowded Main Street of Jerusalem, each now anxious to be home, with family. On some other day, they might have had the time and inclination to enjoy a friendly chat. But not today.

Still, Gray had a good thought. "Here, Nat," he said, reaching into his coat pocket, pulling out a folded copy of the Richmond Whig, handing it to Nat. "I'm finished with it."

"Why, thank you, suh!" Nat said, appreciating the gesture.

"Yes, well ... Be seein' you."

"Yes, suh," Nat said, pocketing the newspaper, alongside the almanac and his Bible. "You take care!"

"You, too," Gray muttered, walking away, lost again in the thicket of his unending troubles.

Bill Bryant

Nat stared at him, with pity.

* * *

As the wagon rumbled off the bridge onto the roadway leading home, Nat made himself more comfortable among the seedbags, and watched Jerusalem receding into the distance.

He did not see what other men might see. He saw Jerusalem, to the extent it was possible, as a man of the Bible saw it.

He did not envision a future such as other men might envision, surrounded by the limitations and constraints of this time and place. He did not agree with the way things were, and therefore could not even begin to imagine that things would remain the same forever.

To the world, he was a slave.

To himself, he was a free man.

And, oh yes, he was special — a man with a great purpose to his life, a man with a mission, a secret truth he had shared only with his wife ... Only Cherry knew about his plan.

The thought of her warmed him as he reached into his coat pocket and pulled out the newspaper, unfolding it in no rush to learn, as usual, how little it contained, of value to a man like him. All newspapers were similar in their inability to surprise him.

Scanning the front page of the Richmond Whig confirmed his expectations, so he turned to the ...!

Stunned ... he thought of the almanac, and quickly reached into his pocket again, pulled out the pamphlet, and opened it — and again was stunned ... and confused ... and downright bewildered!

*Tomorrow Jerusalem: The Story of Nat Turner
and the Southampton Slave Insurrection*

A Circumstance

Bill Bryant

*Tomorrow Jerusalem: The Story of Nat Turner
and the Southampton Slave Insurrection*

**November 1st, 1831
In the Jail at JERUSALEM**

Now, it seemed, the whole world knew the secret truth of Nat Turner.

His very name was on the lips of countless men and women, and even the little children, white and black, free and slave.

Even now, however, more than two months after the great blood loss of August, many important details of what had happened were still missing or incomplete, or in dispute.

Most particularly, the troubled people yearned to know: Why?!

And sometimes, it seemed, the whole world was observing Southampton County, expecting the people who had spawned and experienced the tragedy to be somehow accountable for it, somehow obligated to explain what had really happened.

Of course, only one person in Southampton really knew.

And there he was, finally, where he belonged — sitting on the floor of the rear upstairs cell, his back to the wall, his hands linked by chains, his ankles likewise manacled.

His face, softly illuminated by the late-morning sunlight streaming through the narrow overhead window, was at once impassive yet resolute, captive yet unconquered.

His clothes were dirty, ragged, torn, his floppy hat peppered with buckshot holes.

In the pocket of his coat, reachable even with shackled hands, was his Bible.

Nat was not the only prisoner in the jail. In the other cells upstairs and downstairs were seven other black men, three slaves and four free men — all of them here, where so many other prisoners had come and gone since August ... all because of Nat.

*

Because of Nat, Thomas Gray was also here, sitting on a low stool provided by the jailer, aiming a pencil at a writing pad.

On this chilly but not cold late-autumn day, both men knew what to do. And now, the quiet of the cell disturbed only by the light clanking of chains, both men knew the time had come to do it.

"If you are ready to talk," Gray said, "I am ready to listen."

Nat stirred, slightly, not quite ready to begin. He had agreed to do this because he wanted to do this, not because Gray had asked him. But Gray was a good man, trustable enough in these extraordinary circumstances, whatever his own self-interested reasons for being here ... Still, there was so much to be told, and so little time for telling it.

Gray leaned forward, listening intently to the silence, devoting his whole attention to this man he knew but did not know — this man of great intelligence and startling mystery — this man who doubtless would severely test his ability to do what he had promised to do, for reasons of his own.

Finally, the prisoner spoke ...

Bill Bryant

    You have asked me to give a history of the motives which induced me to undertake the late insurrection, as you call it ... To do so, I must go back to the days of my infancy, and even before I was born ... I was 31 years of age the 2nd of October last, and born the property of ...

* * * * *

October 2nd, 1800
BENJAMIN TURNER Place

    She was born in Africa, in a region of the upper Nile whose people are light olive in color.
    As a spirited young woman, she was enslaved, then transported across Africa, then across the Atlantic Ocean to the United States of America, being unloaded at Norfolk, Virginia, in 1798.
    In 1799, she was purchased in a marketplace by Benjamin Turner, and transported to his farm of several hundred acres along the Rosa Swamp, in Southampton County.
    Here, she was given a new name - Nancy - and became coupled with the son of old Bridget.
    And today, Nancy had birthed a baby boy - and as soon as she could muster the strength, she had tried her very best to kill it.
    "Tried to kill it!" Benjamin Turner declared, describing to neighbor Samuel Francis what had happened in the nearby cabin, where even now old Bridget's son was attempting to comfort the frantic but fatigued, and bound, young woman on the bed.
    Standing near the two white men in the early twilight, old Bridget fidgeted, anxious to be in the main house, where she belonged. "My boy," she said, "he done tied up that African girl real good, 'til she get over this fit she in - An' the baby, he be sleepin' now, up at the house."
    "Good," Turner said, unable to calm his agitation. "Tryin' to kill it like that - tryin' to bash that poor baby's head in - I ... I jus' do not understand human nature sometimes - Bridget," the master asked, "what got into her, to make her behave like that?"
    "Bes' I could figure out what Nancy say, Massuh Turner, she say she don' wan' her baby bein' no slave."
    "Well," Turner grumbled, appreciating her honesty, "it's a fact o' life - an' she'll jus' have to learn to live with it, an' so will the baby ... That's the way it is - the way it's gonna be ... Life mus' go on!"
    "Yassuh, it sho' do."
    "Slave or not, life is too precious to be wasted like that!"
    "Yassuh, it sho' is - I bes' be seein' to that baby boy."
    "Yes, o' course," Turner murmured, staring at the cabin, shaking his head.
    Bridget started for the house, but stopped, and turned around. "Massuh? You make up your mind what name to give the boy?"
    "Yes ... Nat," the master announced. "Nathaniel ... gift o' God."
    "Suh?"
    "Nathaniel - In the language o' the Hebrew people, the people o' the Bible, Nathaniel means gift o' God."

Tomorrow Jerusalem: The Story of Nat Turner and the Southampton Slave Insurrection

"You don' say," she said, nodding, smiling. "Gift o' God — Nat be a special name!"

"Every child," Turner said with wholehearted feeling, "is a gift o' God ... You an' your boy watch that girl closely now, you hear me, Bridget?"

"Yassuh. I knows jus' what to do."

"I'm sure you do," Turner said, convinced of it. Old Bridget was family, and wise in her ways. She probably knew what to do, what needed doing, a lot better than anybody else, including himself. "Go on, now."

"Yassuh."

Watching her hurrying toward the house, Turner said to Francis: "Frost'll be here soon, accordin' to the almanac."

Given an opportunity to talk about the weather, or about something much more interesting and important, Francis opted for the latter: "They'll be hangin' ol' Gabriel Prosser in a few days, an' that should be a lesson to the nigras who've been listenin' to the damned agitators an' stirrin' up the sort o' hellacious fury you've been describin'."

"Oh, I doubt Nancy ever heard o' Gabriel Prosser, 'cept maybe his name — I doubt if she's learned a hundred words o' English since she came off that boat. She's a smart girl, you can tell, but she simply will not accept her condition."

"Needs more o' the whip!"

"Needs none o' the whip — not at my place! 'Sides, I told you where she's from, in Africa. Those people are always less manageable, at first — but they're also more intelligent ... Nancy'll be all right, eventually."

"You are too liberal with your nigras, Benjamin. You give 'em far too many liberties, too much encouragement to better themselves. You let the smarter ones learn to read an' write. You get 'em all excited with religion — I'm tellin' you: It's not good for 'em to make 'em think they can be like us ... A slave is a slave!"

"Even a slave has the right to know Jesus ... I hear your dear wife is with child, again. What are you thinkin' o' namin' it?"

"Depends," said Francis, whose wife had already borne him two sons and four daughters. "If it's a boy, we're thinkin' ... Salathiel, I suppose ... If it's a girl, probably Sarah, like her mother — though I expect folks would call her Sally, like her mother."

"You goin' on patrol this evenin'?"

"Yes ... Can' be too careful, even down here."

"Well, this Prosser scare will soon be over, an' things'll quiet down. You'll see, my friend: Life will be normal again!"

* * *

Gabriel, the well educated 24-year-old property of planter Thomas Prosser of Henrico County, scared a lot of white people in August of 1800, and thereafter.

His conspiracy was extensive, in and around Richmond, the capital city.

The preparations were elaborate, including the gathering and secret storage of guns and gunpowder and ammunition, swords and scythes, clubs and pikes.

Bill Bryant

The plan of attack was practical and direct – aimed, initially, at seizing the arsenal of the state militia.

For months, the conspiracy grew stronger.

And on the appointed day, at the appointed place in the countryside, an army of a thousand black men assembled, and began the march to strike the first blow – before white people could know what was happening.

The white people already knew. Two slaves had told them.

Thus, even as Prosser's army of liberation advanced, Governor James Monroe was leading an army of 650 men to oppose it.

Suddenly – some would say miraculously – a mighty storm arose and erupted. Violent rain lashed at the countryside, making the roads almost impassable ... and flooding out the bridge separating the two armies.

By the time the waters receded, the slaves had learned of their betrayal.

The insurrection dissolved.

All told, 36 black men went to trial and then to the gallows – including, finally, Gabriel Prosser. Captured in Norfolk in late September, he was brought back to Richmond, tried, convicted, and then, on the 7th of October, hung.

Governor Monroe subsequently wrote, regarding the condemned rebels: "They have uniformly met death with fortitude."

And the ever brilliant John Randolph observed: "The accused have exhibited a spirit which, if it becomes general, must deluge the Southern country in blood. They manifested a sense of their rights, and contempt of danger, and a thirst for revenge which portend the most unhappy consequences."

* * *

During the years immediately before and after the birth of Nat, property of Benjamin Turner, there were several other unsettling incidents in Southampton itself – trivial, really, in contrast to the Prosser thing, but nonetheless quite unsettling indeed.

*

In October of 1799, a coffle of slaves passing through Southampton (adding two local men), en route to Georgia, rebelled. Five of the slaves (including the local men) killed the two white traders.

In Jerusalem, four of the slaves were tried and hung. The life of the fifth was spared because of his youth, but he was branded, literally and permanently, as a troublemaker.

*

In 1802, a series of unpleasant happenings shocked the people of the county, amid disturbances throughout eastern Virginia and North Carolina.

Tomorrow Jerusalem: The Story of Nat Turner and the Southampton Slave Insurrection

In February, along a Southampton roadway, a white man chanced to find an unsigned letter darkly hinting at a widespread insurrectionary conspiracy — "precisely by which they succeeded in St. Domingo and enveloped that whole colony in flames." Only a few days later, three slaves killed a hated overseer. Consequently, the three were tried and hung ... Then, in July, a slave tried to kill his master — and soon thereafter two slaves killed another slave. And there were two more trials, and three more hangings.

Throughout the region, within the space of only a few months, there were more than 30 hangings.

Finally, things settled down, restoring folks' peace of mind, more or less.

*

At no time, however, could one entirely escape the dreadful thought of Santo Domingo, where the fierce slave revolt which began on the 20th of August in 1791 had ushered in an era of blood and fire, killing countless thousands and making refugees of countless thousands more.

Some of the refugees found their way to Southampton, and put down new roots. The stories they told, re-enforced by newspaper reports and word-of-mouth accounts of occasional other uprisings in the Caribbean, made Southampton people even more appreciative of the peace they did enjoy.

*

The basic facts of these various trifling incidents and great events were not secrets.

In the Jail at JERUSALEM

In my childhood, a circumstance occurred which made an indelible impression on my mind, and laid the groundwork of that enthusiasm which has terminated so fatally to many, both white and black, and for which I am about to atone at the gallows. It is here necessary to relate this circumstance. Trifling as it may seem, it was the commencement of that belief which has grown with time, and even now, sir, in this dungeon, helpless and forsaken as I am, I cannot divest myself of. Being at play with other children, when three or four years old, I was telling them something which, my mother, overhearing, said it happened before I was born. I stuck to my story, however, and related some things which went, in her opinion, to confirm it. Others, being called on, were greatly astonished, knowing that these things had happened, and caused them to say, in my hearing, I surely would be a prophet, as the Lord had shown me things that had happened before my birth ... And my father and mother strengthened me in this my first impression, saying, in my presence, I was intended for some great purpose, which they had always thought, from certain marks on my head and breast ... My grandmother, who was very religious, and to whom I was much attached, my master, who belonged to the church, and other religious persons who visited the house, and whom I often saw at prayers, noticing the singularity of my manners, I suppose, and my uncommon intelligence for a child, remarked I had too much sense to be raised, and if I was, I would never be of any service to anyone as a slave ...

As time passed, Nat forgot exactly what he had told the other children, to attract so much glowing attention from his mother and father and grandmother and the other older black folks.
Was it something he had merely overheard and remembered later?
Was it something supernaturally inspired?
It really didn't matter.
By the time the child had forgotten the original cause of the commotion, its effect was permanent, its impression deep. He surely would be a prophet — and the older blacks never let him forget it.
He had a destiny, a reason for being alive ... this gift o' God.
The twig had been bent.
For a fact, too, the odd outgrowths of skin which marked the boy's body were regarded, in the stubbornly surviving African beliefs of the older blacks, as a clear sign of great favor — evidence that the marked one was possessed by the Spirit, and thus among the fortunate. By whatever name the old religion was now called — witchcraft, voodoo, conjurin' — it strongly helped to influence Nat's emerging opinion of himself, his specialness.

*

Another powerful early and enduring influence was Christian — or to be more precise: Judaeo-Christian ... Benjamin Turner made certain of that.
Following the collapse of Anglican authority because of the Revolution, amid the inrushing fresh winds and revival spirit of the hitherto persecuted Methodist and Baptist churches, the Turners became ardent Methodists.
Benjamin Turner's frequent family prayer sessions included his black people, who also routinely prayed with the Southampton pastors and traveling preachers Turner encouraged to visit the neighborhood, which had no church of its own.
Thus, as naturally as the seasons flow, the study of God became the focus of Nat Turner's life, the centerpiece of his attention to all other things ... the connecting thread of the complex logic of his life.
God!!!
God in the image of Jehovah — an all-powerful, all-knowing father and great benefactor, exceedingly jealous, vengeful when mightily displeased — demanding obedience.
God in the image of Jesus — a gentle friend ever tolerant of human weakness and error, compassionate and wise and forgiving, liberating — urging love.

Tomorrow Jerusalem: The Story of Nat Turner and the Southampton Slave Insurrection

The God of Africa — a multitude of greater and lesser good and evil spirits manifesting themselves every day in natural ways (if one knew where to look for them and how to interpret them).

In Southampton, as elsewhere, the orthodox and the heretical existed side by side, scripture and superstition competing for the attention and faith of people who wanted, needed, to believe in something, anything, to make life more understandable, more meaningful, more endurable.

Here, as everywhere, the line between the natural and the supernatural was often unclear, for whites and blacks alike.

But for all, God and the Devil were very real.

And for all, the Day of Judgement was coming!

*

Slavery haunted the conscience of religious people.

Consider, briefly, the story of the Reverend David Barrow.

In 1784, having served 24 years as a Baptist preacher in Southampton and in neighboring counties, Barrow rose up in his pulpit and denounced slavery — then freed his own slaves, and headed for Kentucky.

There, in 1798, he published a severe anti-slavery attack, which was widely circulated. The thunderous broadside reached Southampton, of course.

Local folks well remembered David Barrow.

The man was a true inspiration — and a true troublemaker.

* * *

To the slave-child Nat, the spiritual character and fatherly love of Benjamin Turner were blessings which the boy could only dimly appreciate. All things considered, yes, Nat was indeed among the fortunate.

Not so fortunate was another Southampton slave-child — Fed, the property of Betty Moore. In 1805, Fed accompanied his impoverished white folks and their other slaves down to Northampton County, beginning a longer journey ending in Georgia, amid the most cruel and ungodly circumstances of slavery ... with unforeseeable consequences.

In the Jail at JERUSALEM

To a mind like mine — restless, inquisitive and observant of everything that was passing — it is easy to suppose that religion was the subject to which it would be directed. And although this subject principally occupied my thoughts, there was nothing that I saw or heard of to which my attention was not directed ...

Bill Bryant

BENJAMIN TURNER Place

In wonderful springtime, the dogwoods were blooming, the bees were busily at work in Nancy's modest but lovely flowerbed, and the old tomcat was sleeping, as usual, near the cabin door. Nancy was in the kitchen house, as usual.

At her washtub, old Bridget was scrubbing clothes, wringing them, hard, then draping them over the bushes, to dry. All the while, she talked.

Sitting on the ground, Nat watched, and listened.

"Now, the dogwood there, it be small an' crookedy 'cause that the tree they done made the cross from, to put Lord Jesus on - An' that ol' bumblebee over there, you know, chil', he don' make the honey, other bees be doin' that."

"Why he don' make the honey?" the boy asked.

"'Cause at the Creation, when God be tellin' all the critters jus' what they suppose to be doin', the ol' bumblebee he won' payin' no attention!"

Nat tried to imagine it, and laughed.

The master's old Tom approached, closely followed by John Clark Turner, the master's son, a lad of Nat's age. Nat's best friend.

Nat paid them no mind, asking Bridget: "Can I play with the cat now? He done slept plenty long enough!"

"Can' do that," his grandmother answered. "You gots to go with ol' Tom an' young massuh John over to the Francis place - You know, chil'," she had to add, stepping back from the washtub, drying her hands with her apron, this work done, "the cat he be created as our bes' friend - next to Lord Jesus hisself."

"What you mean?"

"God, he make the cat to catch the mice an' rats what eats po' folks' food."

Old Tom laughed. "You fillin' that boy's head with more o' your stories, ol' woman?"

"Every chance I gets!" the old woman chuckled. "Nat gots to know all there be to know, so when the time come for him to serve his special purpose, he know jus' what to do - Now, y'all go on an' leave me be, so's I can get some work done 'round here ... You boys have fun - you, too, ol' man - an' be careful!"

Old Bridget worried about them constantly, of course - especially her Nat, a somewhat frail, sometimes sickly boy who seemed to spend too much time with himself and not enough time with others.

Watching them go, she walked over to the kitchen house, disappearing inside, soon reappearing with her hatchet in hand. Looking around the farmyard for a good victim, she made her decision and headed for it - a properly plump chicken, for Nancy, who was becoming an ever better servant, and not a bad cook.

*

Old Tom and the two little boys reached the roadway and turned in the general direction of the Francis place, the man setting a brisk pace and gesturing with the unbridled enthusiasm which always enlivened his own story-telling. The boys, trying to keep up, listened carefully to every word.

Tomorrow Jerusalem: The Story of Nat Turner and the Southampton Slave Insurrection

"An' so the farmer he look at the man he done bought that there stubborn ol' mule from, an' he say: This here mule won' budge a inch when I tells him to! So the man he pick up a big fence rail, an' he go over to that there ol' mule - an' he whop that mule up side the head! An' the mule he start walkin' - An' the man he say to the farmer: First, you gots to get his attention!"

In the Jail at JERUSALEM

The manner in which I learned to read and write not only had great influence on my own mind - as I acquired it with the most perfect ease, so much so that I have no recollection whatever of learning the alphabet - but to the astonishment of the family, one day, when a book was shown to me, to keep me from crying, I began spelling the names of different objects ... This was a source of wonder to all in the neighborhood, particularly the blacks ...

From infancy, Nat was in the presence of learning.
The master devoutly believed in the personal benefit as well as the practical necessity of education, and therefore actively encouraged it. In addition to all of the white Turners, most of the black Turners - including Nancy - learned, at home, how to read and write, and reckon numbers. The master, the father, would have it no other way.
This was widely known in the neighborhood.
Educational reading was limited - a few basic textbooks with smatterings of history and language usage and moralistic stories, plus occasional newspapers and religious pamphlets, the annual almanacs and, of course, the Bible - all freely available to the family.
This, too, was widely known.
Also common knowledge locally was John Clark Turner's habit of sharing whatever he learned with his constant companion and best friend.
Nat honestly had no memory of learning the alphabet, probably because he had acquired the knowledge so very early and naturally.
Nonetheless, the family was indeed astonished when the boy began spelling the names of different objects in the book he was shown to keep him from crying, thus demonstrating an ability he was not known to possess, an ability uncommon in one so young, white or black.
It was indeed a source of wonder to all in the neighborhood - particularly the blacks. One of their own, the young one already marked for greatness, had really impressed the white folks.
This pleased the boy very much, of course.

* * *

From early childhood, Nat's world was the distance he could walk in a day - and still be home by dark ... And he was truly free to roam.
Some of his playmates in the neighborhood were black. Others were white - notably not only John Clark Turner, but also three of the younger children of Samuel Francis: Sally, born in 1801; Salathiel, born in 1803; and Nathaniel, born in 1805.

Bill Bryant

The Turner and Francis youngsters played together often and well, and sometimes prayed together at the local religious gatherings.

The families were even more closely linked in 1806, when Benjamin Turner's older son Samuel married Samuel Francis' older daughter Esther.

* * *

Not all of the days of Nat's youth were free of care.

One day, his daddy ran away.

The event cast Nancy and old Bridget into a quiet, angry grief, and greatly upset the master, for weeks.

Nat, his mother told him, was much too young to understand just why it had happened. Someday, she promised him, he would understand it all.

Some of the older blacks in the neighborhood whispered that Nat's daddy had become troublesome to ol' man Turner, and had been sold away.

Late Summer 1809
BENJAMIN TURNER Place

Sitting close together on the ground, leaning back against a haystack, the master and the slave stared up at a cloudless star-sprinkled sky dominated by a full Moon.

Patiently again, more like a parent than a teacher, the man had lectured the boy regarding the Earth, where we live, and our Moon and our Sun — and the other planets circling our Sun — and the uncountable stars beyond — each and every one of them a sun in its own unimaginably vast neighborhood.

As unimaginable, in fact, as it all was, the boy did not doubt the truth of the man's words. Faith alone made every claim a fact.

Since the day the boy was born, and almost died, Benjamin had taken a very special interest in Nat, even more so after the boy's daddy went away. The master tended to yield easily to the slave's wishes and whims, and truly enjoyed cultivating the boy's bright young mind — as he did the minds of his own children.

Nat, needlessly to say, was devoted to the man, with an affection more like a son's than a student's.

And this evening, it seemed, the two had never been closer — making this as good a time as any for the boy to be bold.

Nat had heard — overheard, actually — certain stories, or rather bits and pieces of certain stories, told in a whispering way which naturally challenged Nat to know more. Whispers hid secrets, obviously worth knowing.

So Nat was curious, and bold enough now to try his luck with the master — and smart enough not to be too direct, at first.

"Massuh Benjamin?"

"Yes, Nat?"

"Do there be slaves, an' massuhs, in Heaven?"

"I sincerely hope not, Nat ... I pray not."

"Then why do there be slaves, an' massuhs, on Earth?"

Tomorrow Jerusalem: The Story of Nat Turner and the Southampton Slave Insurrection

"Because this is not Heaven. An' it's jus' the way things are, an' have to be, for some people – black an' white – to survive ... It's kind o' hard to explain, Nat – I don' even understand it, some o' the time, an' it disturbs me, more than you can imagine – But o' course, you cannot imagine it, can you? You cannot be expected to understand, at such a tender age."
"When I be ol' enough, massuh?"
"Soon enough, Nat ... soon enough – Someday, it'll all make some sense to you, I hope – An' then," he lightly laughed, "you can explain it to me!"
Briefly, there was silence.
Then: "Massuh?"
"Yes?"
"When I was a baby, why my mama try to kill me?"
Benjamin hesitated, only briefly. "She was out o' her mind that day, Nat – But she loves you now, an' that's all that really matters, hard as it may be for you to understand what happened that day."
"Yassuh ... Massuh?"
"Yes?"
"My daddy run away? ... Or you sell him?"
"He ran away ... an' that's the truth."
"My daddy a good man?"
"Most o' the time – But it was very upsettin' to all o' the family when he ran off like that – very upsettin' indeed. You play the cards you're dealt in this life, Nat, an' you try not to disappoint the people who depend on you – That's the way I reckon it ... Can you understand that, boy?"
"Yes, massuh ... Massuh?" Nat began, debating if he dared to ask the other question, deciding that he did not dare.
"Yes, Nat?"
"Tell me again 'bout the ... the 'clipse."
"E-clipse, Nat ... E-c-l-i-p-s-e."
"E-clipse."
"Always be as exact in your language as you can, Nat, as exact as you need to be to make sure folks understand you."
"Yes, suh."
"The eclipse is a phenomenon ... "

* * *

Nat had no better luck with his mama the next day, while she prepared the noontime meal for everybody.
"Mama?"
"Yes, Nat? – Fetch me the salt over there."
"Yes'm," he said, fetching the box of salt. "Mama?"
"Thank you – Yes, Nat?"
"You're welcome – Mama, when I was a baby, why you try to kill me?"
She knew he was bound to ask that question someday. But that didn't mean she was ready to answer it. The time would come for him to know the whole truth. But not today, not from her own lips. "I be out o' my mind that day, Nat ... 'Sides, it happened a long, long time ago ... I loves you, Nat ... You knows I do."
"I knows it, mama ... Mama?"
"I needs the pepper now."

35

Bill Bryant

"Yes'm," he said, fetching the box of pepper. "My daddy really jus' run away?"

"You gots to stop listenin' to other folks gossipin' - Pay 'em no mind!"

"Did he jus' run away - or did the massuh ...

"Yes, Nat. Your daddy jus' run away ... really." She had to be patient with him. The boy was smart enough that someday he would understand it all, better than she could ever hope to explain it. For now, the best the mother could do was make her son ready to understand.

The son did not even think about daring to ask the other question - and she certainly wasn't going to say a word about it. Because she was his mother. Instead, he asked her to tell him more about Africa, which she did, happily and unhappily, as usual.

All of the Africans - the real Africans - he met were willing to discuss their experiences, even with a boy, though much of it he did not, could not comprehend. The Africans did not speak quite the same language he spoke, sometimes using words which had no meaning whatsoever to him, and often seemed to be talking more to revive their own memories than to teach the boy anything. Still, they were willing to talk, and he was eager to listen.

With Nancy, the wounds of separation were yet fresh, the pain of loss too great to be ignored, or ever forgotten, even for a moment. But she had resigned herself to the fact that she would never again see her homeland, never again feel the embrace of her family there, never again laugh in the language of her youth. And in her resignation she had resolved to make her son know what she was missing.

The boy could not possibly imagine how she felt, deep down. But he must know, for a fact, that her people were a proud people, a free people ...

Early Autumn 1810
SAMUEL TURNER Place

Typhoid had claimed the life of Benjamin Turner, today laid to eternal rest in the family plot at the old homeplace.

Here, gathered in the living room, several neighbors were comforting Samuel and Esther, who was trying to make cheerful conversation.

Nancy came into the room with a glass of water for Samuel Francis, who nodded his thanks. She paused to smile at her son, sitting quietly on the floor reading a book, then left.

"Nancy," Esther said, "has become such a good servant. Benjamin's patience with her was well rewarded ... It was a nice funeral, wasn't it?"

"Yes," Turner replied, distractedly. "Yes, it was."

"Very nice," Francis agreed. "This accursed epidemic has taken away so many good people ... Samuel, you are the oldest man in your family now. Jus' tell us what you want us to do, to help build Benjamin's church. He donated that acre o' land for a purpose, an' the sooner we get started, the better ... You are now the overseer o' this project - an' we do need a church."

Turner wasn't ready to talk about the church. "Nat," he said to the boy in the corner of the room, "you enjoyin' that new book?"

*Tomorrow Jerusalem: The Story of Nat Turner
and the Southampton Slave Insurrection*

"Yes, massuh," Nat said, looking up, eyes wide in wonder. "I likes this book a lot."

"Nat," Esther said, "is such a smart little boy, an' always so polite – an' he was so very respectful durin' the funeral ... Benjamin was like a father to him."

"Yes," Turner said. "Yes, he was."

"Well, if you ask me," Francis said, "he won' be much use to you as a field hand. Hasn't got the muscles for it. Doesn't have the right 'attitude' to be a good slave, in the bes' definition o' the word. You might consider bein' a little stricter with the boy than Benjamin was."

"Shush," Esther softly protested. "He'll hear you."

"Don' get me wrong," Francis said. "He's a nice boy, or I wouldn't let him play with my own children. But he is a slave, an' you have got to be practical, if you expect him to pull his own weight 'round here."

"He is only a boy," Esther said.

"He will be a man someday," Francis said. "Samuel, I naturally assume we are in agreement that whoever we invite to preach in our soon-to-be-built church, he should prepare his sermons with the whole congregation in mind – to tell all o' our slaves what we do want 'em to hear ... We cannot be too careful."

"No," Turner said. "No, we cannot ... Nat, go fetch me a glass of water, please."

"Yes, massuh," the boy said, closing the book as he stood up, carrying it with him as he went to do what the master asked.

* * *

In life, Benjamin Turner had done well.

At the time of his passing, his cultivated land included 60 acres planted in corn, 30 in cotton, 15 in tobacco, several in vegetables, plus the orchards. The final inventory of his other property listed a carriage and assorted saddlery, a flax wheel, three spinning wheels, a loom, tools and equipment for a carpenter, a blacksmith, a barrel-maker and a stiller, with barrels enough for 1,500 gallons, plus 14 oxen, six horses (including several trained jumpers for the fox hunt) and 30 slaves ... Nat and his mother, and the girl Cherry, were now among Samuel's new possessions.

In death, too, Benjamin did well.

Along a roadway leading through his land, a church was built by the people of the neighborhood – Turner's Meeting House – Methodist, of course.

Most of the local families began attending services whenever they could – meaning whenever the weather allowed it, whenever someone was available to do the preaching, whenever there wasn't a special service or a big camp meeting elsewhere worth attending.

Many of the local slaves also attended.

And the congregation heard the message the elders wanted them to hear, and believe in – basically the hope of salvation and Heaven, through the discipline of earthly obedience, amen!

* * *

Bill Bryant

During the years of Nat's passage from boyhood to early manhood, from play to work, the United States of America fought another war against Great Britain.

And as their fathers and uncles had done during the War for Independence, many of the white men of Southampton, some accompanied by their black servants, went away, to help defend the soil of Virginia, and the Republic.

Except for the awful risking of the lives of its sons, Southampton had no direct contact with the reality of this war.

But the white people did know fright when the British suddenly raided into the Chesapeake Bay, did sadly learn of the British bombardment of Norfolk, did angrily hear of the British cruelties in Hampton, did hatefully respond to the hateful British appeal to the slaves of the Tidewater to run away to freedom — or rise in rebellion.

Some of the black people did not share the feelings of the white people.

* * *

In 1813, a Southampton farmer by the name of David Davis died.
His Bible made its way into Nat's hands.

* * *

At war's end, Samuel Turner engaged the services of a tutor for his children Rebecca Jane, Polly and John.

When Nat was free from his chores, he would sit down with the other pupils and share their books, wherever Gilliam Jones was conducting his class — in the main house, or out in the open yard, under the shade of a great oak tree. Samuel Turner, in his liberality, was a lot like his father.

* * *

In 1815, Samuel Francis died, making his widow responsible now for raising the youngest of their 10 children.
Soon after, Esther Turner died.

In the Jail at JERUSALEM

I was not addicted to stealing in my youth, nor have ever been — yet such was the confidence of the Negroes in the neighborhood, even at this early period of my life, in my superior judgement, that they would often carry me with them when they were going on any roguery, to plan for them ...

Tomorrow Jerusalem: The Story of Nat Turner and the Southampton Slave Insurrection

Autumn 1815
CABIN POND

Spiriting away the freshly baked apple pie had proved to be a simple deed, not half as difficult or as daring as the other two boys bravely considered it to be.

According to the plan, one boy went to the door of the kitchen house to distract the cook while another boy dashed from the bushes to the windowsill - to snatch the pie! - while Nat merely waited and watched, from a safe distance, enjoying the sport.

Now, following the other boys along a narrow pathway through the swampy land surrounding Cabin Pond, the leader of the raid was having second thoughts about the wisdom of it.

No, stealing the pie wasn't his idea; and no, he wasn't the one who snatched it; and no, nobody had really been hurt by the petty theft. But yes, he had in fact helped to make the raid possible; and yes, the Bible did say thou shalt not steal ... And yes, the cook was his mother - and oh yes, she surely would take a switch to him if she learned of his involvement in the evil deed.

So Nat tried to concentrate on how good the pie would taste - soon, if this path ever ended.

The boy showing the way told the story of the place they were going, which explained why the path seemed so unused: "An' they say he took his massuh an' he flogged him - So the white men, they grabs that nigger, an' they brings him here to Cabin Pond - kickin' an' screamin' - 'til they gets to this clearin' we's goin' to. An' then they ties him to a spit jus' like a pig - an' they roasts him ... real slow ... An' that's why nobody hardly ever comes here, 'cause the ghost o' that ol' nigger still be here - still kickin' an' screamin' an' ... "

And there, suddenly, it was - a small clear patch of higher ground, at the edge of the pond ... truly peaceful ... truly secret.

Nat immediately loved this place.

VICKSVILLE

At one end of the merchandise-crowded porch of John Denegre's store, Samuel Turner and Peter Blow were engaged in what would probably be their last conversation.

At the other end were Nat and a little black boy, Sam the property of Peter Blow, and two young white girls and a white boy, the children of Peter Blow.

"You have been a good neighbor," Turner said, "an' a good friend. I hate the very idea o' your leavin' Southampton, an' Virginia."

"You are mos' kind, Samuel. I hate the idea as much as you do - But a man's got to know when it's time to quit, an' cut his losses. That land o' mine is all played out, an' new land, good land, don' come cheap 'round here ... It's time to be movin' on."

"I'm sure you know what's best - Nat!" Turner called out. "You an' Mister Blow's children, an' little Sam, go off somewhere an' play. Mister Blow an' I got some business to transact with Mister Denegre."

Blow's youngsters, closely followed by Nat, scrambled off the porch and then around the corner of the building - literally running into a black man Nat had previously seen, but not met, a stranger whose remarkable story Nat had already vaguely heard, along the grapevine.

Bill Bryant

"Whoa!" the man said, reclaiming his balance. "Where you young peoples goin' in such a hurry?"

"They jus' in a hurry to play," Nat said, eager to hear the man say more, in that unfamiliar accent. "Sorry, suh," he added, using politeness as his bait. "You know how young'uns be!"

The man smiled at him. "What your name?"

"Nat, suh ... Nat Turner."

"Well, I be Philip Denegre - a free man ... servant to Monsieur Denegre."

Nat, glancing at the children at play, knowing he was expected to watch them, carefully, could not let this opportunity pass. "How you be free?"

"Now, that be a long story, if you got the time to listen to it."

"I got the time."

"Very well ... Let's go sit on the porch."

"Yes, suh!" Nat instantly agreed, though he realized he wouldn't be able to see the children from the porch. But he did not worry. He could still hear them. And besides, Mister Blow's youngsters always behaved well, and never got into any mischief. They watched over one another.

Philip found a spot on the edge of the porch, and sat down. Nat sat next to him.

And the man, who had told his story many times, began, with great pleasure, to tell it again. "Back in '93, I be Monsieur Denegre's slave. We be livin' down in Santo Domingo, when the slaves rose up again - Oh, it was a terrible, terrible time it was ... But I warned Monsieur Denegre, an' we got hold of a small boat, an' we escaped. An' Monsieur Denegre, he so thankful to Philip he make Philip free man! ... Now, back in '93 ... "

"If you be free, how come you still with Mon- ... Monsieur Denegre?"

Philip smiled. "'Cause we get along together real good - better than me an' my wife get along, I tell you. I reckon it make as much sense to stay with him as it do to leave him ... So I stays."

"Tell me 'bout the risin'."

"Well, like I jus' say, it was terrible ... Back in '93, before Toussaint L'Ouverture ... "

"Who?" Nat asked, thinking he should know but not recognizing the name from the sound of it.

Philip could not help but smile and shake his head at the same time. The boy knew so little, had so much to learn, apparently. "Toussaint L'Ouverture - Boy, you ever hear tell o' Moses?"

Of course! "L' ... L'Ou-ver-ture, he was the great general - Not even Napoleon could beat him! - An' yes, suh, I knows 'bout Moses, too - Moses be right here, in my Bible," Nat proudly declared, patting the pocket of his coat.

More than a little surprised but hiding it well, the man stared at the unseen Bible. "Got your very own Bible," he said, more to himself than to Nat. He looked at the young man with new respect. "One day, you know, I saw him ... "

"Moses?" Nat had to ask.

Philip laughed, and so did Nat, who in that moment knew this would not be their last conversation. "No," Philip finally answered. "Not Moses ... The General!"

*Tomorrow Jerusalem: The Story of Nat Turner
and the Southampton Slave Insurrection*

SAMUEL TURNER Place

Along the split-rail fence near Nancy's cabin, the abundantly overgrowing honeysuckle and the ambitious morning glories met and intertwined, in a harmony of such pure sweetness and gentle color.

Inside the cabin, Nancy was reading recipes when her son appeared at the open door.

"Mama?"

"Nat ... what you doin' here? Thought you had chores."

"Chores done. Jus' come to visit."

"Sit yourself down."

He did, then went straight to his purpose: "Mama ... Tell me 'bout the day I was born ... An' tell me 'bout what happened to my daddy."

She looked at him, long and hard. The questions were not questions now, but expectations. She waited, until the right words came.

She thought of Africa, of home, of the great river and the birds of the sky and the creatures of the forest. She thought of her village, her friends and her family. She remembered the day of her capture, the long walk across Africa, the long voyage across the ocean, the chains, the day she was bought at auction by the old master. And looking now at her boy, she saw the whole meaning of her difficult life, the only compensation for all of the sadness she had known.

"Yes, I try to kill you the day you was born - an' I wasn' out o' my mind. I knew 'xactly what I was doin' ... My people - your people - a proud people. Not meant to be slaves! I try to kill you 'cause I don' wan' my baby to be a slave ... So I don' regret tryin' to kill you ... An' I sure don' regret failin'! You knows I loves you, right?"

"Yes, mama."

"Your daddy did run away - for a fact ... He was a good man, but he don' like bein' a slave, an' he always givin' the massuh at leas' a little trouble, 'bout this thing or that - Oh, I done heard the stories, too, 'bout how he got caught, 'bout the massuh takin' him down to Murfreesboro, an' sellin' him. Well, the ol' fools tellin' that story be the same ol' fools sayin' your daddy be Benjamin Turner - An' what they know? Was they there? ... You jus' pay 'em no mind, you hear me?"

"Yes, mama."

"Stand up."

He did.

Then, slowly, she stood.

"Nat ... All these years, since you was a baby, I been tryin' to mold you in my way. But you ain' a chil' no longer. You becomin' a man ... Nat?"

"Yes, mama?"

"Be a man!"

* * *

Entering manhood, Nat worked.

He worked in the fields, of course, when necessary. He didn't enjoy it, but knew that the labor was putting food on the table, so he did his share.

Mostly, he worked around the homeplace, making a point of becoming handy at the chores which kept him out of the fields.

Bill Bryant

Early on, he developed particular skill as a carpenter.

*

And he played.
The games of childhood were at an end, but there were other games for a mind like his to play. Experiments, actually.
When not engaged in his master's work, Nat experimented in a variety of manufactures. He cast molten metal into earthen molds, trying to make useful objects. He tried to make paper. He tried to make gunpowder.
He perfected none of these. But each experiment convinced him that he could achieve perfection, if only he possessed the right tools and materials to do so.

*

And he prayed.
Either alone or at Turner's Meeting House, Nat applied himself to religion with an enthusiasm uncommon even among very religious folks.
Such enthusiasm made him do something remarkable.
He asked the elders of Turner's Meeting House to permit him to be baptized, to become fully and formally a member of the church. The request seemed reasonable, to him.
The elders declined, politely enough, saying it would set a bad precedent.
Nat accepted their decision, respectfully enough, because he had to. But he resented it deeply, and would not forget it.

* * *

In 1816, there was a new life over at Thomaston.
A baby boy was born.
The proud parents named him George Henry Thomas.

* * *

In 1817, full to the brim with confidence in his optimistic idea, Clements Rochelle petitioned the General Assembly of Virginia for the right to establish a new town.
Rochelle already owned and operated a ferry at the site, eight miles downriver from Jerusalem.
The town would be named Monroe, in honor of the President.
The General Assembly approved.

* * *

*Tomorrow Jerusalem: The Story of Nat Turner
and the Southampton Slave Insurrection*

In the spring of 1818, Samuel Turner got married again, exchanging vows with the widow Elizabeth Reese Williamson.

Also, Nat's good friend Sally Francis married Thomas Moore, a farmer.

* * *

Late in 1818, the General Assembly received another petition from down in Southampton — a surprisingly eloquent appeal from the dirt-poor and supposedly illiterate Nottoways.

The tribe asked permission to sell off much of the Indian land (mainly to pay off white creditors) and turn the other acreage into privately owned farms. The petitioners reasoned: "What is more disheartening to a man than to know that the labor of his hands is not to go to the children of his body. And when we know it will, with what energy of industry it animates man, for the happiness of his children."

And the news swiftly circulated in Southampton that there was a new Indian over in Simmons Town — a fellow named William Bozeman, who had gone away from here some years ago, gotten himself an education, and returned.

Bozeman had returned to remind the Nottoways (and the General Assembly) that his grandfather, their chief, had fought and died for the great Washington in the great war for American independence — which should entitle the Nottoways to some consideration, surely.

The General Assembly agreed, and approved the request.

* * *

During 1818-19, a severe economic depression began to grip the South, badly affecting virtually everyone, in one way or another.

The supply of eagerly overgrown cotton exceeded the demand for it, causing the market price of a pound of cotton to begin falling sharply from its recent high of 30 cents — causing, too, a surplus of slaves among the planters of the Tidewater. The coffles moving southward through Southampton became longer, often becoming even longer while passing through the county.

*

All things considered, it was not a good time for Nat to ask Samuel Turner for an understanding enabling Nat to purchase his freedom, by hiring him out to others, for wages.

But Nat did ask for it — and so did John Clark Turner.

Samuel wouldn't hear of it.

Not now.

Bill Bryant

In the Jail at JERUSALEM

Having soon discovered, to be great I must appear so, I therefore studiously avoided mixing in society, and wrapped myself in mystery, devoting my time to fasting and prayer. By this time, having arrived to man's estate, and hearing the scriptures commented on at meetings, I was struck with that particular passage which says: "Seek ye the Kingdom of Heaven, and all things shall be added unto you." I reflected much on this passage, and prayed daily for light on this subject. As I was praying one day at my plow, the Spirit spoke to me, saying: "Seek ye the Kingdom of Heaven, and all things shall be added unto you" - the Spirit that spoke to the prophets in former days - and I was greatly astonished, and for two years prayed continually, whenever my duty would permit ... And then again I had the same revelation, which fully confirmed me in the impression that I was ordained for some great purpose in the hands of the Almighty ...

Summer 1821
CABIN POND

To some, the Spirit that spoke to the prophets in former days speaks in a voice loud and clear and manifestly divine - a voice to be heeded.

To some, the Spirit speaks in a whisper yet distinctly, explosively revealing some basic powerful truth regarding one's self and one's potential in this life - a whisper to be heeded.

The Spirit spoke to Nat.

Nat heeded it.

And the austerity of his life and manners became a topic for remark by white and black.

One could not ignore how "different" he was - not even here, now, with her ... following the path to the secret place.

He had told Cherry about the Spirit speaking to him. He had also told some other people in the neighborhood. The blacks, particularly the folks who already knew that Nat was special, were fascinated. The whites, particularly the folks who already knew that Nat was peculiar, were skeptical.

Cherry, a frail sweet girl of limited ability as a worker but considerable appeal as a young woman, was impressed.

Even here, now, he was trying to impress her, with the truth.

She must know him, she must understand his commitment to the Bible, his constant preoccupation with this matter of the Spirit - why, at this very moment, he confessed to her, a part of him very badly wanted, needed to be alone, somewhere, immersed in prayer and meditation, trying to know himself better.

She understood, she told him. She really did. Still, he seemed so serious - too serious for her, on a nice day like this.

"Cherry ... I don' know what, exactly, I am supposed to do - But I know it's somethin' real important - I know it for a fact! ... Why you laughin', girl?"

Tomorrow Jerusalem: The Story of Nat Turner and the Southampton Slave Insurrection

She was, for a fact, laughing. "'Cause you sounds jus' like a preacher — an' I's the only person in the congregation! ... When you finds out jus' what it is you suppose to do, 'xactly, you tells me?"

"You be the first to know!" he promised her, feeling less serious, indeed reaching deep into the white man's language to display his lighter side: "I shall with proper expedition divulge it to you at the appropriate — What you laughin' 'bout now, girl?" he grinned, knowing the answer and liking it.

"You! — You jus' like a ol' peacock struttin' 'round the barnyard, his big tailfeathers all spread out — You jus' showin' off! Course, I do likes the way you talks so fine when you got a mind to. You knows the right way to talk."

"Ain' no right way, no wrong way, Cherry. All folks talk differently — in the cabins, up at the main house, the ones who've had some schoolin', an' the ones who ain' had none — You got to learn to talk to folks in their own language ... Why you smilin' so pretty?"

"'Cause you gonna be an important man someday, Nat Turner. I feels it ... deep down inside."

And she did.

And she was right, if the early signs were right. Already, at a place in the woods on a neighbor's property, he had begun preaching, occasionally, to gatherings of local blacks. Already, he was just about the best known and most respected slave in the whole neighborhood. It was not hard to imagine him becoming even better known and more respected, well beyond the neighborhood.

Nat now held her hand as they neared their destination.

"And there it is," he proudly announced, pushing back a low tree branch to enable her to lead him into the secret place, "right here!"

In the Jail at JERUSALEM

Now, finding I had arrived to man's estate, and was a slave, and these revelations being made known to me, I began to direct my attention to this great object, to fulfill the purpose for which, by this time, I felt assured I was intended. Knowing the influence I had obtained over the minds of my fellow servants — not by the means of conjuring and such like tricks, for to them I always spoke of such things with contempt — but by the communion of the Spirit whose revelations I often communicated to them, and they believed and said my wisdom came from God. I now began to prepare them for my purpose, by telling them something was about to happen that would terminate in fulfilling the great promise that had been made to me ...

Early 1822
ELIZABETH TURNER Place

The dreamer's vague vision clashed with the slave's raw reality.

Near the cabins, the servants came together.

From the main house emerged a widow in mourning dress — Elizabeth Turner, followed by James Griffin, then by Thomas Moore and his wife Sally.

Bill Bryant

As the white folks approached the black folks, Griffin could be ever more easily heard, reading from the inventory in his hands – "plus 75 bushels o' corn, 87 pounds o' picked cotton, 2,484 pounds o' bacon, 75 pounds o' dried beef, 341 pounds o' lard, 259 pounds o' salt pork – Let's see here – plus 150 hogs, 11 sheep, 17 head o' cattle an' 23 slaves. The will specifies, as I said to you earlier, that ol' Tom an' ol' Bridget are to be cared for the rest o' their lives, an' that Nancy will stay with you."

Elizabeth was grateful. "I am so glad Samuel chose you to be the executor, Mister Griffin. I could not deal with all o' this right now – The very thought o' breakin' up the family distresses me so!"

"You jus' set your mind at ease, Elizabeth."

The widow faced the servants. "I have good news for you! Mister Griffin here is confident it will not be necessary to sell any o' you to the slave traders. He believes he can find homes for all o' you in Southampton!"

The unspoken tension of the moment eased, somewhat.

"Nat!" the executor said.

"Yes, suh," Nat warily responded.

"You are acquainted with Mister Moore here?"

"Yes, suh – an' I know Miss Sally, too – She an' I ... "

"Mister Moore has agreed to purchase you, for $450," Griffin noted. "You are his property now."

"Yes ... suh."

Sally was quick to put the situation in the best light. "Jus' think, Nat! We can gossip every day now! – It'll be like ol' times!"

"Yes'm," Nat smiled. "Mistuh Griffin ... How 'bout Cherry?"

"I think I have a buyer for her, as well," Griffin said. "Mister Giles Reese is prepared to pay $40 for her. Not much, but a fair price, considerin' – Mister Reese an' his wife are good people. They'll take good care o' Cherry. No need for you to worry none."

"Yes ... suh."

*

But Nat did worry.

And so did Cherry.

"It ain' fair!" she declared when she and Nat were finally alone together, in the cabin she shared with Nancy. "It ain' right, breakin' up the family – An' you an' me, how 'bout you an' me?"

"Could be worse," he said, embracing her, trying to comfort and calm her, yes, trying just like Sally, bless her, to put this unhappy situation in the best light possible. "Could be a whole lot worse – Could be headin' over to Cross Keys to go south! ... 'Sides," he added, making an effort to sound pleased with the prospect, "Mastuh Moore's place only 'bout a mile away from Mastuh Reese – We be seein' one another often enough ... It'll be all right ... It'll be all right, girl, I'm tellin' you ... You be hearin' me, Cherry?"

She held him tight. "I be hearin' you ... Oh, Nat!"

The pain and sorrow in her voice made him angry.

So helplessly angry.

Tomorrow Jerusalem: The Story of Nat Turner and the Southampton Slave Insurrection

In the Jail at JERUSALEM

About this time, I was placed under an overseer, from whom I ran away ...

Summer 1822
CABIN POND

Amid the humming, buzzing, whirring, swarming symphony of the insects all around him, Nat heard only the sounds of the words he was reading in the Bible, in Exodus: "And he that stealeth a man, and selleth him ... he shall surely be put to death."

Then he closed the book, and stared at the peaceful surface of the pond.

The problem wasn't Thomas Moore. The problem was the overseer Moore had felt it necessary to employ, to help increase the productivity of the farm.

The master was just being practical, the master explained to his grumbling slaves: These are hard times for everybody, what with the price o' cotton still fallin' — But if we can increase productivity, we won't have to sell off anybody. Which made some sense.

But the hired man not only made all of Moore's black people work a lot harder and longer, but also re-enforced his like-it-or-not attitude with a short whip he kept tucked inside his belt. He treated the people like dirt — and was obviously quite ready to treat them worse.

Nat could not bring himself to kill the man. But he could understand why some other slave might gladly perform the service.

Finally, he made up his mind what to do ... what needed doin'.

But first ...

GILES REESE Place

Giles Reese had proved mimself to be, during these past few months, a good master. He had decided that he liked Nat — had decided, too, that he liked the idea o' Nat someday marryin' Cherry, an idea Reese's wife also approved.

Now, Reese's Cherry and Moore's Nat sat on the bench behind her cabin.

"It ain' Christian o' me," he said, "but I truly hate that overseer! I wish I could do somethin' to get rid o' him!"

"Better'n Massuh Moore goin' broke an' sendin' you over to Cross Keys."

"Cherry ... I be goin' away."

"What you mean?"

"I mean ... Partly, I jus' got to get away from that overseer. An' partly, I jus' got to know what it's like to be free. An' partly ... I jus' got to be by myself."

Truth be told, he wasn't entirely sure why it had to be done. Running away was a radical, and risky, solution to the problem. But it had to be done ... The only real alternative was not to run away, which would solve nothing. And he was not willing to do nothing.

"Where you go?"

Bill Bryant

"I don' know ... I'm not sure."
"They gonna put the nigger dogs on you."
"I doubt it - 'Sides, you know me: If I don' want 'em to find me, they ain' gonna find me!"
"When you goin'?"
"Soon - real soon ... If I stays 'round here, you know where I'll be ... if you really need me."
"Well," she said, cheering up, "I ain' plannin' on goin' anywhere anytime soon, so I be here ... in case you needs me!"
In the agony of his decision, he had to smile.

In the Jail at JERUSALEM

And after remaining in the woods 30 days, I returned, to the astonishment of the Negroes on the plantation, who thought I had made my escape to some other part of the country, as my father had done before - But the reason of my return was that the Spirit appeared to me and said I had my wishes directed to the things of this world, and not the Kingdom of Heaven, and that I should return to the service of my earthly master. "For he who knoweth his master's will, and doeth it not, shall be beaten with many stripes, and thus have I chastened you" ... And the Negroes found fault, and murmured against me, saying that if they had my sense they would not serve any master in the world ...

THOMAS MOORE Place

They had not put the nigger dogs onto Nat's scent. Sally Moore absolutely would not hear of it.
Nor did Nat have to fear the overseer's whip if he returned. Sally insisted that if Nat did return and did have to be whipped, she would not allow the overseer to do it and did not want her husband to do it, she would do it herself - and Thomas Moore absolutely would not hear of that.
So as the runaway slave came walking up the lane, with the white folks and the black folks alike drifting toward the spot where the confrontation would soon occur, Nat had less to fear than he could know. Certainly, he was prepared for the worst.
"Thought you might come back," Moore called out to the approaching figure with authority. "Sally here, she's been sayin' all along that she knew you'd be returnin', eventually."
"Had some serious thinkin' to do, Mastuh Moore," Nat said, noticing how very pleased with herself Sally seemed to be.
"Maybe so," Moore said, lowering his voice as the distance between them decreased but attempting to be no less stern, "but you know perfectly well I cannot afford to let my nigras go runnin' off for a month at a time jus' 'cause they got 'some serious thinkin' to do' - There's work to be done 'round here! - You're my slave, an' I'm your master, an' we both got duties to perform! I cannot jus' ignore what you have done."
"No, suh," Nat said, firmly but softly, standing face to face with Moore. "Like the good book says: 'For he who knoweth his master's will ...'"

Tomorrow Jerusalem: The Story of Nat Turner and the Southampton Slave Insurrection

"'An' doeth it not,'" Moore continued, "'shall be beaten with many stripes, an' thus have I chastened you' – Exodus 21:16 – You ain' the only one 'round here with a Bible ... Actually," Nat's earthly master said, retreating toward the compromise he had negotiated with his wife, "Sally an' I are agreed that you are gonna have to work even harder, to atone for your absence – An' you are not to set one foot off this farm for the next 30 days, for any reason – any reason whatsoever! ... Understood?"

Nat nodded, slowly comprehending what had just been said. In one sense very relieved, in another sense he almost wished for the overseer's whip.

Thirty days!

Oh, Cherry ...

Autumn 1822
GILES REESE Place

He had returned because he knew – even if the Spirit had not told him so – that his place was here, in Southampton, doing not only his master's but also his Master's work.

He had his reasons for going.

He had his reasons for coming back.

Now, one of them was at his side, and together they were ready to make the great leap into the married life.

And in the presence of family and friends, they did make the great leap over the broomstick on the ground – and Nat Turner and Cherry Reese did become husband and wife in the eyes of the people of their world.

The blacks who murmured against him now congratulated the newlyweds, as did the owners of the groom and the owners of the bride.

Sally was so happy for both of them.

Winter 1822-23
SOUTHAMPTON COUNTY

Before the first snowflakes gently fell, from the finest homes to the crudest cabins, even the most isolated and the most ignorant folks were well aware of what had happened down in South Carolina, in Charleston.

Details of the conspiracy were only sketchily reported, but the conclusion to the incident was certain enough – the hanging of 35 blacks for attempting an insurrection.

Another potential Santo Domingo had been avoided, again because the plotters were betrayed by other blacks.

Several white men were implicated in the matter.

The leader: Denmark Vesey, who had purchased his freedom in 1800 with money won in a lottery – a privileged black, a man who knew how to read and write, an artisan, a seaman who had visited other countries and spoke other languages – a faithful reader of the Bible, fond of the African traditions ... a militant man.

* * *

In the late spring of 1823, to the east of Southampton, militiamen were sent against a gang of black bandits who were raiding farms near the Dismal Swamp, the bandits' lair, where hundreds of escaped slaves and displaced Indians resided in virtually impenetrable security.

On the 25th of June, the militiamen captured the leader, Bob Ferebee.

His fate was preordained.

* * *

During 1823, the price of cotton fell to 10 cents per pound.
With predictable consequences.

* * *

Southside militiamen were active again in 1824, when some farms along the boundary between Virginia and North Carolina experienced raids by another gang of black bandits, led by Bob Ricks.

Ricks and another Southampton slave had been added to a coffle destined for Georgia, but with 17 other slaves had broken away.

The militiamen managed to chase Ricks and his men into freedom, finally, in the Dismal Swamp.

* * *

Also in '24, the merchant ship Cyrus sailed from Norfolk for Liberia.

Among its passengers were 13 members of the free black Clarke family, from Southhampton.

* * *

In 1825, word circulated that the Creeks and the Cherokees were becoming more restless in Georgia and in Alabama.

* * *

Also in '25, the merchant ship Hunter sailed from Norfolk for Liberia, with 15 Southamptonians aboard.

* * *

Tomorrow Jerusalem: The Story of Nat Turner and the Southampton Slave Insurrection

And during the early and mid-1820s, beyond the United States of America:
British abolitionists campaigned aggressively against slavery in the British West Indies.
National liberation movements flourished in South America.
Revolutions shook Poland, Turkey, Greece, Italy, France and Spain.
It was in the newspapers.

In the Jail at JERUSALEM

And about this time, I had a vision, and I saw white spirits and black spirits engaged in battle, and the Sun was darkened, the thunder rolled in the heavens, and blood flowed in streams — and I heard a voice saying: "Such is your luck, such are you called to see, and let it come rough or smooth, you must surely bear it" ... I now withdrew myself, as much as my situation would permit, from the intercourse of my fellow servants, for the avowed purpose of serving the Spirit more fully ...

Thus, even as the world of Nat Turner was slowly but surely expanding, the range of his roaming and the scope of his ministry steadily increasing, his influence spreading, he was putting an ever greater distance between himself and the people around him, his family included, though to a lesser extent.
Outwardly so ordinary, inwardly he struggled daily, his questioning mind in constant motion, considering again and again and again his limited options, praying continually for the insight, or the revelation, or the sign, to tell him what to do.
He was known now to many as Nat the Preacher, fundamentally a Methodist. He preached among the people in his own neighborhood, and he preached among the people at the Peter Edwards place, the Porter, Williams and other places, including the farm of childhood friend Nathaniel Francis.
Many of the folks to whom he ministered accepted as the gospel truth Nat's claim of special purpose, though all of them remained as ignorant as he confessed himself to be regarding what that purpose might be.
Whatever it might be, he told them, repeatedly, he and they would know it when the time came.
It was so vague ... but it was a promise!

*

Perhaps, he thought, he was meant to establish a school, or even a town, for his people — using his considerable talents to win the white folks' approval and cooperation ... Yes, he could be a great teacher and builder of minds!
Or perhaps, better yet, he was meant to lead a powerful revival — his faith so profound, his message so sensible that his voice would be heard and respected not only among the black people, but also among the white people ... Yes indeed, he could be a great reacher and saver of souls — to advance the holy cause of freedom!

Bill Bryant

Perhaps.
Insurrection ... ?
He thought about it.
He thought about it a lot.
God's will be done.
If it be known!

December 24th, 1825
BLACK CREEK MEETING HOUSE

Here in the Baptist church where the Reverend David Barrow had denounced the practice of slavery in 1784, now the Reverend Jonathan Lankford was in trouble.

He had expected opposition – but not such hostility.

"Please hear me out!" the embattled minister appealed to his unruly congregation. "In making this necessary announcement, I am mindful – as many of you are mindful – of the example provided to us by David Barrow, who ... "

"His bad example!" someone in the pews yelled.

"And," the man in the pulpit persisted, "we should all be mindful, friends, of the letter Pastor Barrow circulated in '98, asking if it is a righteous thing for a Christian to hold or cause any of the human race to be held in slavery – I say ... "

"How dare you!" someone shouted as the unhappy muttering surged throughout the church.

"I say – Now let me finish – I say his question remains to be answered – And it must be answered – And I know, and you know, that many of you agree with me!"

"Not as many as you'd like to think!" someone cried out, triggering another surge of angrier muttering.

"I have been a member of this fine congregation for 25 years, my friends," Lankford declared, standing his ground, determined to finish this message, "and I have been your pastor for seven of those years – and I mean it when I say to you that I cannot, and I will not, administer the ordinances of the gospel if to do so requires me to depend on the contributions of members whose prosperity is based upon the ownership of other human beings!"

Hearing the challenge again only made it more offensive, to some.

Amid a storm of objections, the Reverend Jonathan Lankford with effort made his way through the congregation, out the door, mounted his horse, and rode off.

*

On the eve of Christmas, no less, the man had shamelessly, inexcusably insulted the Christianity of his own people – his friends!

Therefore, that very day – indeed almost before the dust kicked up by the pastor's horse had come back to rest in the churchyard – certain members of the Black Creek Meeting House began discussing how best to remove the pastor from his pulpit permanently. It was, after all, their pulpit, really.

Even Lankford's sympathizers in the congregation, who shared the passion of his private sentiments but not the zeal of his public

*Tomorrow Jerusalem: The Story of Nat Turner
and the Southampton Slave Insurrection*

conviction, had to agree: By next Sunday, what had just happened here would be known in every single nook and cranny of the county, and beyond, exposing all of them to criticism among the white people while encouraging false hopes and dissatisfaction, needlessly, among the black people.

Something had to be done, soon, to restore the unity and integrity of the church.

The pastor had stirred up a hornets' nest.

*

Of course, Nat heard about it.
Who didn't?

1826

Throughout the United States of America on the 4th of July, people joyfully celebrated the 50th anniversary of the Signing of the Declaration of Independence, with so much to celebrate! The young nation, now five times the size of France, had already grown from 13 states to 24, its population from well under four million to well over 12 million — with so much growing sure to come.

Within the week following the 4th, it became generally known that not only Thomas Jefferson but also John Adams had died on the sacred day.

The awesome coincidence was widely interpreted as a sign from God, affirming the Providential great purpose of the American people and their unique experiment in self-government and human rights.

Amen to that, most folks agreed, then went back to whatever it was they were doing.

* * *

In Richmond, the elected representatives of the people of Virginia received a petition from one Anthony Blunt of Southampton County.

Blunt, a recently manumitted ex-slave more than 60 years old, simply asked the General Assembly for permission to live out his remaining years in Southhampton, a wish which required an exception to recent legislation requiring newly freed blacks to leave the county where they were given their freedom.

The General Assembly rejected the petition.
Blunt, saying he had nowhere to go, went.

*

Incidentally, the new Southampton member of the Virginia House of Delegates was Vicksville storekeeper John Denegre.

Bill Bryant

* * *

In Southampton on the 1st of December, in the struggling town of Monroe, a boychild was born to the wife of Fielding Mahone.
The baby was tiny and weak.
The worried parents named their new son William, and prayed that little Billy would live.

* * *

Old Bridget passed on.
Old Tom, too.
From time to time, Nat visited with his mother, now apparently for all intents and purposes content to be living and cooking at Elizabeth Turner's place. He tried sometimes to imagine the circumstances which would permit Nancy to return, someday, to her own people. But the exercise always defeated him. He did not enjoy being defeated.
He spent as much time as possible - not nearly enough considering his duties to master and Master - with Cherry, who now shared her cabin with their infant son Redic.
Sally Moore, too, was now a mother. The little boy's name was Putnam.
Nat saw less and less of John Clark Turner, a fine figure of a man with a farm and family of his own. But their reunions were always most friendly, as though only a few days had passed since boyhood.
Not as friendly as in youth, but civil, were Nat's relations with Salathiel and Nathaniel Francis. Sally's kid brothers were now a couple of lanky bachelors with modest farms but much ambition (especially Nathaniel).
The many black folks who knew and trusted Nat included a few men he himself knew and trusted well enough to justify some lessening of the distance, some lowering of the wall, he customarily maintained. Even a prophet must have friends.
Some of these were slaves, notably: Richard Porter's Henry, a solid man faithful to his convictions and loyal to his friends, in all weather; Jacob Williams' Nelson, a clever fellow known as a conjurin' man, a fact Nat did not let stand in the way; and boyhood playmate Sam, now the property of Nathaniel Francis.
Others were free men, notably: Thomas Haithcock, who lived with his wife and stepdaughters on a small farm adjacent to Moore's; Will Artist, who lived with his slave wife and their six children on a small farm near Benjamin Turner's old place; and Berry Newsom, then hiring himself out as a laborer but hoping to convince somebody someday to indenture him as an apprentice craftsman - no small hope, mind you, for a black man. (Newsom, and Artist, happened to be very light-skinned, so much so that at a certain distance either might be mistaken as white.)
From time to time, of course, new folks would enter Nat's life, some jus' passin' through, some bound to stay.

*Tomorrow Jerusalem: The Story of Nat Turner
and the Southampton Slave Insurrection*

Early 1827
CROSS KEYS

Thomas Moore had purchased a new slave, then sent Nat here with the wagon to fetch the property and bring it home.

Moore hadn't intended to buy a new man so soon, but couldn't resist this one. And Nat could understand why, just looking at the man emerging from the shadows of the back room of the storehouse — a prime field hand, surely worth every penny of the $425 paid for him — tall, powerful, perfectly proportioned — impressive, to say the least.

Hark, the man told Nat when asked, as they walked from the storehouse into the daylight, heading toward the wagon. Hark was his name — named, he matter of factly explained, by his mama and her master after Hark the great black warrior general of the great king of Arabia. Plus, the man then noted with quiet pride, he could read and write and reckon numbers.

Yes, Nat was impressed, and by the subtle expression in his face clearly let Hark — Hark Moore now — know it.

As Nat and Hark settled onto the seatboard of the wagon, Nat noticed several men walking in the roadway toward the storehouse. Though restless to be starting for home, away from this sometimes unfriendly place, he waited for them. All of the faces were friendly, including the one he had not seen before.

The familiar faces belonged to Thomas Haithcock, Will Artist and Nathaniel's Will, an often angry young man occasionally too outspoken for his own good.

As for the other face, a face with distinctly Indian features ... "William Bozeman," the rather shabbily dressed but proudly mannered older man said, offering his hand up to Nat. "As I was telling your friends here, I must be heading home — But they insisted that we meet."

Nat accepted the offer and shook hands with the man, firmly enough to underscore the sincerity and meaning of his reply: "This is a real pleasure ... I have heard o' you, Mistuh Bozeman."

"And I have heard of you — although, I must confess, I do not know how much of it to believe!"

Nat shared the Indian's smile. Haithcock, Artist and Will Francis grinned. And Hark observed.

"Suh," Nat said, "that was a good thing you did for your people."

"Well, if it means the Nottoways will be around for a few more generations, on our own land, then it will be a good thing. In the meantime, we'll just try to keep surviving, like most other people."

For some reason (if any reason was really needed), Bozeman's simple statement was enough to trigger Will's temper: "White man treat the Nottoway jus' like he be treatin' the black man — like dirt! Make you sell off your bes' lan', leavin' you with po' lan' — Rich white people got all the good lan'! — You an' all the other Indians shoulda wiped out the white devils when you had the chance!"

Bozeman briefly hesitated to respond. The man was uncomfortable, obviously — yet so poised.

"Well," the Nottoway said with great care, "the times the other tribes made the attempt, they failed — and my people had enough good sense not to join them. It does help to be more numerous and better armed than your enemy. War," Bozeman began, but quickly stopped himself and hastily retreated. "Personally," he said, seeking higher, safer ground, "I think it best to consider the white man not as an

Bill Bryant

enemy, but as a reluctant partner — For example, I do not doubt that your people will be emancipated, someday, and then ... "

"'Mancipation!" Will Francis growled, not caring who might hear him. "White man's fancy word, meanin' he ain' gonna be in no God-damn hurry 'bout it! I hates that word!"

In the awkward silence, Bozeman made his final move, again offering his hand to Nat, who again accepted it, more firmly than before. And with the briefest of farewells, the Nottoway walked away, toward home.

"'Mancipation," Will muttered. "Jus' a god-damn lie! Be a cold day in Hell — cold enough to freeze your ... "

"Speakin' o' the weather," Nat said, "it'll be rainin' cats an' dogs later on today, you jus' wait an' see."

Will thought about it. "Sorry 'bout my cussin', Preacher Nat."

"Ain' no big thing, Will — God does damn, every now an' then — An' a cold day in Hell is hard to imagine, for a fact ... An' as for freezin' your hands an' your feet, well ... "

The men, including Hark, laughed.

"Nat," said Haithcock, "you still comin' by my place tomorrow? The wife, she be needin' your prayers."

"I be there."

"An' don' forget," Artist reminded him, "my young'uns expectin' you to talk to 'em from the Bible again, soon."

"Soon," Nat promised him. "Gentlemen ... Massuh tol' me to get back home by nightfall, so we got to go ... Y'all take care o' yourselves!"

Amid cheerful goodbyes, Nat flicked the reins and started the wagon homeward.

*

Along the way, Nat turned to Hark, studying the man, who understandably had a lot on his mind right now.

"You don' say much," Nat observed.

"Don' have much to say."

"Those men back there ... What did you think o' 'em?"

Hark, staring ahead, shrugged. "Got no real opinion o' 'em ... 'cept maybe for one thing."

"What?"

Hark turned to Nat, and without even a subtle expression in his face declared: "I know who their leader is."

Yes, Nat was very impressed.

* * *

In April of '27, down in Murfreesboro, Southampton residents Howell Francis and Nancy Hill got married — much to the consternation of virtually everyone who heard about it.

The groom was 16.

The bride was 70.

News of their improbable union set many tongues to wagging, in delicate yet playful conversation as well as in bawdy speculation.

*Tomorrow Jerusalem: The Story of Nat Turner
and the Southampton Slave Insurrection*

* * *

Nathaniel Francis went for a visit to the town of Suffolk, in Nansemond County to the east, and unexpectedly returned with a new slave.

A Southampton-born mulatto named Nelson – better known as Red Nelson – had caught Nathaniel's attention in the marketplace and pleaded to be purchased, to be saved from the trip south, promising to be the best slave the young master had ever owned.

So Nathaniel bought him.

Red was more thankful than words could describe.

* * *

Then there was that incident involving the Negro preacher, who – in addition to claiming publicly to have experienced strange visions – had gone and done the hitherto unthinkable.

The claimed visions were a mystery at best, to the outsider. How else could one view such extraordinary assertions by such an ordinary man?

But what the man actually went and did was ... well, amazing!

In the Jail at JERUSALEM

I sought more than ever to obtain true holiness before the great Day of Judgement should appear, and then I began to receive the true knowledge of faith. And from the first steps of righteousness until the last was I made perfect. And the Holy Ghost was with me, and said: "Behold me as I stand in the heavens" – And I looked and saw the forms of men in different attitudes, and there were lights in the sky to which the children of darkness gave other names than what they really were – for they were the lights of the Savior's hands, stretched forth from east to west, even as they were extended on the cross on Calvary for the redemption of sinners ... And I wondered greatly at these miracles, and prayed to be informed of a certainty of the meaning thereof – And shortly afterwards, while laboring in the field, I discovered drops of blood on the corn, as though it were dew from Heaven. And I communicated it to many, both white and black, in the neighborhood ... And I then found on the leaves in the woods hieroglyphic characters, and numbers, with the forms of men in different attitudes, portrayed in blood and representing the figures I had seen before in the heavens ... And now the Holy Ghost had revealed itself to me, and made plain the miracles it had shown me – For as the blood of Christ had been shed on this earth, and had ascended to Heaven for the salvation of sinners, and was now returning to earth again in the form of dew – and as the leaves on the trees bore the impression of the figures I had seen in the heavens – it was plain to me that the Savior was about to lay down the yoke he had borne for the sins of men, and the great Day of Judgement was at hand.

Bill Bryant

!

>About this time, I told these things to a white man on whom it had a wonderful effect. And he ceased from his wickedness, and was attacked immediately with a cutaneous eruption, and blood oozed from the pores of his skin. And after praying and fasting nine days, he was healed – And the Spirit appeared to me again, and said: As the Savior had been baptized, so should we be also ...

Naturally, the notion that a local slave might be experiencing mystical (meaning unconfirmable) visions met with a wide range of reactions in the neighborhood, from skepticism to ridicule among the whites, from skepticism to respect among the blacks. (Nat showed some of the leaves to Sally, who of course could make no sense of their peculiarities, no sense whatsoever, and therefore could only smile indulgently, profess her sincere interest, really, but confess her utter ignorance of such things, unfortunately.)

Somewhat more credible, but no less odd, was Nat's story about the truly awful afflictions and seemingly miraculous healing of the white man.

The man had a name – Etheldred T. Brantley, a fellow from down in Northampton working as an overseer up in Southampton.

Respectable in the eyes of some, to others Brantley had become a mean drunkard and a harsh overseer. That any self-respecting slave would even consider befriending such a "wicked" man made their relationship most unusual from its beginning.

Yet it was a golden opportunity for Nat the Preacher, who, once the relationship began with a chance encounter and a simple accepted offer of human kindness, determined to go as far with it as he could.

As for the overseer's reported afflictions: A doctor, asked for an explanation of the hearsay healing claim, said he could understand the "cutaneous eruption" – the bad rash – but that the alleged oozing of blood from the pores of Brantley's skin did not correspond to anything within his knowledge of medicine.

But Brantley was, in fact, cured – of whatever it was that ailed him.

And he did, in fact, cease from his wickedness.

*

The story might have ended there.
But it didn't.
Then came the hitherto unthinkable.
Incredibly to many – even to some who approved of the idea – Nat Turner and Etheldred Brantley now openly requested permission to be baptized together, in and by the church: Turner's Meeting House, now pastored by the Reverend Richard Whitehead. The elders at their next meeting would have to make a decision without local precedent.

To be baptized together, in and by the church! Or not!

*Tomorrow Jerusalem: The Story of Nat Turner
and the Southampton Slave Insurrection*

Well, the very thought of such a thing bred a spirited discussion (and sometimes angry debate) which continued for several weeks, not only within the congregation of Turner's Meeting House, but also, of course, among many other people in Southampton. Word traveled a little faster than usual this time.

Amid this struggle of conscience, Nat and Etheldred kept themselves busy with their daily chores, and waited.

Nat could imagine the discomfort of the white folks. He did not imagine the pleasure of the black folks. He could see it.

CROSS KEYS

Thomas Moore had no problem with the proposed baptism, but tried not to become involved in the controversy.

On the other hand, Sally expressed her opinion quite often and publicly.

Indeed, she became Nat's advocate.

Yet however righteous the cause, her position was not comfortable, especially during an unpleasant exchange in front of the general store at Cross Keys.

As she boosted young Putnam up onto the carriage seat, a man in a small group of men nearby barked at her his own opinion in the matter: "Tell 'em no! - Y'all been talkin' 'bout it for weeks now, an' that's long enough! Be done with it! Tell 'em no!!"

Poised to board the carriage, Sally tried to ignore him.

But the man kept barking: "Y'all are jus' encouragin' the niggers! You hear me? - Your brother Nathaniel is chairman o' the elders, an' you can tell him for us we're expectin' ... "

"My brother," Sally snapped, digging in her heels and turning to confront the man, "needs no advice from you! He will make up his own mind, in his own time! An' the Bible says ... "

"The Bible, madam, can be interpreted in many ways," the man growled, "which is why we have preachers - ordained preachers, not nigger exhorters - an' why we have boards o' elders, to decide the right ways! The niggers ... "

"The Negroes," Sally proclaimed, "are human beings, too! - They have got as much right to get into Heaven as we do!"

"Well, in my church, the closest they'll ever get is 'nigger heaven' - up in the balcony!"

"You ... "

"An' I mus' say, madam, you're not helpin' your own chances o' gettin' into Heaven by takin' up your nigger's cause!"

"But if you knew Nat ... Oh, move over, Putnam," she said to the wide-eyed little witness to this scene. "You cannot argue with ignorance!"

* * *

The elders made their decision, and promptly communicated it to the slave and the overseer - and, along the grapevine, to everyone else interested in the issue.

Bill Bryant

There would be no baptism of Nat Turner and Etheldred Brantley in and by the church, Nathaniel simply explained, because the elders just couldn't see how anything good could come of it.
End of discussion. End of argument.

*

And the story might have ended there.
But it didn't.

In the Jail at JERUSALEM

And when the white people would not let us be baptized by the church, we went down into the water together, in the sight of many who reviled us, and were baptized by the Spirit ...

PERSON'S MILL POND

However great the mystery surrounding the origins of the incident, there could be no questioning what happened next, in the waist-high water near the shoreline of the mill pond near the old Meherrin Baptist mission.
There were witnesses – well more than 100 of 'em, at least, maybe as many as 200. No one counted.
Some of the planters (including Nathaniel) would not let their people go to the gathering. But many other blacks came, among them Cherry and Redic, and Nancy. Hark, too.
Sally Moore came, and so did many other whites – mostly men, mostly there to mock and jeer and damn to Hell the two men at the center of the uniquely peculiar spectacle.
No one saw the dove which Nat predicted would come and sit on his shoulder, as the Spirit like a dove had descended upon Jesus following his baptism by John in the waters of the Jordan.
However:
Everyone saw the black man and the white man wade into the water, together.
Everyone heard Nat's brief prayer invoking the blessing of the Spirit.
Everyone watched Etheldred baptize Nat by full immersion. Extraordinary!
Everyone watched Nat baptize Etheldred by full immersion. Unthinkable!
Done!!
It was as simple as that ... And the crowd – the congregation – soon began dispersing, in every direction.

*

The witnesses testified, wherever they went.

*Tomorrow Jerusalem: The Story of Nat Turner
and the Southampton Slave Insurrection*

And within a few days, almost everyone in Southampton knew about it.
Of course.

In the Jail at JERUSALEM

After this, I rejoiced greatly, and gave thanks to God ...

When he was a boy becoming a man and the elders of Turner's Meeting House rejected his request to become a member of the church, Nat had not fully understood what he was asking of the white men or why they said no, and was therefore bitterly disappointed.
Good Christians they might be, but not good enough, he reasoned at the time.
This time was different.
This time, he fully understood what he was requesting – challenging – daring the white men to do. He expected them to say no, and was not disappointed.
Yes or no, he could not lose.
He had questioned – challenged – defied the way things were, and succeeded in creating a public discussion and debate. He had made the white people think.
He had sown new seeds of doubt among the white folks, and new seeds of hope among his own people.

*

Thus did the name if not the person of Nat Turner become more widely known.
The details were sketchy.
But the fact remained: That black man, that slave, that preacher, that exhorter, that Negro, that nigra, that nigger had actually baptized a white man – in the sight of many.

* * *

Increasingly, Nat prayed and fasted.
Increasingly, he turned to the words of the Prophets.
Increasingly, he felt the passion.

Bill Bryant

The Revelation

Bill Bryant

Tomorrow Jerusalem: The Story of Nat Turner and the Southampton Slave Insurrection

November 2nd, 1831
At the Jail in JERUSALEM

Bright an' early, at the crack o' dawn, Thomas Gray again made his way through the murmuring crowd, toward the apprehensive guards.

Both the crowd and the guards seemed more numerous and tense this early morning than late last night.

Gray had spent a restless and disturbing night with little sleep – made more difficult by the occasional excited voices elsewhere within the inn and out in the town – and had forced himself out of bed only to answer the call of nature, and of duty. Having visited the privy, he returned to the inn for a light breakfast, then headed straight for the jail.

The day was just beginning, and already he was bone-tired – yet oddly eager for the coming exercise.

Special deputy Collin Kitchen unlocked the door, and led the lawyer into the jail.

Much of the night, Gray's mind had been relentlessly searching through misty memories of the times, prior to August, when he and Nat had chanced to meet, and talk. But no matter how hard he tried – and he had been trying very hard indeed since August – he simply could not remember many of the details of those casual encounters and conversations.

Failing to remember merely reminded him of the distractions, the pain, he had been suffering in recent years, which added to his current torment.

*

Much of the night, between brief lapses into uncomfortable sleep, Nat had been remembering everything. What else was there to do?

Now, sitting on the floor with his back to the wall, he waited for Gray.

The constant presence of at least one guard prevented the special prisoner in the rear upstairs cell from speaking freely, even in whispers, with the prisoner in the adjoining cell – Thomas Haithcock, that good and faithful friend. The answers to so many questions were only a few feet away ... yet out of reach.

The cell door opened, and closed.

"Good mornin'," Gray said, settling onto the stool.

"Good mornin'," Nat replied, stretching his legs, his chains tapping against his chamberpot, near the tray with the remains of his simple but satisfying breakfast. The whites were feeding him well enough, certainly better than he had been feeding himself during most of the past 10 weeks. And if he hadn't been getting a lot of sleep since his capture, soon there would be plenty of time for sleeping. Soon, he would be at perfect peace.

For a moment, the two men just stared at one another, without expression, in clear communication of their shared fatigue, and their shared resolve.

Gray, alone again with the contriver of the great insurrection, thought again of the suddenness of that bloody rage, the way it had struck without warning. Or were there warnings, unwisely, foolishly, fatally ignored? – what of the slave Nelson's peculiar "prophecy" to

Bill Bryant

his overseer? Or the persistent brotherly advice at which Sally Travis had persistently scoffed? Or Nat's strange behavior on occasion?

Why could no one — except Nat and then his few confederates — see what was coming?

* * * * *

**Late Winter 1828
Near CROSS KEYS**

The unannounced icestorm, with its spectacular beauty and constant cracking sounds and shattered fallen tree limbs, and then the smothering snowstorm, with its gentle embrace, had frozen life throughout Southampton for fully a week.

Finally, after several days of thawing and drying, the roads became passable again.

Not feeling well, not well at all, Thomas Moore insisted on riding the wagon over to Cross Keys, to fetch supplies, and Sally insisted that Nat accompany him. She understood her husband's need to get out of the house, to escape the confinement of recent days, and she knew how stubborn he could be, so she did not protest too strongly. But Nat would go along!

Nat amiably agreed, but in a sense dreaded the trip. He, alone, had privately welcomed the storms and the paralysis they caused. When people couldn't move about, neither could the latest gossip — and Nat knew it was only a matter of time until Thomas heard about his slave's odd encounter with a white man in Jerusalem a couple of weeks ago; unless, he hoped, the shock and duration of the storms had made people forget that truly trivial incident.

The ride over to Cross Keys was uneventful and quiet, though the master, when he did speak, displayed an impatience and grouchiness not normal for the man. Nat tried to be patient and cheerful, but the testing became harder as the wagon neared Cross Keys and the master became more talkative, and the talk turned to slavery.

Now, Thomas Moore was in fact a good master, with many doubts about slavery, and much sympathy for the slaves. But on this day he was in no mood to deny either the practical benefits of slavery or the impracticalities of emancipation.

And Nat was in no mood to let the master's words go unopposed. Their lively "discussion" ended in front of the general store at Cross Keys, when Nat declared: "The slaves ought to be free, an' someday will be!"

Which created a problem.

The problem wasn't with Moore, who had heard such words before, at home.

The problem was with the small crowd of rowdy young white men who overheard the slave's defiant remark — during an apparent argument with a white man — and immediately began expressing their displeasure.

To defuse the situation, Moore loudly promised the nigger a good flogging as soon as they got home, then turned the wagon around, and got away from there.

The ride home was one long, angry lecture from the master.

Nat endured it, burning inside but determined not to make matters worse.

*Tomorrow Jerusalem: The Story of Nat Turner
and the Southampton Slave Insurrection*

Thomas was right about one thing: Nat was going to get himself into a heap o' trouble one o' these days if he didn't learn to keep his opinions to himself!

As soon as they got home, the master went to bed.

Early Spring 1828
TURNER'S MEETING HOUSE

Thomas Moore God bless him was dead and in his grave and may he rest in peace forever but life must go on, Sally was attempting to reason with Salathiel outside the church some time after the service inside had ended on this wonderfully warm day.

In addition to which she breathlessly continued after the briefest of pauses Putnam had strayed off somewhere, God knows where, and it was time for her to begin collecting her people for the ride home, really, and besides ...

"My point exactly!" Salathiel declared, at the first opportunity. "Now that Thomas is dead, God rest his soul, I'm tellin' you, Sally, you must be more careful!"

Salathiel, who worked his small farm and shared his tiny house with one ever obedient slave (Nathaniel's Red Nelson), could variously be described as wild and reckless, or as powerful and brave and resolute, depending on the need and impulse of the moment. Sally had to listen to him. He was, albeit younger and less mature, her brother.

"Dear brother, what more can I say on the subject? I think you are too distrusting o' other people - You were like that as a boy, too - But now, for you to call Nat a 'person o' bad character' - Really!" she laughed.

"Dear sister, I am merely sayin' I wish you would be more cautious in your dealin's with him. You been knowin' Nat even longer than me, an' I do recall you yourself sayin', more than once, he had a streak o' mischief in him when he was a boy - An' as the twig ... "

"Oh, Nat might've gone along with the other nigra boys, but he was always jus' their 'thinker' - not one o' the ones doin' the real mischief. Why, I doubt if he has ever stolen anything in his whole life - or, for that matter, done anything else to be much ashamed of. Good Lord, Salathiel, the man is positively notorious for his good habits!"

"He ... "

"You're right, I've known him longer - an' I understand him better - than you. When we were children ..."

"That was then. This is now! You're an intelligent woman, Sally, an educated woman - Open your eyes! This 'friend' is goin' aroun' tellin' people he has seen 'mystical figures' in the sky, an' 'bout how he has found 'drops o' the Savior's blood' on the corn, an' tree leaves with 'hieroglyphics' on 'em, an' - I swear, I cannot for the life o' me make any sense out o' what he's sayin', when he gets to talkin' like that!"

"Well, it doesn't make much sense to me, either, sometimes - But it's not a crime to believe in miracles. An' besides, I take it as a compliment that Nat feels he can share these 'revelations' with me - An' you should take it as a compliment, too! Does it ever occur to you that maybe he's jus' tryin' to continue bein' your friend?"

Bill Bryant

"I doubt it," Salathiel scowled. "More like he's throwin' his 'revelations' in my face! - If you ask me, there's no difference 'tween Nat an' some conjurin' man, no difference whatsoever!"

"Oh, there's a world o' difference!" she laughed, to hide her impatience with her brother's ignorance.

"An' there was that business with Etheldred Brantley! The man's had to go back to North Carolina 'cause o' people shunnin' him since that 'baptism'!"

"Jonathan Lankford would have baptized them."

"If he still had a church - None o' his people followed him out o' the Black Creek Meeting House - nary a one!"

"He was a good man."

"That's not what the elders said - They said he had 'yielded too much to the delusions o' Satan an' thereby lost sight o' the duties o' the gospel'!"

"You always had a good memory, too, when it suited your purpose - Nat means well, he really an' truly does."

"An' when it suits your purpose, you can be mighty forgetful - How 'bout the time Nat ran away?"

"He came back! - An' we were glad to have him back ... He seemed the better for it, too."

"You are impossible!"

"You are uncompromisin'!"

"An' how 'bout what happened at Cross Keys, when he told Thomas - in front o' other white men - the slaves ought to be free an' someday would be?"

"Nat is hardly alone in that opinion!"

"Can' stop him from thinkin' whatever he wants to think, but he had no right sayin' that to his master's face with other men listenin', an' watchin' - He put Thomas in a tight spot that day!"

"I confess, there are times when I wish Nat was not so ... outspoken."

"I suppose you heard 'bout what happened in Jerusalem a few weeks before Thomas died?"

"No," Sally said, feeling a twinge of worry, wondering what Nat had decided not to share with her. "What happened?"

"Nat back-talked a white man!" Salathiel declared, sensing, finally, an advantage in this otherwise hopeless argument.

"What did Nat say? - An' what did the white man say to provoke him?"

"The man merely remarked that Nat surely was lucky to have such a good master, an' Nat jus' grinned at the man an' said: 'Have we any other master but Jesus Christ alone?' - An' then Nat turned his back on the man an' walked away - jus' walked away - Mighty peculiar behavior!"

"Doesn't sound like a back-talker to me - Sounds like a Methodist!"

"It was the way he said it - an' the way he turned his back on a white man, an' jus' walked away!"

"Salathiel ... I really must be goin' - I do sincerely appreciate your concern for my welfare, especially now that Thomas is gone. I know that you insist on aggravatin' me on this subject because you love me - An' I love you - But I think I know Nat a lot better than anybody else knows him, except maybe Cherry. I grant you, Nat is unusual ..."

"He's strange! ... You need to be cautious - please!"

"But what am I supposed to be cautious about? Nat does his work, he's honest, he's sober, he's wonderful with Putnam and the other

68

neighborhood children — An' he has made a good family with Cherry. Marriage does settle a man down, dear bachelor brother of mine!
"Well ..."
"An' for your information," she had to say, seeing him retreat an inch, "Nat has told me, on more than one occasion, that he does not believe in conjurin', or any o' those African superstitions — He places his faith entirely in the same good book we do — An' that tells me all I really need to know about him!"
"Sis ... He's a born trouble-maker — Nathaniel and I both think he might even become, well, dangerous."
"Salathiel!" she laughed, her loyalties really tested now, forced to confront his true point of view. "To hear you talk, I swear, one would think my very life is at some risk! — That is pure nonsense!"
"What I'm tryin' to say ..."
"I do not want to hear ..."
"Damnation, Sally!" he said in acute frustration, with her, with himself, not knowing how to make any real progress with these admittedly vague apprehensions. "You would not survive a day down in Santo Domingo!"
"This is not Santo Domingo!" she said, then, softening her tone to calm both of them: "This is Southampton County. Our people know an' trust one another. Our lives are all woven together. We depend on one another, all the time."
"Sis ..."
"When was the last time a black person killed a white person in Southampton? It jus' does not happen here!"
"Tell that to the two slave traders who got killed!" he felt compelled to note even as he tried to control his temper.
"They were traders," Sally said with contempt, "an' the men who killed 'em were properly punished," she reminded him, "an' besides, that was a very long time ago, before your time."
"Sally ..."
"Salathiel, I do not intend to spend the rest o' this beautiful day arguin' with you ... If you cannot trust Nat, trust me. I know Nat. He is as harmless as they come — outspoken, yes, perhaps too much so for his own good, sometimes — unusual, yes, perhaps even peculiar — but harmless ... He is family!"
And with that, she smiled, turned her back on him, an' jus' walked away.

PREACHING PLACE

Only a few of the people remained, including a shy young woman and a spry old man, both unknown to him, both now approaching him.
Today, he had preached and prayed with the folks regarding forgiveness, but it had been hard for him to concentrate his thoughts and feelings in that direction, and he wondered not if but how much he had disappointed their expectations. The years of trying to strengthen their fragile hopes for the future generally, and specifically to build up their faith in him, had done little if anything to improve their daily lives, and he knew it, and they knew it, too, yet continued to believe in his special purpose.
"Preacher Nat," the girl said, her voice a notch above a whisper, "can I jus' hol' your Bible a spell? I can' read or nothin', but I never even done touched the holy book."

Bill Bryant

Nat handed his Bible to her, envying the bliss on her face, the awe and joy in her eyes, the rapture, pure and simple and beautiful to behold.

"Moses," the old man said to him. "My name be Moses, Preacher Nat. I be livin' over in Nansemond County. Been hearin' 'bout you. Walked a mighty long way jus' to see for myself."

"To see what for yourself?"

"To see if you's the prophet they says you is - the real Moses, the one gonna lead our people out o' Pharoah's lan'!"

In the Jail at JERUSALEM

And on the 12th of May 1828, I heard a loud noise in the heavens, and the Spirit instantly appeared to me and said the Serpent was loosened, and Christ had laid down the yoke he had borne for the sins of men, and I should take it on and fight against the Serpent ... for the time was fast approaching when the first should be last and the last should be first ... and, by signs in the heavens, that it would make known to me when I should commence the great work - and until the sign appeared, I should conceal it from the knowledge of men ...

May 12th, 1828
GILES REESE Place

"You as crazy as your mama was the day you was born!" Cherry nearly shouted as she bolted from her chair at the table across which Nat was holding hands with her when he made the announcement.

But his hand still held hers. "Keep your voice down. You'll wake Redic - Jus' sit down, please," he calmly asked. And she did, slowly, though her face lost none of its anguish. He knew she would be alarmed, and opposed, at first, Spirit or no Spirit. But he had to tell her. She did deserve to know. And he did need someone, other than the Spirit, to share with him this awful burden. "My mama had good cause to do what she did that day ... She wasn't crazy."

"Your mama a fine woman. I don' mean her no disrespect, you knows that."

"I know," Nat said gently. Cherry herself had become a fine woman. He knew she still admired and loved him as she did when she was younger, but could understand how her fierce loyalty had been tempered by the years of being married to such an uncommon - and, yes, sometimes admittedly difficult - man, who surely loved her but surely loved Him more. So he expected her to challenge him, and he welcomed the challenge, he needed it. Because if he could not convince her, of all people ...

"Nat, you been talkin' 'bout your 'special purpose' for as long as I can remember - But you been talkin' 'bout startin' a great revival, or gettin' the white folks to help you open a school for our people - But this ... Oh, Nat!"

"Cherry ... "

"Lately, you been prayin' more, fastin' more, spendin' less an' less time with me an' Redic - An' Lord knows we don' get enough time

Tomorrow Jerusalem: The Story of Nat Turner and the Southampton Slave Insurrection

together as it is — not to mention all the time you spends preachin' an' visitin' from one end o' the county to the other — An' now ... this!"

She had just been told that he had been picked, by God, to lead an uprisin' o' the slaves, yet here she was, worryin' an' complainin' 'bout how little time they spend together! But she must understand, she must be made to understand. One step at a time. "I got to be alone a lot, to think, to pray, to let the Spirit speak to me — An' I got to go out an' about, to spread the good word to our people, to help 'em in their miseries, to give 'em some hope, to prepare 'em."

"Prepare 'em for what, Nat? — To get 'em killed?!"

"Keep your voice down! ... Someone might hear you."

She paused, to compose herself, but did not stop. "But why, Nat? — An' I don' wanna hear 'bout how the Spirit is tellin' you to do this — I wants to know why you think it has to be this way — 'cause I knows you, Nat Turner. I knows you got your own reasons for thinkin' the Spirit must be right."

"Cherry ... There's a limit to what I can do, bein' a slave. You know that. White folks're not gonna listen to any slave preachin' a message that tells 'em to free their slaves. White folks're not gonna help me open a school ... I jus' been dreamin', thinkin' it was possible."

"But they be such nice dreams."

"Yes ... Yes, they were."

"Nat, if you needs your freedom so badly, ask Miss Sally to set a price — You a smart man, with lots o' free time to hire yourself out. You could buy your freedom."

"I don' belong to Sally," Nat bitterly reminded her. "I belong to Putnam. I am the property of a nine-year-old boy! ... 'Sides, with Thomas in his grave Sally is dependin' on me more an' more. Now's not the time to be askin' her."

"You could run away ... I won' blame you none."

At this moment, when she was willing to snuff out the flame of her own candle to light his, he loved her more than ever — which was probably the real reason why, why it had to be this way. "The way things are, I am gonna be a slave 'til the day I die. Ain' nobody gonna give me my freedom — an' your freedom, an' Redic's. An' it ain' likely I could ever earn enough money to buy my freedom, an' yours, an' Redic's ... An' I can' jus' run away, 'cause here is where I am meant to be ... 'cause I loves you," he explained, as simply as he could.

"An' I loves you. But you still ain' answer my question ... why?"

"Cherry ... It ain' jus' me an' you an' Redic — It's all o' our people — It's our problem, an' our only solution is to rise up, an' fight for our freedom! ... An' the Spirit will be with us — Trust me."

"I trusts you, but ... I's scared."

"I don' blame you ... I's scared, too," he softly confessed — then firmly added: "But I shall do what the Spirit says. What else can I do? ... I am meant to do some great work. What other great work is available?"

She could not answer his questions. And so she yielded to this frightening new fact of life, and to his comforting embrace.

Bill Bryant

PREACHING PLACE

On his way home as the Sun began to rise, Nat paused to sit on the fallen tree trunk where he often sat, alone or among his people.

He opened his Bible to the Book of Ezekiel – Chapter 9 ... Verse 4.

He could easily have recited the words from memory, but chose instead to go to their source.

And in the dawning light, he read ... "Go through the midst of the city, through the midst of Jerusalem, and set a mark upon the foreheads of men that sigh and that cry for all the abominations that be done in the midst thereof. Go ye after him through the city, and smite. Let not your eye spare, neither have ye pity: Slay utterly old and young, both maids and little children and women. But come not near any man upon whom is the mark. And begin at my sanctuary. Defile the house, and fill the courts with the slain: Go ye forth ... And they went forth ... and slew in the city."

He slowly closed his Bible, put it in his coat pocket, stood up, stretched, and continued on his way home, in no hurry.

Perhaps – probably – he had always known it would come to this. Indeed: What other great work was available, to a man in his unique situation?!

*

The compulsion within him now had a very specific direction, his vision a very fine focus, his life a very great meaning.

Oddly, he thought, even as the prospect of insurrection did in fact scare him, it also excited, empowered and emboldened him – and brought to him a special peace of mind, free from the aimless urgency of the years of wondering and worrying, free from the shackles of ignorance.

Now, knowing for a certainty the will of the Spirit, he could devote himself not to vague speculations, but to specific plans for action. Now, even if he dared not even faintly hint at what was coming, everything he said and did among his people would be designed to help prepare their minds and souls for the inevitable day of action.

Still, it was one thing to know what to do, quite another thing to know how to do it. The task of planning would take some time (and surely the Spirit would give him enough time to form a good plan). He would have to be patient, of course – and much more careful not to provoke the white people, not to attract attention, though it would be difficult at times.

So: While waiting for the Spirit to give him a sign in the heavens (and surely it would be not only manifest but also convincing), he would proceed with the usual routines of his life and work and ministry.

One small voice within him persistently whispered that maybe, just maybe, the Spirit was preparing him for a mission he might never be required to perform. Maybe, just maybe, the white people in the near future would see the light and experience a miraculous change of heart and begin making meaningful progress toward general emancipation ... It was possible. Anything was possible – God willing!

But if God could work such a miracle among the whites, why would He need Nat Turner?

*Tomorrow Jerusalem: The Story of Nat Turner
and the Southampton Slave Insurrection*

October 5th, 1829
JOSEPH TRAVIS Place

It would be confusing for a little while, Sally explained to her overseer as they strolled down the lane toward the road on this exceptionally pleasant afternoon, escaping from the happy scene behind them – the noisy reception following the quiet wedding at Turner's Meeting House.

The former Sally Francis, once the widow Sally Moore, was now Sally Travis.

Legally, mind you, this place was still hers. But for all practical intents and purposes, this was now her husband Joseph's place, as head of the family.

Sally was radiant with happiness, and Nat was in good spirits, too. All around them, the exquisite beauty of autumn in Virginia was becoming ever more obvious – indescribably lovely already, the friends agreed.

"Joseph," she noted, "will be movin' all o' his tools an' equipment here, o' course, we hope by the first o' the year. An' you could not ask for a better master, Nat."

"Glad to hear you say it," he said, needing no confirmation of what he had seen and decided for himself. Joseph Travis was a hard-working but easy-going man, a good Christian, a natural friend. "What if Putnam tells me to do somethin', an' Mastuh Travis tells me to do somethin' else?"

"Listen to Joseph," she said with a smile.

"Glad to hear you say that, too," he laughed.

"An' you can learn carriage-makin'!" she joyfully added, in her enthusiasm for the new life awaiting all of them. "You should enjoy that immensely. An' Joseph agrees with me, that you should keep the name Nat Turner. Joseph says everybody already knows who Nat Turner is, but nobody would know Nat Travis!"

"I'm grateful to Mastuh Travis."

"Joseph."

"Joseph?"

"He says you may address him as Joseph – in private circumstances."

"O' course."

"He is such a good man, Nat, an' from such a good family – Why, the Travises were at Jamestown!"

"Jus' so long as he's good enough for you, Sally."

They reached the end of the lane. "I do adore this time o' year," she observed. "I think God gives us the autumn to make all the hard work worthwhile ... which is not very theological, I suppose, but it makes some sense to me."

"Me, too ... We bes' be gettin' back to the house – Folks'll be wonderin' if the bride done run away with the overseer!"

Their laughter was silent, and wholehearted.

* * *

Beginning in October of 1829, continuing through the dramatic winter months, a special convention met at the Capitol in Richmond, to create the new Constitution of the Commonwealth of Virginia.

Bill Bryant

Great expectations abounded, especially among the western Virginians who came to the Capitol loudly demanding a larger share of the political power in Virginia, righteously brandishing words like "liberty" and "equality" – fightin' words!

The convention raised expectations among the blacks of Virginia, too, particularly among the slaves, many of whom had a pretty good idea of what was happening in Richmond and hoped and prayed that in such a spirit of democracy the cause of emancipation might be significantly advanced.

The delegates represented the best of Virginia – prominent among them former President Monroe and former President Madison and Chief Justice Marshall, and the eccentric but brilliant John Randolph, the latter-day Patrick Henry – not to mention some of the finest citizens of Southampton County.

Such wise men!
Such important issues!
Such high hopes!

When the work was done, the western Virginians did possess a larger share of the political power, though not enough to satisfy them.

The convention did not advance the cause of emancipation one inch.

At the time, the white people did not realize how very hopeful the black people had been – or how very disappointed they were – or how very embittered many more of them became.

In the Jail at JERUSALEM

> And on the appearance of the sign, I should arise and prepare myself, and slay my enemies with their own weapons ...

The sign did not appear, but Nat made ready for it, patiently, carefully.

It wasn't easy.

His initial sweet peace of mind began to erode, into a stream of new wondering and worrying, more constant and more difficult than before. The pressure, instead of decreasing, increased.

To show the way to others, he himself must know the way.

To be the leader of a rising of the slaves, he must be more than the Preacher. He must also be the General.

He drew a crude map of Southampton County.
He started a list of names.
He hid the map and the list.

He endlessly reviewed all he knew which might be helpful, an optimist feeding hungrily on every trifle, and realized how little he knew about some things – how much he must try to learn.

Every problem he identified, and every opportunity, became a seedling in his mind, growing into branches and limbs and twigs and leaves, and the future became a forest of possibilities.

There were so many details to think about. And if any detail mattered at all, it mattered a lot.

Thus, his life proceeded.
It wasn't easy.

* * *

*Tomorrow Jerusalem: The Story of Nat Turner
and the Southampton Slave Insurrection*

Eleven-year-old Lucy Travis, of Brunswick County, had fun during her family's visit with her uncle Joseph in Southampton.

Lucy met her new aunt Sally (visibly with child) and her new cousin Putnam, whose slave Nat had a real knack for entertainin' young'uns.

Besides knowing how to tell a good story well, the craftsman who repaired tin buckets and old yard bells and helped with the carriage-making in Joseph's shop had a talent for taking strips of iron and scraps of wood and transforming them into playful objects - a simple cradle for a girl's doll, a harmless sword for a boy's imagination.

Back home in Brunswick, in a letter she wrote, she well remembered Nat, that humble and kind Negro, who enjoyed privileges almost equal to the whites.

* * *

Another visitor to the Travis place, one who came and went and eventually came and stayed, was young Maria Pope.

Maria rubbed Nat wrong in many ways.

Sally didn't like her, either.

Maria was superior to Nat and to the other servants, and she knew it, and her behavior always reflected it. She scorned the blacks. She enjoyed commanding them. Maria was no child. She was old enough and smart enough to know better, but didn't, and her ignorance was no excuse for her arrogance. She was asking to be hated. An' somebody, somewhere, was gonna take her down a peg, or two, someday.

Nat's feelings about the girl became deeply personal, so uncharitable as to be unworthy of his Christian better self.

To put it bluntly: If ever he did what the Spirit told him to do, Maria Pope would experience the wrath of Jehovah.

Her name, he vowed, would be at the top of the list of the utterly slain.

* * *

Early in 1830, a rumor of impending insurrection circulated among the slaves of Solomon Parker, and among other slaves in that neighborhood.

But nothing happened.

* * *

Eighteen-year-old Charlotte Elizabeth Musgrave, who had married Doctor Robert Musgrave in 1829, presented him with a baby boy in '30.

The doctor, with much effort, and much love, surprised and delighted the new mother with a fine pianoforte, made in England.

* * *

Bill Bryant

From the port of Norfolk, in '30, the merchant ships Montgomery and Valador set sail for Liberia, among their passengers 42 Southamptonians.

* * *

The rumor spread that certain whites – probably Quakers – had organized a way to help the slaves of the South escape to the North, and that the conspiracy was now active even in Southampton.

* * *

It was a fact, sketchily reported along the grapevine, that the free blacks of the North during the summer of '30 conducted a "Negro Convention" in Philadelphia, far away from the fields and forests and realities of Southampton.

And it was a fact, likewise sketchily reported, that a free black named David Walker in '30 published his thoughtful pamphlet "Walker's Appeal" in Boston, likewise far away.

The convention was brief and orderly, and soon forgotten by most of the people who heard of it.

The pamphlet was shocking. Its circulation was limited, naturally – but its reputation spread like a wildfire through the South.

Walker, while damning in no uncertain terms the "unjust, jealous, unmerciful, avaricious and bloodthirsty" whites of the world, sent a legion of insurrectionary messages to the slaves of the South – plus a conciliatory message to the whites of America.

To the slaves: "Never make an attempt to gain our freedom or national right, from under cruel oppressors and murderers, until you see your way clear ... God will give you a Hannibal ... If you commence, make sure work – do not trifle for they will not trifle with you ... One good black man can put to death six white men ... Fear not the number and education of our enemies ... This country is as much ours as it is the whites', whether they will admit it now or not, they will see and believe it by and by."

And to the whites: "Remember, Americans, that we must and shall be free and enlightened as you are. Will you wait until we shall, under God, obtain our liberty by the crushing arm of force? Will it not be dreadful for you? I speak, Americans, for your good ... Throw away your fears and prejudices, then, and enlighten us and treat us like men, and we will like you more than we do now hate you."

* * *

Joseph and Sally Travis became the proud parents of a baby boy – little Joe.

Nat Turner and Cherry Reese became the proud parents of a baby girl – Charlotte.

* * *

*Tomorrow Jerusalem: The Story of Nat Turner
and the Southampton Slave Insurrection*

The Caribbean continued to seethe.
And the news, borne by the grapevine and by refugees, continued to flow upward through coastal North Carolina to Southampton, and was rarely encouraging, to the ears of the white people, who tried not to think about it too much.

* * *

In the autumn of '30, the old Jerusalem Jockey Club was re-established, with William Goodwyn as president and Alexander Peete as secretary.
The first races would be run on the 9th of November, not far from town, the prizes ranging from $100 to $500 — with substantial personal wagering, of course.
Beginning in May of '31, the horses of Southampton would be running over at Lawrenceville in Brunswick County, and then in Norfolk.
The club's rebirth greatly displeased some people, who strongly objected to the gamblin' an' the drinkin' an' the cursin', an' whatever other evils could be even loosely connected to the sportin' life.

* * *

Nathaniel Francis, a fervent Democrat and supporter of Andy Jackson, in 1830 could and therefore did on occasion boast that he and his people — including 15 slaves of all ages and a family of six free blacks living on his property — were now farming 300 acres, at a profit.
On the 11th of October, 25-year-old Nathaniel exchanged wedding vows with 17-year-old Lavinia Diana Matilda Rollins Hart. (Noteworthy to people who noted such things: The bride, a Northampton County girl, happened to be a granddaughter of Etheldred Brantley Sr., whose son Etheldred Brantley Jr. had worked for some time in Southampton, as an overseer — You remember him, the one who got involved with that Negro preacher ... The baptism ... You remember!)
At year's end, Lavinia was with child.

* * *

Also, in 1830:
In France, the people, in another revolution, ousted the elitist King Louis Philippe and replaced him with the populist King Charles. Americans applauded.
In Poland, the people continued to rebel against the hated occupying Russians. Americans raised funds for Polish relief.
In the United States, the people elected General Andrew Jackson to become the new President. The Democrats cheered. The Whigs were outraged.

Bill Bryant

* * *

At the Capitol in Richmond, Doctor John Floyd — a brigadier general of the state militia, a veteran of the Virginia House of Delegates and the United States House of Representatives — recited the oath of office and became Governor of the Commonwealth.

Floyd was determined, indeed resolved, to do whatever he could do during his administration to promote the idea of general emancipation, to rid Virginia of its economically harmful reliance on slave labor.

The time for more aggressive action, he believed, had come.

* * *

Still, the sign did not appear.
Which gave Nat plenty o' time to think about it, an' pray.
Among all of the details and problems and doubts which assailed him daily, one in particular nagged at him with unsettling uncertainty.
There could and should and must be no doubt that he and the other fighters for freedom would have blood on their hands when the fighting was done. All of 'em.
But could he himself kill?
When the time came, would he kill?
There couldn't, shouldn't, mustn't be any doubt in his mind.
Yet there was, an' it nagged at him fiercely.

In the Jail at JERUSALEM

And immediately on the sign appearing in the heavens, the seal was removed from my lips, and I communicated the great work laid out for me to do, to four in whom I had the greatest confidence ...

February 12th, 1831
SOUTHAMPTON COUNTY

He knew it was coming.
But still!
He had learned about it in the Richmond newspaper Thomas Gray had kindly given him in January, in Jerusalem — and had quickly confirmed it in the almanac he had purchased for Joseph.
There, on the second page of the newspaper, was the crude illustration and the announcement of the lecture to be delivered at the Capitol.
And there, on the second page of the almanac, was another simple drawing — and a detailed explanation of what would soon be happening.
He fully expected it.
But still!
The Sign!
On this clear cool day, the Moon did pass between the Earth and the Sun — beginning at 10:50 a.m.
The instant he detected a distinct difference in the light surrounding him and looked up in the sky and saw — briefly in the

Tomorrow Jerusalem: The Story of Nat Turner and the Southampton Slave Insurrection

blinding glare – the first proof of it, Nat slowly knelt in the middle of the roadway, awestruck by the impending glory of it.

Devoting little time to silent prayer, he rose to his feet, and continued on his way.

He was wasting no time. He had places to go, people to see.

The Sign!

As the eclipse of the Sun increased, throughout Southampton the chickens went to roost, cows started mooing for their food, pigs squealed, the air became cooler.

She, too, knew it was coming. Nat had told her.

But still!

When, finally, her curiosity overcame her fear and she left her darkening cabin and looked up and saw it well in progress, Cherry staggered against a nearby tree, groaned in great pain, and began crying, uncontrollably.

No one saw her, to ask her why.

The Sign!

The phenomenon peaked at 12:25, in peculiar cold twilight – a perfect circle of flames dancing around the pitch-black Moon – a so-called annular eclipse, the most complete ... visible in its totality only along a path passing directly over Southampton County, Virginia.

It ended at 1:53.

Many people, especially the better educated, had known it was coming.

But still!

No artwork in a newspaper or almanac could have prepared anyone for the sheer visual drama and emotional impact of it, the overwhelming majesty of the phenomenon, the awe-inspiring heavenly power of it. Only the blind were not impressed – and, yes, they heard all about it.

If it was difficult for the people only partly prepared to try to comprehend the scientifically predicted and described phenomenon, you can just imagine the bewildered reactions of the many other people – especially the ignorant, the superstitious, the fanatically religious, the easily spooked – to whom the eclipse was a complete surprise, the rudest of shocks. You would've thought the world was comin' to an end!

*

In January, during that long cold wagon ride from Jerusalem back to the homeplace, Nat had grappled with a perplexing question: Because this celestial display would be natural, explainable and widely known in advance, would it be any less the "sign in the heavens" promised to him by the Spirit?

By the time the wagon had come to a stop in the farmyard, he had arrived at the probable answer: Of course, God could send the whole world a sign whose message only he would immediately understand ... Of course!

On this 12th of February, he was spectacularly convinced.

Therefore ...

PREACHING PLACE

Ready to begin, Nat sat on the fallen tree trunk.

Bill Bryant

In the chill of the late afternoon, four other slaves settled onto the ground in front of him, wondering what this most unusual meeting was all about. Nat had chosen:

Hark, of course — Hercules — a big, powerful man beyond comparison even with most other big, powerful men. Hark was smart and decisive, in a quiet, self-confident way. More loyal than the best of friends, a true believer in Nat, Hark would be the second in command.

Sam, the property of Nathaniel Francis — a bosom companion of Nat since boyhood. Sam was a steady-handed, level-headed man, with a sharp eye for details. He was influential among the blacks at and near the Francis place, a born leader.

Henry, the property of Richard Porter — a hard-working man, always eager to please, able to keep a promise, and a secret. Henry, too, was well regarded in the area where he lived. He was a stubborn man, next to Hark perhaps the most loyal to Nat.

Nelson, the property of Jacob Williams — a sly and clever fellow. Nelson seemed capable of great daring and bravery. But he was a voodoo man and something of a braggart. The former did not overly concern Nat, but the latter did. Nat was mindful, for example, that Nelson's sister was the wife of old Jeff the faithful overseer at the Peter Edwards place — and old Jeff was one of the people Nat least wanted to hear a whisper of what was coming.

As different as each man was from the others, all, in Nat's judgement, shared one vital quality: They would approach this task as seriously as he, and would see it through to the end ... come it rough or smooth.

*

He began by telling them what they already knew — how, since childhood, he had been clearly marked for some great purpose in his life, how he had spent many years struggling to understand what his purpose might be, how he had prayed constantly for guidance and enlightenment.

Then came the hard part of the explanation, as simple as it now was.

He told them he had known his purpose for several years, in fact, but had been waiting for a sign in the heavens telling him to share the knowledge.

The eclipse, he said, was the sign.

Then he began to describe the revelation he had experienced on the 12th of May in 1828, how the Spirit had appeared to him, and ... and by the time he got near to the point of this meeting, they already knew.

"We're risin'," whispered Hark, who had suspected this for quite some time.

"Santo Domingo!" Nelson declared.

In the Jail at JERUSALEM

It was intended by us to have begun the work of death on the 4th of July last ...

*Tomorrow Jerusalem: The Story of Nat Turner
and the Southampton Slave Insurrection*

Pickin' the day was easy.

The worst slave-tradin' day o' the year ('specially over at Cross Keys) — the day massuh was mos' likely to sell you an' put you in his pocket — seemed to Nat, an' to the others, to be the mos' fittin' time, to add a whole new meanin' to the white folks' Independence Day.

Makin' a plan was not easy.

That first meeting at the Preaching Place was devoted more to mutual encouragement than to the details of the insurrection. And subsequent occasional meetings at Cabin Pond, and other secluded locations, gradually revealed to the new conspirators the exquisitely elaborate difficulties with which Nat had been privately struggling, every day, for years.

A few decisions, like the date, required little discussion. The most important decision, Nat dictated: This must be our secret! — Gabriel Prosser and Denmark Vesey failed only because they were betrayed, because their plans involved too many people for too long. Their way led to disaster! — Therefore, though it made the task harder in many details, no one else must know. No one!

Such a task — to create, almost from scratch, an army able to fight its first great battle on its first day, able to sustain itself through a long war, able to win that war.

So many details!

From bulldogs to the prospect of victory, the problems confounded the plotters.

The two mean ol' bulldogs belonged to Giles Reese, and would surely challenge any strangers, especially at night.

The prospect of victory — the very idea of establishing a black republic in the South, a stronghold the whites must respect, a nation with law and order and justice and prosperity — hovered over every discussion like an angel of hope, yet received little of their attention. It was almost beyond imagination, amid the immediacy of preparing for the first battle.

So many details!

Men ... Soldiers could not be recruited now, but a few other trustworthy men could be asked, innocently, in the right circumstances: What if? — And when the time came, a few could be told to be ready. Otherwise: No one else must know. No one!

Guns, gunpowder, ammunition, swords ... The whites must provide the weapons of war, sufficient to arm every black before the battle.

Horses and mules ... Early on, some of the men must walk. All must be mounted before the battle.

The path of the insurrection ... Toward Jerusalem in good time, initially the rebels must go where it would be better to recruit men and obtain weapons and mounts. Choosing in advance among the interweaving roadways and pathways and traces and lanes was a dizzying ongoing exercise.

Who to kill, who to spare ... if anyone.

To rise up would be easy. To win would be hard. The distance from the beginning to the end would be vast. Throughout, blood would flow.

There was no other way.

And the days became weeks and months of planning, of meeting in secret, talking in secret, thinking, feeling, dreaming in secret ... praying, in secret. Nat prayed a lot.

The task would take much time. Much patience, much care.

What if?!

Bill Bryant

THOMAS GRAY Home
JERUSALEM

Joseph Travis, being truly a good and giving man, had decided to give his legal business to the troubled Thomas Gray.

Joseph, wanting some questions answered regarding his last will and testament, had jotted them down and handed the paper to Nat to deliver to the lawyer, seein' as how Nat was goin' into town anyway, for somethin' – Needn't wait for a reply ... No reason to hurry.

Hitchin' the ol' mule to a bush, in the shade, Nat soon found Gray where he expected and hoped to find him, at his desk upstairs in his seven-gabled home and inn at the eastern end of the Main Street – conveniently, through a window, within easy sight of the field where scores of infantry militiamen were already assembling for a semiannual drill.

When Nat entered Gray's office, the man was chuckling, obviously at something he was reading in the newspaper.

No older than the black man, the white man appeared older than he was, weighted by care and distracted by melancholy. At some point, Nat knew, he must address his own questions to Gray – but not now. Instead: "What you laughin' at?"

"Oh, Nat, hello – An item here in the Whig, 'bout an apprentice boy runnin' away from the Whig office – Robert Starbuck, known in his old neighborhood as 'Bad Bob' – Listen to this: 'A dollar will be given for apprehending him, which is more than he is worth' – Ha!"

Nat smiled in appreciation. Gray, even in his depressing circumstances, did on occasion display a good sense of humor, which helped one to like him. "You'd think," said the slave, "even a 'bad' white boy would fetch a higher reward."

"You'd think so ... Here – You're welcome to the newspaper. It's an old copy, from February, but things don't really change much, from month to month, do they?"

"No, suh ... Thank you, suh."

"What can I do for you today, Nat?"

Folding the newspaper and putting it in the pocket of his coat, alongside his Bible, then pulling out Joseph's note and unfolding it, and extending it to Gray, Nat said: "Mistuh Travis asked me to give this to you. Said he's already mentioned the matter to you."

"Yes, he has," Gray said, accepting the note. "You jus' tell Mister Travis I'll prepare some written answers to his questions, an' he, or you, or somebody else can pick 'em up the next time one o' y'all comes to town, or I'll drop 'em off if I get down your way – An' you be sure to thank him for me."

"I surely will ... Mistuh Gray," Nat began, pausing to make a final choice of words, knowing his own question to be rather bold, but not at all afraid to ask it, with this man. "A couple o' years past, you said you had a real strong feelin', deep down, 'bout emancipation comin' ... How you feelin' 'bout it nowadays?"

Gray was not at all taken aback by the black man's directness, which merited directness in reply. This black man could be trusted to understand. "I am not quite so optimistic now, Nat, to be truthful with you – Don't get me wrong, you know how I feel 'bout slavery, but ... But a man's got to be reasonable, an' realistic, an' responsible. Lord knows, I have tried to change other people's minds regarding the issue. Even tried to change my daddy's mind, once too often – but ... But one person can do only so much, an' agitatin' the issue jus' gets

Tomorrow Jerusalem: The Story of Nat Turner and the Southampton Slave Insurrection

folks riled up - 'specially my daddy - So I say, for the time bein' at least, it's better to leave well enough alone ... Mind you," Gray thought to add, "our new governor is said to be favorably disposed to emancipation, so progress is possible - I dare to say, Nat, within your lifetime you will witness at least the beginning of general emancipation ... if that's any consolation to you, considerin' my earlier pessimism."

"Some," Nat said, with an apparent lack of conviction, understanding the man's point of view but nonetheless understandably disappointed with it - but also knowing, of course, that within a few months the whites would be dealing with a problem far more immediate than emancipation.

"Naturally," Gray said, feeling the need to be more encouraging, "I, an' others like me, we'll continue to raise the subject, at the right times an' places - An' I assure you, there's a lot o' support for the Colonization Society. An' I, for one, would be only too happy to help any man arrange in his last will an' testament to free his slaves - Has Mister Travis expressed such an interest?"

"No," Nat said softly, with a sudden unseasonable chill in his voice. "I belong to Miss Sally's boy, Putnam."

"Ah, well," Gray murmured, slightly taken aback.

Nat tried a different approach to the subject. "What with General Jackson now bein' the President, ain' that a good sign? - I mean, po' folks understands other po' folks, an' I hear ... "

"Andy Jackson might've been born in a log cabin, Nat, but he lives now in a fine mansion - surrounded by slaves! Don't you be misled by Jackson's plain ways - An' don't you let your people get their hopes up, 'cause o' him - He'd sooner own you than lift a finger to help set you free!"

"I didn't know," Nat muttered, slightly taken aback.

"Well, now you do. Not gonna be any easy solution to the problem soon."

"You suppose," Nat ventured, staring through the window at the disorderly young men forming ranks in casual response to the strong urging of their leader, "there be slavery in Heaven?"

Gray smiled even as he shook his head. "You should be the one to answer that particular question. You're the preacher. I am merely a simple country lawyer ... I do suppose we may pray together for the same answer."

Nat smiled. "Amen to that, suh." The young men seemed more like boys, really, more interested in playing some sort of game than in training for war. "You are a good man, Thomas Gray."

Gray smiled. "Thank you, Nat."

Following a respectful pause, Nat observed: "Militia beginnin' to drill."

"Such as it is," Gray said, looking through the window. "Now, when I served in the militia, we drilled more often, an' the state provided good rifles an' sidearms an' - These lads, they mean well, but jus' look at 'em. Too many years have passed since the war. We've half-forgotten how to soldier properly. Oh, I reckon if these boys did have to fight the British, they'd give a good account o' themselves, in the end - But there's a big difference 'tween believin' you can do somethin', an' actually doin' it!"

"Do you think the British ... "

"O' course, there is one day o' the year when the lads look smart an' ready - the 4th of July! Captain Middleton'll be workin' 'em hard so they can impress all the folks who'll be in town on the 4th. You

Bill Bryant

know, Nat, if you've never been to one o' our Independence Day shindigs, you should come!"
The 4th!
Suddenly, Nat felt uneasy, unwell - and with an abruptness verging on gross discourtesy, he mumbled his thanks again for the newspaper, and left, to go home.
Gray, puzzled but only briefly disturbed, returned to his real worries.

* * *

In June, certain new laws became effective throughout Virginia.
It became a crime to teach free blacks to read and write. An offending black teacher could be punished with no more than 20 lashes of the whip, a monetary fine up to $50, and up to two months in jail. An offending white teacher could be fined up to $100.
It also became a crime for free blacks to conduct mass meetings - anywhere - anytime - "under whatsoever pretext."
To some, this was jus' more handwritin' on the wall.

In the Jail at JERUSALEM

Many were the plans formed and rejected by us, and it affected my mind to such a degree that I fell sick ...

July 4th, 1831
GILES REESE Place

Very many were the plans the five slaves had formed and rejected since the 12th of February, including the new plans made necessary when Nat realized that not only in Southampton but also everywhere else in the region the militiamen would be coming together on the 4th - o' course!
That detail alone did not mean that the insurrection could not be attempted on the 4th, but it did vastly complicate the planning and visibly discourage the other conspirators, and the whole overwhelming problem made Nat ill, weak in body and mind and soul.
It scared him, too, to think how close he had come to leading his followers - his friends - into probable disaster ... not to mention Cherry, the children, himself.
To get as far away as possible from his inner misery and theological confusion, he had to come here, to be with her.
And here, with her, he had spent an endless, sleepless night following yesterday's painful announcement to the other men - not canceling the Judgement Day, he insisted, only delaying it. It was still meant to be, he assured them, an' if it was meant to be, it would be ... in good time ... when they were ready.
Cherry did comfort him, some, to the best of her limited ability in these disheartening circumstances, encouraging him simply to believe what he had asked the others to believe. Which reminded her: "Hark come by while I was outside teachin' Redic."
"What he say?" asked Nat, looking up from his Bible.

*Tomorrow Jerusalem: The Story of Nat Turner
and the Southampton Slave Insurrection*

"He say jus' you take care o' yourself, not to worry yourself 'bout nothin' — 'cause everything's gonna be all right. He say there be another time ... He say you knows what you's doin'."

"Do I? ... Maybe you was right 'bout me bein' crazy ... Maybe me an' the others, we jus' been imaginin', dreamin' we could do it!"

"Nat Turner! You jus' imagine the Spirit talked to you? — You jus' dream all that up? — Was we all dreamin' we saw that 'clipse o' the Sun?"

"Maybe I jus' failed. Maybe my faith was not strong enough — God made the Sun stand still for Joshua!"

JERUSALEM

Evening approached, with its promise of modestly ambitious Roman candles and other fireworks in brief yet spectacular, pleasing display.

The considerable crowd, which had been observing the duly impressive militia review and drill, now began gradually moving toward the front of the courthouse — adorned by the ladies of the town in red, white and blue bunting — to be inspired and entertained by some traditional oratory. The program would include a reading of Mister Key's great patriotic poem "The Star-Spangled Banner" and, naturally, a reading of Mister Jefferson's Declaration of Independence.

Red Nelson stood faithfully at the carriage near which Nathaniel Francis was conversing amiably with several other white gentlemen — his brother Salathiel, Caty Whitehead's son Richard, the prosperous planter and chief magistrate Jeremiah Cobb and the lawyer James Strange French. (The presence of the latter testified there was a temporary truce in effect on this day. More than once, bitterly, Nathaniel Francis and James Strange French had clashed on the subject of Andrew Jackson.)

"So Lavinia finally decided not to come," Nathaniel was explaining. "She is a hard-workin' wife, with lots o' vigor an' determination, when she puts her mind to somethin' — But she's still only a woman, an' lately this pregnancy's been slowin' her down a bit."

"I'm confident," Cobb said, "you'll give her a good account o' the celebration when you get back home — Ah, there is Colonel Mahone ... "

Across the street, mathematician-scholar-storekeeper-colonel Fielding Mahone, a most humane and good-natured man, was strolling toward the courthouse, holding a hand of little Billy Mahone, whose other hand was playfully waving a small American flag.

"That boy o' his," Nathaniel noted, "sure is a little'un."

"The boy's a runt!" Cobb more accurately observed. "But smart! I was in Monroe the other day, an' happened to overhear Billy talkin' 'bout the railroad, with his daddy ... The lad can be sassy an' mischievous, too, so I've heard — But jus' give him some growin' time. He might surprise us!"

"He's got a lot to try to live up to," French said, "bein' the son of Colonel Mahone."

"When," Whitehead asked, of anyone who cared to answer, "do you reckon the railroad will come through Southampton? Twenty years from now? Thirty years?"

"Sooner than that," Cobb replied. "Much sooner — more like five years, I would reckon, accordin' to my sources o' information — An' mark my words, gentlemen, mark 'em well: when the railroad comes, we

85

shall never be the same again! ... The railroad changes things, a lot o' things, wherever it goes."
 "Five years!" Whitehead declared in amazement. "That is certainly good news!"
 "I shall share with you some other good news," Cobb said, slightly lowering his voice and leaning forward as though to draw the other men closer, which it did, just enough to lend an air of importance and confidentiality to what he was preparing to divulge. "President Jackson has authorized the transfer of five companies of infantry from the North to Fortress Monroe."
 "Really!" French exclaimed. "I have seen no reference to such an action in the newspapers."
 "Nor will you," Cobb said. "The authorities don't want the slaves to think we take seriously the prospect o' insurrection - an' they do not wish to disturb the white population, by suggestin' we might need more federal troops in Virginia."
 "Virginia can take care o' herself!" Salathiel said with pride, and scorn.
 "You must not have been observing the militia closely," Cobb lightly jested, to the amusement of the others. "Seriously, in view o' the recent reports o' unrest in Delaware, Maryland an' the Carolinas - not to mention the Caribbean - I think it is a wise precaution to strengthen the federal garrison."
 "Gentlemen," French said with a grin, "as much as I detest Andy Jackson - No, today, in the spirit o' the occasion, I shall merely dislike the President, intensely - I must agree that we cannot be too careful. Seems like there's a new crop o' abolitionist agitators up North. They are becomin' bolder, gentlemen!"
 "I have been told, by one o' our people," Whitehead reported, "there's a lot o' grumblin' among the slaves 'cause o' the failure o' the Constitutional Convention to take any action toward emancipation."
 "Slaves are always grumblin' 'bout one thing or another," Salathiel said. "When they stop grumblin', that's when I'll worry!"
 "How," Cobb honestly wanted to know, "can they reasonably expect emancipation until we figure out how to pay for it? If the slaves are smart enough to complain 'bout the Constitutional Convention, they should be smart enough to appreciate our dilemma!"
 "You cannot expect a child to understand economics," Whitehead said. "Like my mama says: You cannot negotiate with a two-year-old!"
 "Well," Nathaniel said, glancing toward the courthouse, where the oratory was beginning, "there is, thank God, a great distance 'tween grumblin' an' risin' up." He turned toward the carriage. "Red! Reach into the rig an' fetch me that bottle o' brandy."
 "Yassuh!"
 "Good man," Nathaniel said to Red, then to the others: "Glad I bought him - best man I'll ever own. An' I'm sure Salathiel shares my opinion."
 "I do," Salathiel said. "Red is a model slave ... I cannot say the same," he felt compelled for some reason to add, "'bout Nat Turner!"
 "The preacher?" Cobb inquired, knowing the name but not the man.
 "He is not a preacher," Whitehead sternly protested, being properly ordained to make the distinction, and the judgement. "That nigra has neither the background nor the training to be considered a preacher. He's nothin' but a common exhorter! - He may think he's a preacher, but ... "

*Tomorrow Jerusalem: The Story of Nat Turner
and the Southampton Slave Insurrection*

"No tellin' what's in that nigger's mind," Salathiel scowled. "You know, he's been preachin' to the blacks that the eclipse was a sign from Heaven!"

"A lot o' people," the truth forced Whitehead to note, "put that interpretation on the phenomenon – One o' the Northern newspapers said that a man in New York City prophesied that the lower end o' the city was gonna sink into the sea, an' some fools actually rushed to the upper end! ... If Turner has exhorted the nigras to believe that the eclipse was a sign o' the Judgement Day bein' near, he has not been alone in doin' so."

Red handed the bottle of brandy to Nathaniel, who offered it to Cobb, who with a smile accepted the kind offer.

"I suppose," Nathaniel said, "Nat is merely tryin' to encourage his people, in his own way, an' ... "

"I say," Salathiel said, "it's dangerous to give the slaves any encouragement, in any way – My dear brother here still permits Nat to call him by his first name – even in public. I declare, I think Nat does it to embarrass Nathaniel, to show his disrespect – pretendin' to be Nathaniel's equal!"

"I'm not sure anymore," Nathaniel said, "what he means by it. You have to keep in mind: Nat an' I used to be the best o' friends, when we were children. More an' more, as we've grown older, we've changed – an' we've had some differences 'bout certain things."

"The illustrious Patrick Henry," Cobb remarked, "once said that honest men may honestly differ."

Salathiel could not ignore the opportunity. "He also said 'Give me liberty, or give me death' – an' a smart nigger preacher, or exhorter, or whatever, can figure out a way to interpret that wrongly, too!"

"Still," Nathaniel said, pausing to take a sip of brandy, "one bad grape doesn't make a wine bad." He passed the bottle to Whitehead, who passed it to Salathiel.

"One bad apple," Salathiel reminded them, "spoils the barrel!"

"Perhaps," Cobb conceded. "But I do not worry 'bout the likes o' this Nat Turner o' yours. I worry 'bout the real hot-heads, the born trouble-makers – An' you can always tell who they are. At the worst, one might steal your valuables an' your best horse an' go high-tailin' it to the Dismal Swamp. You jus' got to keep your eyes on that sort, all the time. An'," he added with a gravity befitting Southampton County's chief magistrate, "we must be ever vigilant against outside agitators!"

"Agreed," said the preoccupied James Strange French, "although I cannot imagine an agitator havin' much success in Southampton. If I were a slave livin' hereabouts, I would count myself among the fortunate – Gentlemen, I submit to you that this is perhaps the last place people need to be worryin' 'bout any serious disturbance o' the peace by the Negroes."

Cobb saw it first, and said: "Hartie Joyner decided to buy that colt."

The others saw it, too – the very spirited colt, with Joyner in the saddle, and another man walking alongside.

"Who is the other man?" Whitehead asked.

"That young fellow," Cobb said with special respect, "is, in my expert opinion, perhaps the finest horseman in all o' Southampton County – Thomas Jones! Man loves horses, treats 'em like women ... I never thought anybody could separate that colt from its mother."

"Gentlemen," French said, "I must be goin'. I have some packin' to do – I shall be startin' for the Natural Bridge in the mornin', to

Bill Bryant

visit some o' my kinfolk there. Nathaniel," the zealous Whig said to the zealous Democrat, "I trust you are enjoyin' the disreputable an' thoroughly reprehensible behavior o' your new President Jackson an' his cronies?"

"I am!" Nathaniel proudly affirmed, with a grin to prove it.

"Enjoy it while you can!" French loudly proclaimed, with a greater grin. "'Cause the fat's in the fire!"

Then, with a nod to the other gentlemen, French departed, in a hurry, as though he had somewhere important to go, something important to do.

Nathaniel shook his head. "Now what do you suppose he meant by that?"

"Peculiar man, sometimes," Cobb said. "Good lawyer. He expresses himself poorly in writing, but his knowledge of the law cannot be faulted."

"Nathaniel," Salathiel said, "you still want to borrow Red next week?"

Nathaniel laughed. "How can I borrow what is mine? ... Yes, I do."

"Nathaniel," Whitehead remembered to inquire, "will you an' Lavinia be comin' to our place next weekend?"

"Certainly," Nathaniel replied, certainly hoping so. "We wouldn't miss one o' your dear mother's social gatherin's for all o' the cotton in Georgia! We are still talkin' 'bout the last time we visited with y'all. But we won't be able to stay very long. Lavinia, you know."

"Yes, o' course," Whitehead said, with an appropriate tone of sympathy, sincere sympathy because he had seen his mother and one of his sisters in Lavinia's present condition and well understood the joy and the danger of it. "You an' Lavinia hopin' for a boy or a girl?"

"A boy, o' course!" Nathaniel happily exclaimed. "We need more workers!"

The laughter of the gentlemen, and of Red Nelson nearby, put a pleasant mask on the awful unspoken truth o' the matter: Nathaniel and Lavinia Francis were hopin', an' prayin', mostly that she an' the baby would survive the birthin'.

Late July
LEVI WALLER Place

Four groups were gathered at Levi's as Nat slowly approached along the Barrow Road, slowly because the mule was in less than its usual no hurry on this smotheringly hot and humid day.

The Sun was utterly merciless, except a little in the shade, and even there it reached, relentless, demanding of mind and body and spirit ... and it wasn't even August yet.

Near the main house, Levi's wife was saying something to her two very attentive young sons and very inattentive infant daughter, the toddler trying to hide under the large apron of her loving black nanny.

Near the school, a dozen or so carefree boys and girls and their teacher were enjoying a brief playful recess - a picture of childhood innocence and simple fun.

At the still, Levi was conversing with several of Rebecca Vaughan's kin - her sons George and Arthur, who helped the widow farm her land further down the road, toward Jerusalem; her brother-in-law Harry, a wealthy innkeeper in Jerusalem; and her daughter Mary's husband John

Tomorrow Jerusalem: The Story of Nat Turner and the Southampton Slave Insurrection

Thomas Barrow, who more than any other man (as he rightly boasted on occasion) made this road. All of the men were armed with shotguns, ready for the hunt.

At the well, Levi's Yellow Davy, Albert and Davy were sharing a ladle of fresh cool water with another slave, Marmaduke, who lived near here.

Nat went to the well.

Dismounting at the watering trough, he thankfully accepted the ladle offered by Marmaduke, and thankfully drank.

He knew these men. Yellow Davy, Albert and Marmaduke he considered to be likely recruits for the army of liberation, if only he were free to recruit. Of blacksmith Davy's loyalty, he was unsure.

When it was evident that Nat had finally satisfied his thirst, Marmaduke asked: "You be preachin' hereabouts anytime soon?"

"No. Won' be preachin' anywhere 'til next month, on the 14th, down at the Barnes Meetin' House — Y'all look like you need some religion. Y'all're welcome to come on down. Should be very interestin'," he said, sending the strongest signal he dared.

"Maybe I come," said Marmaduke, clearly meaning it.

Yellow Davy and Albert at least briefly nodded. Davy seemed completely indifferent.

"Preacher Nat," said Yellow Davy, casually but with unexpected and therefore surprising directness, "you be hearin' any good news lately 'bout Santo Domingo?"

"No," Nat said, with attempted disinterest. Nor did he now want to hear anything said 'bout Santo Domingo — or anything else even remotely relating to the cause which obsessed him. So he decided to change the subject himself. "Y'all ... "

"Maybe," said Marmaduke, not angrily but with an ever so slight, possibly knowing smile which made Nat uncomfortable, "there be a risin' someday in Virginia ... What you think, Preacher Nat?"

Damn him! "I think," said Nat, glancing at the hunters, "a man could get himself in a heap o' trouble jus' thinkin' 'bout it ... Sure is hot today!"

"You ever give it any thought?" Albert asked.

Damn him, too! Was this just idle risky talk? Or had these men heard something they should not have heard. "If I have," Nat replied, laughing and shaking his head, "I sure wouldn't be standin' here now talkin' with you 'bout it — 'ticularly with all o' those white men with shotguns standin' right over there. Be a good way to get myself whipped, or sold, or sent off to the Lunatic Asylum up in Williamsburg — An' my mama didn't raise no fool!"

The men laughed, but Davy then spoke seriously: "You boys better listen good to Preacher Nat — an' shut your big mouths! You get us all in trouble!"

Amid the grumbling surrender to Davy's good advice, Nat hastily said his farewells and mounted the mule, and rode away, slowly.

*

Was it indeed just idle risky talk?

Or had they indeed heard somethin'?

He made himself stop thinking about it, finally, by making himself start thinking about the message he must deliver on the 14th, at Barnes.

Bill Bryant

Only a massive thunderstorm that Sunday would prevent a goodly crowd of whites and blacks alike from converging on the meeting house down near the North Carolina border. Sally's uncle the Reverend George Washington Powell would be in the pulpit, inside. Outside, under the arbor behind the church, Nat would be preaching.

And it would in fact be interesting, Nat knew even now.

If by then he could, he would make it known - by some inspired choice of words which only the faithful would understand - that the day of liberation was at hand.

Or maybe, he thought in a fleeting moment of weakness against which immediately he fought hard, he might be too ill on the 14th, to go to Barnes - a cowardly thought, quickly conquered, for now.

The people would be awaiting him ... awaiting his message.

Whatever words the Spirit inspired him to say, he must not fail the people.

CATHERINE WHITEHEAD Place

Not expecting any visitors today, Caty Whitehead responded with her usual cheerful efficiency and dispatch when the guests began arriving.

By the time the first carriage finished its dusty journey up the long lane leading through the cotton fields to the main house, a second carriage had been sighted in the lane, closely followed by two men on horseback.

The visitors - Joseph and Sally Travis and little Joe, Nathaniel and the very expectant Lavinia Francis (who as soon as she arrived went upstairs to rest), Jeremiah Cobb and William Parker - all just happened to be passing through the neighborhood and, of course, just had to stop and say hello and pay their respects to one of the most hospitable hostesses in all o' Southampton.

The crowd was sudden, but the widow was used to it, and knew what to do. Even with most of the servants at work in the fields, she would manage. She always did.

While her son Richard and her man Hubbard made the guests comfortable inside the house, Caty and two of her daughters went to the garden to pick vegetables, another daughter went with a hatchet to the chicken coop, and yet another daughter tended to the preparation of the liquid refreshments. Only Caty's first grandchild, asleep in the cradle, was spared a task.

With the ladies of the house thus engaged, Richard instructed Hubbard to fetch a pitcher of water and some glasses, then sat down and started a polite conversation, with an innocent reference to the recent dry weather and its unhealthy effect on the crops.

Within a minute, the conversation took a wrong turn, into politics, and beyond.

Joseph, a man with little interest in politics, mentioned the unpredictability of Virginia weather - which caused Jeremiah, a candidate confident of election in mid-August to the Virginia House of Delegates, to make a comment mildly critical of Andy Jackson's dealings with the unpredictable British - which caused William, who prior to becoming a lawyer had served along the Canadian border during the last war, to offer a terse but conciliatory opinion of the British - which caused Nathaniel, whose pro-Jackson fervor was exceeded only by the fierceness of his anti-British sentiments, to declare his complete and absolute distrust of the Mother Country.

*Tomorrow Jerusalem: The Story of Nat Turner
and the Southampton Slave Insurrection*

The conversation quickly veered toward the undeniable evil of the British during the wars – especially their incitement of the slaves to rebellion – damnable, the men had no problem agreeing.

At which point, a woman's voice was heard: "We should emancipate them," Sally said with quiet conviction and simple logic, gently cradling in her arms her sleeping baby. "Then we would not have to fear rebellion."

In the brief perfect silence, Joseph frowned a little. His wife was a woman of strong and usually reasonable opinions, accustomed to speaking her mind, especially at home, and he loved her all the more because of it. But she was nonetheless a woman among men who better understood such matters, and this was really not the right time or place to begin venturing into that particular thicket. "My wife ... "

"My dear lady," Jeremiah said with a condescending smile, to Joseph's annoyance, "it is not as simple as that."

"Why not?" Sally simply asked. "It seems obvious to me ... "

"Because," said Jeremiah, who had been thinking about the whole vital issue even more intensely since becoming a candidate for service in the General Assembly, "it is an extremely complicated, difficult proposition – more so than you may imagine."

"My dear sir, I ... "

"Madam, accordin' to the census last year, there are upwards o' 470,000 slaves in Virginia, easily a third o' the wealth o' Virginia – the very foundation o' the economy which sustains us all, Negroes as well as whites. Now, the original sin o' introducin' slavery to Virginia may not be ours – you can blame the British for that crime, too – an' a lot o' people may disapprove o' slavery, but it is as much a fact o' life as the air we breathe."

"It still seems obvious to me ... "

"Let me finish, dear lady ... Emancipatin' the slaves is a noble idea. But how are we to obtain the many scores o' millions o' dollars to compensate their owners – or the many more scores o' millions o' dollars required to transport 'em to Africa, an' insure their safe settlement there? – An' I am speakin' only 'bout the slaves o' Virginia!"

"But the Colonization Society," Sally said, pausing to accept a glass of water from old Hubbard. "Thank you ... But the Colonization Society ... "

"Has done a mountain o' fine work," Jeremiah countered, "an' managed to resettle only a couple o' thousand blacks."

"The states o' the North managed to abolish slavery," Sally persisted, to Joseph's increasing discomfort.

"The North," Jeremiah said, evidently impatient, "had far fewer slaves, an' far less dependence on 'em."

"The South, Sally," said Nathaniel, "is different. You know it as well as we do. The slaves may be in bondage to us, but we are in bondage to the economic system – I frankly wonder where we would be without the slaves. If we do emancipate 'em an' send 'em back to Africa, white men an' women sure ain't gonna replace 'em as workers, not in sufficient numbers – or buy our land, not with so much cheaper, better land out to the west o' Virginia. No, this is not the North, Sally."

"Sally," William noted, "a lot o' those Northern slaves were not emancipated, but merely sold into the South – probably at a profit," he laughed, "knowin' those people."

"The Northerners," Jeremiah added, "made their real profit shippin' the slaves over from Africa, an' up from the Caribbean – An' I can

91

Bill Bryant

assure you, my dear lady, havin' so nobly eliminated slavery, the Northerners now have no higher opinion o' their remainin' free blacks than we entertain toward our own - a mostly ignorant, idle class o' people, to whom 'liberty' means bein' free to do nothin'!"

"Well, what do you expect?" Sally flared, waking the baby. "Who do you suppose is responsible for their ignorance? Who writes the laws limitin' their opportunities to improve their condition?"

"Those laws," Nathaniel firmly reminded his sister, "are meant to protect our interests."

"Only because, when all is said an' done, we fear the slaves," Sally as firmly reminded all of them. "But if we emancipate 'em ... "

"There would be chaos!" Jeremiah exclaimed. "Emancipation, if it comes..."

"If?!" Sally said with disbelief, again disturbing the baby, as Joseph squirmed.

"When it comes," Jeremiah conceded, for the moment, "it will take a great many years to accomplish. Do not delude yourself to the contrary - An' please do not misunderstand me, dear lady. I am not unsympathetic to the condition o' the Negroes, an' I have given much thought to numerous emancipation proposals. But I have not found one that'll work!"

"Surely," Richard said, more than ready for his mother to make her appearance, "even the slaves - the intelligent ones - are capable o' understandin' the problem we face. Our slaves do."

"Sally," Nathaniel could not resist saying, "has at least one intelligent slave who might not ... "

"You jus' leave Nat out o' this!" Sally snapped.

"Nat?" Jeremiah inquired.

"Nat Turner," Nathaniel answered, "Sally's ... "

"The preacher," Jeremiah noted, leaning forward.

"Yes," Nathaniel affirmed, "the preacher, Sally's ... "

"The exhorter," muttered Richard.

"Sally's best friend," Nathaniel said, rather sorry he had raised the subject, as her face reddened.

"Yes, he is!" Sally said with proud defiance, then glanced at Joseph and thinly smiled. "Next to my beloved husband, o' course."

"Thank you, my dear," Joseph said, an almost pained expression on his face.

"As a matter o' fact," Sally sternly continued, "I would much prefer to have Nat for a friend, or a neighbor, than some o' the white people I have encountered in my life." She paused, then with an even thinner smile added: "Present company excepted, o' course."

"O' course," Jeremiah said on behalf of them all.

"Friends you may be," Nathaniel grumbled, "but do you think Nat ever forgets - for even an instant - that he is your slave?"

Sally glared at her brother.

"Several years ago," William said, as anxious as the others to find some way out of this awkward conversation, "I heard a doctor compare slavery with a cancer of the body. The cancer might kill the patient, eventually - but the surgery to remove it surely would ... The choice is not simple."

"Gentlemen!" Caty Whitehead declared as she entered the room, finally. "Sally! I trust everyone is comfortable?"

"Yes," said a chorus of relieved voices.

"Fine!" Caty grinned. "An' I do hope Richard has not been puttin' you to sleep by rehearsin' the sermon he's preparin'!"

*Tomorrow Jerusalem: The Story of Nat Turner
and the Southampton Slave Insurrection*

"Indeed!" Jeremiah said with great interest, grateful for the new direction, at last. "When an' where will you be preachin'?"

"Next month," Richard replied, "on the 21st, down at Barnes ... George Powell will be preachin' there on the 14th," he added with a tone of mischief, "in company with the Reverend Nat Turner."

"That exhorter?!" Caty laughed.

Sally seethed, yet hid it well, Joseph observed.

Early August
PETER EDWARDS Place

In the roadway at the beginning of the lane neatly flanked by cotton fields, Nat stopped, reluctant to walk even one step further.

He stopped not because he was too tired to proceed, although he had in fact come here by a very roundabout route, meandering, thinking, worrying.

He stopped not because he was arriving too early, for him. He was in fact late, even for him. He could see, and hear, the jubilee gathering well in progress.

He stopped because right now he wanted to be alone, not here among so many folks he knew - the inescapable focus of the attention of almost every man and woman here, including most if not all of his confederates, for whom he had no new ideas ... no solutions, no answers to their repeated questions, which demanded answers, soon.

Suddenly, someone at the gathering started playing a banjo, with an enthusiasm, a joy which raced across the cotton field, someone with real talent - probably old Jeff, the master's overseer, husband to Nelson's sister - Jeff, whom Nat respected as a man, distrusted as a friend, rejected as an ally.

Earlier, while walking along a woodland pathway through the property of Doctor Robert Musgrave, Nat had been attracted to the distant yet distinct appeal of someone playing a pianoforte. Choosing to forget where he was supposed to be, he had detoured into the woods, seeking the source of the music, getting near enough to the doctor's house to glimpse through an open window the doctor's wife, thoroughly enjoying herself. He had lingered there at the edge of the woods only long enough to begin thinking about some of the simple pleasures denied to his people, remembering where he was supposed to be, and why. And then abruptly he had left.

Now, where he was supposed to be, wishing to be elsewhere, he started walking up the lane, briskly.

Every day of delay and indecision added to the weight upon him - the wondering how his four carefully chosen men were really handling the continuing strain. As well as he did understand each man, each man was a challenge to understand as fully as he needed to. There were limits to what he could ask, boundaries to what he could know. One man can't get but so deep into what another man is truly thinking. Go too deep, and the other man's thoughts become a swamp, a thicket, the way in and the way out known only to that man. Nat knew that truth well.

Every day of secrecy increased the risk of accidental discovery, or deliberate betrayal.

Besides the four, how many others now knew, or had good reason to suspect, that a plot was in motion? How many others could sense an uprisin' in the wind? He himself had strongly hinted at the

Bill Bryant

possibility, with Thomas Haithcock, and with Berry Newsom, and a few others he trusted with his life – leaving out all of the details of when and where and how, if only because he did not know when, or where, or how.

Every day of uncertainty fed his frustration.

Still, his faith in the Spirit was firm.

Still, the war of liberation had to begin somewhere.

And as his mama had told him more than once, when he was a boy, learning to work, you go until you got to stop, you do until you can't do no more.

It was good advice then, he had long ago decided, and it was good advice now, he reckoned as he quickened his pace and placed a confident smile on his face.

Finally, better late than never, he was where he was supposed to be.

*

Peter Edwards could be demanding or generous, hated or loved.

Today, the master was generous, and loved, for now.

Several times, during the afternoon of feasting and entertainments, he emerged from the main house, roamed among the scores of celebrating blacks, consulted with old Jeff, then returned to the house, a smiling and self-satisfied man.

Once, he spoke briefly with Nat, who with Peter's blessing occasionally preached here.

Nat spent most of the afternoon well off to the side of the scene of jubilation, with the people closest to him – his mother, who had walked over from Elizabeth Turner's place because she hadn't seen her son in several weeks and just wanted to know how he was doing, and all four of his special men, plus Nathaniel's Will, Sam's close friend.

If this group included only Hark, Sam, Henry and Nelson, Nat would have been inclined to talk in whispers about the plan, or lack of plan. But Nancy was here, and Will. So the conversation was empty of hidden meanings.

Toward the end of the festivities, old Jeff wandered over, today more holier-than-thou than usual, and in jest asked Nat: "Found any interestin' leaves lately?"

"No," Nat smiled in reply, "not lately – How 'bout you?"

Jeff just grinned, and walked away.

Nat did not like the overseer's question – jestful, yes, but an untimely, unwelcome reminder of the notoriety which followed the preacher everywhere. There were times when he almost regretted the incident with the leaves, because of the doubters who would not forget, troublesome people in his present circumstances. Fact or falsehood, he had claimed to see what others didn't, and the claims had defied reason – and disturbed the serenity of some.

Preparing to leave, Nat mentioned, again, that he would be preaching on Sunday the 14th, down at Barnes, and expected all of them to try to attend. All promised to be there.

As he walked away, Henry tagged along, followed by Nancy.

With Henry, quickly in their brief privacy, he nailed down one trivial detail of the great plan. No, he did not agree that an army of volunteers living off the land would really need a paymaster; but

*Tomorrow Jerusalem: The Story of Nat Turner
and the Southampton Slave Insurrection*

yes, because Henry insisted, Henry would be the paymaster. Henry, happy, went away.

With Nancy, Nat tried to be as patient and as caring as a son should be with his mother, without revealing what was on his mind and in his heart. If she knew him as well as he figured she did, she already knew he was up to somethin'. But the less said about it, the better for her.

"Son, I ain' been seein' much o' you lately."

"Been busy, mama."

"You takin' good care o' yourself?"

"Yes, mama."

"You eatin' enough?"

"Almos' enough, mama," he smiled.

"You spendin' enough time with your family?"

He hesitated. No sense tryin' to lie, with her. "No ... But Cherry, she understands."

Nancy shook her head in disapproval. "Serve you right if Massuh Reese's bulldogs forget who you is, an' eats you up!"

Nat laughed. "I'll do better, mama."

"What you gonna say to the people at Barnes?"

"Don' know ... Can' decide," he said, with a sudden glance across the cotton fields and a slight frown which to her betrayed him.

"Nat," she said, like a mother offering wisdom and a friend offering advice, "I got only one thing to say to you. Life ain' gonna wait for you to decide what's bes' to do ... Life gonna happen with or without you. An' sometimes, you jus' got to go with what you knows, an' feels, deep down inside."

"Mama ... "

She silenced him by embracing him, tightly, briefly, letting go only because she had to. "You take real good care o' yourself, Nat - an' come by an' say hello to your ol' mama every now an' then!"

"I will, mama ... I will - I promise."

She smiled warmly, then turned her back to him, and went away.

He stood there and watched her go.

She had given life to him, had done her best to take it away from him, then had done her best to nurture her baby into the man he had become, a man who made her proud to be herself.

He had given so little to her, except his love.

Soon, he promised her with a prayer, he would give Nancy the greatest gift she could imagine - the gift which would make her enslavement and her years of bondage almost worth their terrible cost - the gift she wanted most, deep down inside.

The freedom of her people!

* * *

There wasn't much news to report in the Richmond Enquirer's edition on the 2nd of August.

Inconspicuous among the many small advertisements was the offer of a $20 reward for the return of a slave to his master in Cumberland County.

The runaway Stephen Price, a mulatto approximately 30 years old, was a ditcher, a stonemason, a carpenter, a fiddler - "and, indeed, he is so ingenious that he is good at almost any thing."

That was one way to get your name into the newspapers.

Bill Bryant

* * * * *

November 2nd, 1831
In the Jail at JERUSALEM

Silently, together, the two men had hungrily dined on the leftover fried chicken and bread and soft cider jailer Collin Kitchen had brought into the cell late in the afternoon.

Gray's eyes burned. His right wrist was stiff and sore from the scribbling of notes always in a hurry to try to keep pace with Nat's rambling words. Gray's head ached. His back ached. His whole body ached.

Nat felt little different than he had the day before, or the day before — better rested, better fed, more at peace than he had felt at any time since ...

"Nat?"

"Suh?"

"What you said earlier, 'bout the time fast approachin' when the first should be last an' the last should be first ... Do you not find yourself mistaken now?"

Nat considered the question, but not for long. He had asked himself that very question countless times during the past two months, and each and every time he had been compelled to the same answer.

The prisoner glanced down at his Bible, on the floor at his side, then looked deep into the lawyer's tired yet expectant eyes, and asked the question which to him answered everything:

"Was not Christ crucified?"

*Tomorrow Jerusalem: The Story of Nat Turner
and the Southampton Slave Insurrection*

The Rising

Bill Bryant

*Tomorrow Jerusalem: The Story of Nat Turner
and the Southampton Slave Insurrection*

! !

It wasn't in the local newspapers, but it happened.

From mid-July into early August of 1831, the Earth experienced massive convulsions — at two places, widely distant.

On the island of Babuyan, north of Luzon in the Philippines, an already active volcano erupted with especially violent energy.

And in the middle of the main shipping channel in the Mediterranean, between Sicily and Malta, a rumbling which began in mid-June exploded into sudden existence a new island — which the great nations of Europe began scrambling to claim.

The great columns of ash reached high into Earth's atmosphere, and spread with the winds.

! ! !

And a strange, unexplained fog did soon cover the Earth, briefly — with spectacular heavenly effects, everywhere.

It was in the local newspapers.

! !

Bill Bryant

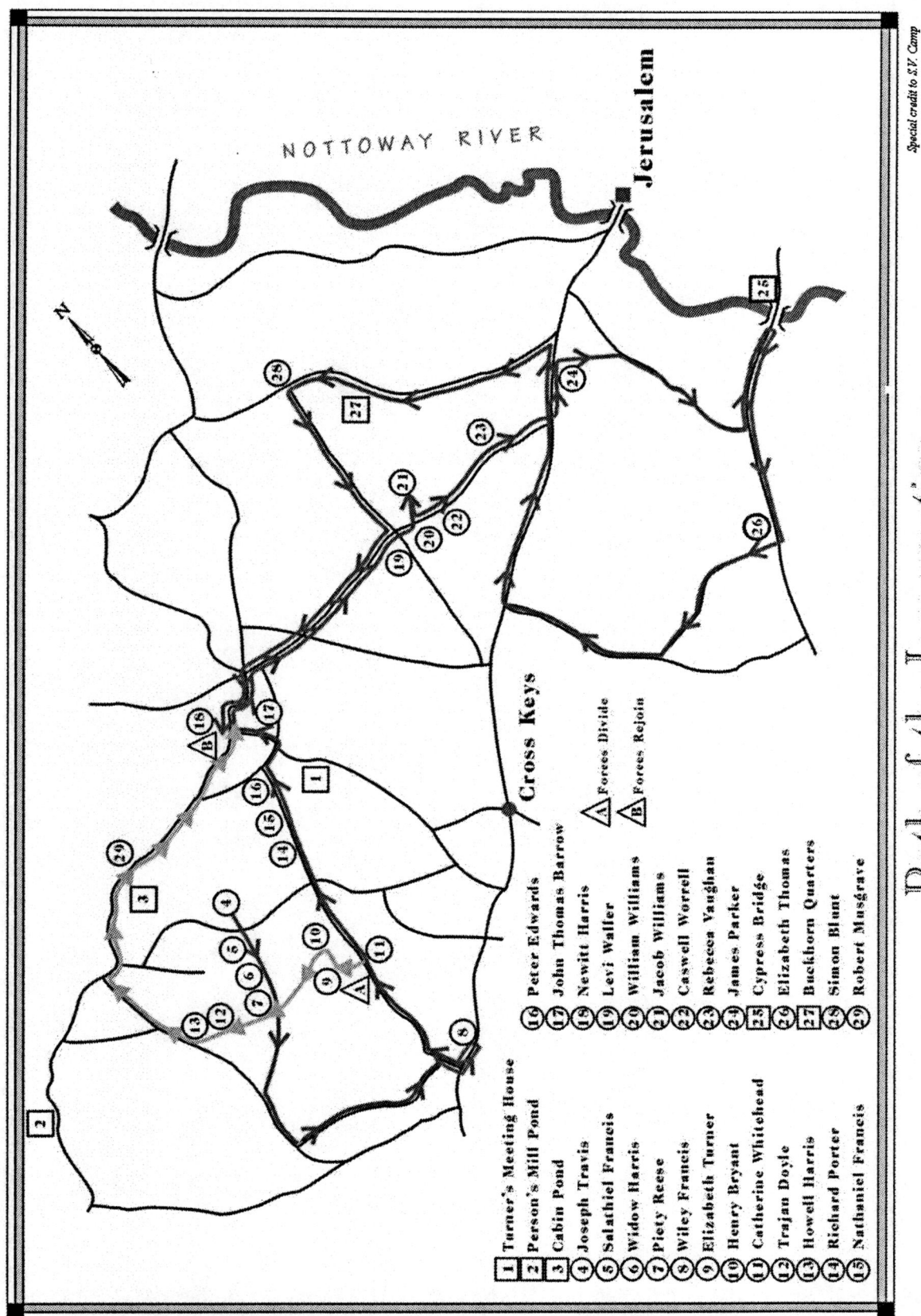

Tomorrow Jerusalem: The Story of Nat Turner and the Southampton Slave Insurrection

Path of the Insurrection

1. Turner's Meeting House
2. Person's Mill Pond
3. Cabin Pond
4. Joseph Travis
5. Salathiel Francis
6. Widow Harris
7. Piety Reese
8. Wiley Francis
9. Elizabeth Turner
10. Henry Bryant
11. Catherine Whitehead
12. Trajan Doyle
13. Howell Harris
14. Richard Porter
15. Nathaniel Francis
16. Peter Edwards
17. John Thomas Barrow
18. Newitt Harris
19. Levi Waller
20. William Williams
21. Jacob Williams
22. Caswell Worrell
23. Rebecca Vaughan
24. James Parker
25. Cypress Bridge
26. Elizabeth Thomas
27. Buckhorn Quarters
28. Simon Blunt
29. Robert Musgrave

A. Forces Divide
B. Forces Rejoin

Special credit to S.V. Camp

Bill Bryant

Tomorrow Jerusalem: The Story of Nat Turner and the Southampton Slave Insurrection

In the Jail at JERUSALEM

And the time passed without our coming to any determination how to proceed — still forming new schemes and rejecting them — when the sign appeared again, which determined me not to wait longer . . .

SATURDAY
August 13th, 1831
SOUTHAMPTON COUNTY

The Sun began to rise at 5:23 ... and the future began to change.

At the Travis place, awakening at dawn, Nat soon emerged from his cabin, into an oddly moist and hazy atmosphere. He paused, stretched, accustomed his eyes to the unfamiliar soft early light, then, in no hurry, proceeded with his chores, thinking about tomorrow.

His people, particularly his chosen men, would be expecting strong words of encouragement — and he could not disappoint them.

Inevitably, as the Sun rose above the eastern treeline, Nat saw it.

The Sign!

The early-morning Sun was of a pale greenish tint, and did not offend the eyes.

Seeing it, pausing to stare at it, in pure wonder, Nat did not think to stop what he was doing, to pray. The sight was indeed strange and impressive, but not persuasive.

So he continued with his chores, trying to concentrate on Sunday's message, occasionally glancing upward.

As other folks at the place observed the Sun and asked his opinion of it, Nat merely shared their natural curiosity and ignorance, then returned, thoughtfully, to his work.

The mid-morning Sun was a light blue, with a strong hint of green, and did not offend the eyes.

At the Reese place, Cherry saw it, of course — with gradually increasing alarm.

She continued with her chores, thinking of Nat, worrying about him, and about what he might be thinking now.

The late-morning Sun was silvery white, and did not offend the eyes.

Throughout Southampton, people saw it, of course ... and became ever more puzzled, and troubled, as the spectacle persisted.

In farmyards and fields, along the roadways in the countryside and in the streets of Jerusalem, folks assembled in small groups to stare at the unexplainable phenomenon and talk about it.

Their faces, enshrouded now in a dull and gloomy light, had an odd, ghostly appearance.

Nat, increasingly persuaded, but not convinced, worked harder, faster.

*

Bill Bryant

The Sign!
The afternoon Sun was polished silver - with a black spot prominent in the lower left - and did not offend the eyes.

Whatever was happening, folks agreed, it was ominous - perhaps a warning of impending doom - a sign that the Day of Judgement was near!

And with the pace of life slowing almost to a halt, a sense of dread crept among the people.

Convinced now beyond the shadow of doubt, Nat finished his chores, early. Having managed during the day to share the deepening concern of the others without betraying his mounting inner excitement, he went to the main house, to get Joseph's almanac, then headed toward Cabin Pond ... to be alone with tomorrow, and beyond.

*

The Sun set at 7:02.
The Sign!
And for more than an hour thereafter, the western horizon was rimmed with a curtain of brilliant scarlet.

Arriving at the Reese place in the afterglow, at peace with himself and at peace with the Spirit, Nat played with his children, then went to bed, early, with Cherry in his arms.

She knew.

Elsewhere, following a day etched deeply and forever in memory, the people talked about it and thought about it and worried about it well into the evening, in candlelight and lamplight and in the soulful darkness of their bedrooms.

Sleep came uneasily.

* * * * *

SUNDAY
August 14th
BARNES MEETING HOUSE

The Sun was almost normal again - but not the people, who anxiously flocked to the churches of Southampton in search of explanation, guidance, comfort.

The scene at Barnes was a dusty, noisy confusion of horses and carriages and wagons and several hundreds of white people and black people converging from all directions, intermingling, separating.

There was a certain frantic quality to the scene, as though the people knew that yesterday had been historic in some way yet to be revealed, and suspected that today would be memorable, too. The blacks especially seemed to be in an excited, one might even say agitated, mood.

The white men and boys entered the church by one door, the white women and girls by another door, filling every pew and lining every wall, eager to sing the reassuring songs of faith and glory, impatient to hear the Word of God from the man in the pulpit - the Reverend George Washington Powell.

*Tomorrow Jerusalem: The Story of Nat Turner
and the Southampton Slave Insurrection*

The black folks assembled around the grape arbor behind the church, making a path for the arrival of the Preacher, and his family.

Nat - more than a little surprised and more than a little concerned by the size and energy of his uncommonly expectant congregation - noticed here and there red scarfs and red sashes and other glimpses of red, a silent eloquent conspiracy of color, which, he thought, surely the whites could not help but notice, too.

Yes, it would be a day to be remembered.

Because on this day, at this place, Sally's dear uncle George and Sally's dear friend Nat were men with missions.

*

Inside the hot church, confronting his kinfolk and friends and neighbors in one of life's moments of truth, George Powell did what the phenomenon of yesterday had resolved him to do today.

When the singing was done and the time came, he spoke from his whole mind and heart and soul - and dared to preach, without constraints, against the evils of slavery ... even as the rising enthusiasm of the blacks at worship outside drifted inside the open doors and windows of the church.

He damned in uncomfortably explicit detail the abuses and ill effects and moral wrongs of slavery - interpreting the strange Sun as a bold manifestation of heavenly disfavor, a call to repentance. And the disturbing echoes of more than a century of debate and discussion and prayer in Southampton were heard in his words as he tried to breathe new meaning and urgency into the memorable but ignored appeals of David Barrow and Jonathan Lankford, and others who had failed.

Finally, much to the relief of his sweltering congregation, George Powell reached the end of his fervent assault, having done the best he could do.

"I declare unto you, my brothers in Christ," he appealed, to one side of the church, "and unto you, my sisters in Christ," he appealed, to the other side of the church, "that the day is coming when we shall all be held accountable for our sins! ... And slavery is a sin!! . . . And the sooner we eliminate it from our lives, and from the life of our beloved nation, the closer we shall be to God and Heaven when the Day of Judgement comes - and it is coming!!!"

And the congregation, with sharply mixed feelings, responded: "Amen!"

*

In the windless hot shade of the arbor, the Preacher neared the end of his own fervent but heavily veiled message.

Even now - especially now - he dared not be explicit.

But all had seen the Sun - *The Sign!*

With his Bible firmly in hand and no need to open it, now, he spoke to his enraptured listeners from the Book of Revelation, Chapter 6, Verse 2: "And I saw, and beheld a white horse. And he that sat on him had a bow. And a crown was given unto him ... And he went forth conquering ... and to conquer ... and fight against the Serpent ...

Bill Bryant

For the time is fast approaching when the first should be last ... and the last should be first!"

He paused, and as he slowly turned his head to stare into the eyes of his people he said it again: "For the time is fast approaching when the first should be last ... and the last should be first!"

Then, from his own whole mind and heart and soul, Nat spoke: "However great your burden – whatever it may be, today – know this: Tomorrow ... is another day!"

And the congregation shouted: "Amen!"

And the Preacher, holding high his Bible now, said: "Yes! – Tomorrow is another day! – And it is fast approaching, oh yes! – That day of glory, praise be to God! – That day when the first should be last, and the last should be first, praise be to God! – That Day of Judgement! – Praise God!!"

And the congregation roared: "Amen!!!"

And the Preacher whispered: "Amen."

*

As the services ended, the excited congregations again intermingled outside the church, some of the people planning to picnic, some ready to begin the long ride or longer walk home – thinking, hard, about what each had just heard ... And briefly, the whites and blacks became one large loud crowd of the faithful – two realities co-existing on this day surely long to be remembered, after yesterday.

Two white men pondered the scene.

"George might be right," said one. "He certainly did offer us some food for thought ... 'specially considerin' yesterday."

"Food only for them that can stomach it," grumbled the other.

"Ol' Nat sure got 'em stirred up today."

"For a fact! – An' a lot more o' 'em than usual, too."

"I don' know whether it's Nat or this infernal heat or the Holy Ghost – or what happened yesterday – but some o' the nigras've been actin' mighty ructious today – One o' 'em like to rode over me with his wagon comin' in here!"

"After what happened yesterday, a lot o' white folks've been behavin' real peculiar, too ... Mighty – I mus' say it – mighty God-damn strange – that Sun yesterday!"

"Yes, sir, ol' Nat must've preached up a storm ... What do you suppose all o' the red means?"

"Now that you mention it, I've been wonderin' the same thing myself ... It mus' mean somethin'!"

In front of the white men passed ol' Moses from Nansemond – a bright red bandanna tucked tightly inside the rope belting his waist – beginning the walk home, smiling at the white men and nodding his head, then grinning, knowing ... Soon!

*

"Soon," Nat assured Hark and Henry and Sam and Nelson during their brief encounter in the relative seclusion of the trees behind the privies.

"When?" asked Hark.

Tomorrow Jerusalem: The Story of Nat Turner and the Southampton Slave Insurrection

"Very soon," Nat promised them, wanting to trust them fully — particularly now — but now more than ever unwilling to risk the enterprise with remarks which could be overheard by the wrong person.

"When?" asked Henry. "We in this together."

Nat glanced around them, warily, then told them as much as they needed to know: "We'll meet next Sunday afternoon, at Cabin Pond ... Be there."

They understood.

In the meantime, he instructed them — quickly, because he could see Sally in the distance, searching for him, to begin the ride home — maintain absolute secrecy, be inconspicuous, work hard for your masters during the week to be sure you are free on Sunday.

"On Sunday," the Preacher said, "we all be free!"

They understood.

* * * * *

**MONDAY
August 15th
SOLOMON PARKER Place**

Leaning against a cabin, Becky chanced to overhear the conversation among Jim and Isaac and Preston.

It sounded like a conversation she had overheard here some 18 months ago. But this time, it had an extra urgency to it.

So she edged closer to the cabin's open door as the discussion heated up.

"I heard 'bout it over in Sussex County!" Jim declared.

"An' it be happenin' soon," Isaac said, "right here in Southampton!"

"Praise Jesus!" Preston proclaimed.

"If they comes my way," Jim said, "I be joinin' 'em — an' killin' all the white people I can find — I be ridin' with 'em to the Promised Land!"

Just then, Jim thought to go to the door, to look outside — just in case. And thus he discovered Becky, immediately grabbing her arm and pulling her into the cabin.

The men told her to promise them she would not say anything to anybody about what she might have overheard.

Considerin' the circumstances, she did not hesitate. She promised.

* * * * *

**THURSDAY
August 18th
GILES REESE Place**

Morning breezes played through the nearby cornfield as Nat and Cherry sat on the bench behind her cabin.

Bill Bryant

"Best you keep these," he said, with great seriousness, handing her a packet of well folded sheets of paper. "Hide 'em, somewhere good ... who knows?" he brightened. "Maybe they be important someday!"
"Maybe," she said, trying to smile. "You hungry?"
"I'm fastin', remember?"
"You should be eatin' ... You needs your strength."
"The Lord is my strength."
"You knows what I means."
"I know ... I knows," he said softly.
"Nat ..."
She could not speak.
"Cherry ... "
He could not speak.
His right hand reached out to her.
Her left hand reached out to him.
Their fingers touched, and tightly intertwined.
Finally, she found the courage to ask the question both of them had been avoiding: "When?"
"Sunday ... Sunday night ... The Moon be full an' high in the sky early on, so we can see our way ... Lot o' the white folks'll be down at the camp meetin' in Gates County - includin' a lot o' the militiamen, so I hear."
She gripped his hand more tightly, then relaxed her grasp, then tightened it again.
"I be prayin' for you, Nat Turner."

JACOB WILLIAMS Place

Heavily perspiring in the glaring afternoon sunlight, Jacob Williams' slave Nelson and his overseer Caswell Worrell paused while working on opposite sides of the split-rail fence being repaired midway the lane connecting the main house with the Barrow Road, a few miles from the road into Jerusalem.
"I jus' be tellin' you what the signs say," Nelson said.
"That we white folks might look out an' take care o' ourselves," Worrell half-jokingly replied. "That somethin' is gonna happen!"
"Yassuh - an' befo' too long."
"Signs say that, too, do they?"
"Yassuh."
Worrell stared at the slave. Nelson was a peculiar sort of man - but this talk was peculiar even for Nelson. He could not ignore it. "You know, Nelson," he began, trying to sound stern without seeming to be alarmed, which he wasn't, "there are masters - an' overseers not as understandin' as I am - who would speedily put the whip to you for talkin' like that ... Got half a mind to do it myself!"
Unafraid but sensible enough not to go too far with this contest of words, Nelson retreated. "Now don' you be blamin' me for what the signs say ... Any conjure-man hereabouts tell you the same thing."
"Witch doctor!" Worrell snorted, thankful for a convenient way out of this awkward conversation. "You an' your 'supernatural insights' are gonna get you into a mess o' trouble one o' these days - Now conjure me up that next rail!"
"Yas, suh," Nelson grinned, "massuh!"

Tomorrow Jerusalem: The Story of Nat Turner and the Southampton Slave Insurrection

* * * * *

SATURDAY
August 20th
JOSEPH TRAVIS Place

    Sitting up in bed, his open Bible on his lap, Nat looked up quickly when Hark knocked softly on the open door.
    "Nat," said the powerful man, filling the doorway, "supper be ready up at the house ... You sure you wants to stay here?"
    Nat breathed deeply, and sighed. "I'm stayin' ... I cannot face her, Hark, knowin' what's comin' ... I jus' can't ... You understand?"
    "I understands."
    "Jus' tell Miss Sally I be feelin' poorly."
    "Whatever you say."
    "Now you be sure to run all your 'errands' this mornin'. You know what to do, an' what to say to 'em."
    Hark nodded. He knew exactly what to do, and what to say to the other men. There was really no good reason to linger, yet he hesitated. "Nat ... Ain' no man more ready than I am, for what's comin' - 'cept you, o' course - but ... But what if we loses this war?"
    The older man cast a thin smile toward the younger man. The question did not surprise or concern Nat. He had asked it many times himself - but not since the 13th, when the Sign convinced him of victory in the conflict to which the Spirit compelled him. He would not, could not allow the thought of defeat to distract him now. And besides, his mind was already moving, slowly but enjoyably, toward the tasks beyond the battles immediately ahead. "Don' be worryin' yourself 'bout losin'. Worry 'bout this: What if we wins the war? ... But first," he conceded, "I suppose we got to put the boat in the water, an' see how well it floats."
    Hark nodded, and slowly walked away, thinking about it, encouraged.

*

    Still sitting up in bed, his open Bible still on his lap, Nat quickly looked up when Sally gently rapped on the door.
    "May I come in?" she cheerfully inquired.
    Startled but rapidly coming to his senses and regaining his composure, Nat closed his Bible, set it down on the bed, and stood up. "Sally - why, o' course, do come in, please."
    She entered, carrying a small but abundantly filled tray. "I'm so sorry to hear that you're not feelin' well - But you need to eat!"
    "You are mos' kind, Sally ... mos' kind."
    She gracefully placed the tempting tray on the table. "You eat some o' this now, you hear?"
    "I will."
    "You promise?"
    He managed a smile, for her. "I promise."
    "Be a shame to throw such good food to the pigs!"
    "Yes'm," he had to agree.
    "You preachin' anywhere tomorrow?"
    "No ... Not tomorrow."

Bill Bryant

"I suppose you're not goin' down to the big camp meetin' - So many people are."
"No ... Jus' gonna stay 'round here - You an' the family goin' over to Barnes in the mornin'?"
"Yes - except for Miss Maria. I swear, Nat, that girl can be so ... so, pardon my language, so damned exasperatin' at times! She is bound an' determined to have her way about everything - includin' goin' into Jerusalem for a visit - again!"
"I'm mighty sorry to hear that," Nat muttered.
"What did you say?"
"I say, I'm sorry to hear that she is bein' her usual self - after all that you folks've done for her."
"There are times," Sally tried to laugh, "I jus' want to take a big switch to her - an' be done with it!"
"I understand the feelin'," Nat grimly agreed, imaginin' the switch.
"Well, she can do what she wants, we don't own her - The rest of us will be goin' to Barnes, to hear Dick Whitehead preach, then do some visitin'."
"Y'all have a good time ... a real good time."
"We shall - Nat ... Are you all right? - I mean, you haven't quite been yourself lately - for a couple o' months, truth be told. I can't put my finger on it, but ... "
"I'm fine," he weakly smiled. How had he been betraying himself? What had she been wondering? What could she possibly know? How could she possibly know it? "I'm fine, believe me."
"Nat Turner, I have been knowin' you a long, long time, an' I can tell when somethin's botherin' you ... If there's a problem ... "
"I'm fine," he said again, unsmiling. If only she would stop being so damned concerned about his well being - his problem!
"If you say so," she said, not believing it but knowing him well enough to know when to stop trying. One could get only so close to Nat Turner. "You goin' over to Mister Reese's later on?"
"Yes," he said, relieved.
"Give my love to Cherry - an' hug the little ones for me!"
"I'll do jus' that, Sally ... You give little Joe a hug for me."
"It'll be my pleasure ... Well! You take care now."
"You, too ... An' thank you for the food."
"You are very welcome."
She began to leave, paused at the doorway and turned around, and began to speak, but stopped, smiled, and walked away.
Nat stared at the empty doorway, sat down in the chair at the table, looked at the food, and pushed the tray away.
He wanted to cry, but did not, because he could not - because it was too late to cry, too late even to think about reconsidering decisions already made, much too late.
The Spirit had spoken!
The Sign had appeared!
And the zeal within him flared up to burn out the impulse to think about it all, again.

*

Sitting at the table, Nat was staring at the doorway when Nelson appeared.

*Tomorrow Jerusalem: The Story of Nat Turner
and the Southampton Slave Insurrection*

"Nat, good day! – I jus' saw Hark, up at the house. He be comin' here soon as he's done eatin' – Nat ... We got to talk 'bout who's bringin' what to the meetin' tomorrow, to eat."

Nat smiled and shook his head. A war soon to begin, and he must talk about who's bringin' what to the meetin' tomorrow, to eat. "Sit down, Nelson ... An' help yourself."

BENJAMIN EDWARDS Place

Near the main house, Isham and Hardy and two other men gathered closely.

"Preacher Nat is up to somethin'," Hardy declared. "An' I got a good idea o' what it is."

"I can tell you what it is," Isham said proudly. "I knows it for a fact! General Nat's gonna rise up an' murder all the whites!"

The men moved even more closely together.

* * * * *

SUNDAY
August 21st
GILES REESE Place

Hearing the rooster announcing the sunrise, Cherry, awakening, reached for Nat, who was not there.

She arose, checked on the sleeping children, then went outside.

Rounding the cabin, she found him near the edge of the cornfield, looking at the eastern horizon, his Bible in his left hand at his side.

She approached him, standing to his right.

He extended his arm around her shoulder, and brought her to him.

"You all right?" he asked.

"I'm fine."

Together, they observed the dawn.

BARNES MEETING HOUSE

As the congregation ended the singing of "How happy every child of grace who feels his sins forgiven," the Reverend Richard Whitehead moved purposefully to the pulpit, his well crafted sermon at the ready.

Dick Whitehead did not intend to go anywhere near the delicate topic of slavery today. George Powell had said more than enough – too much, really – last Sunday.

Nor would Caty Whitehead's boy have to be concerned today with the annoyingly distracting noises of a nigra prayer meeting outside. George had seemed to be competing with that "preacher" to rouse his own people – and he had failed.

"Amen!" said the Reverend Richard Whitehead.

"Amen!" the congregation responded.

Bill Bryant

"Brothers," he began, "and sisters — We do not know when our days will end, and we shall be called to judgement. We do not know that inevitable date on which we shall be summoned to the feet of our Creator, and required to account for the time He has given us. We do not know. We cannot know ... And because none of us can know, it clearly behooves each and every one of us to make peace with God! — before it is too late! ... Oh, my brothers, and sisters — Oh, ye children of the one true God ... "

3 p.m.
CABIN POND

Finally, Nat arrived.
In the bright sunlight filtering through the trees and reflecting on the pond, not the expected four but six men were waiting for him.
Hark ... idly stoking the fire beneath what remained of a small pig on a spit.
Henry ... sitting next to a small keg of brandy.
Sam ... leaning against a tree, and munching bread.
Nelson ... squatting near the fire, juggling a baked sweet potato.
And William Reese's Jack — whom Nat knew to be only a tool in the hands of the commanding Hark and surely nowhere near as strong-willed or as decisive, or as brave, as the others he had so thoughtfully selected — Jack ... standing at the water's edge, staring across the pond, glancing only briefly at Nat.
And Nathaniel's Will ... standing very near the entrance to the clearing, waiting.
"Will," said Nat.
"Nat," said Will.
"You know why we are here?"
"I knows."
"An' why are you here?"
"Preacher Nat, my life is worth no more than the lives o' these other men ... An' liberty is as dear to me."
"You plannin' to obtain your liberty?"
"I will ... or lose my life!"
Nat offered his hand, and Will grasped it.
"Where do we begin?" Hark asked.
Nat did not hesitate: "At home."

SOUTHAMPTON COUNTY

As the afternoon progressed, Jerusalem and Cross Keys and the surrounding countryside might just as well have been deserted, considering how few people were going anywhere or doing anything in the merciless August heat, which easily discouraged all but the most necessary activity.
At home, or wherever they happened to be visiting, people mostly relaxed and recreated themselves and socialized, at a deliberately slow pace, with nowhere to go right away, or any time real soon.
Travelin' would be cooler toward evenin'.

*Tomorrow Jerusalem: The Story of Nat Turner
and the Southampton Slave Insurrection*

* * *

At Elizabeth Turner's place, the widow and her overseer and most of the 18 slaves were absent most of the day, visiting.

Nancy stayed close to the kitchen house, keeping herself busy.

Constantly, she thought about Nat, and worried.

She had seen the look on her boy's face while he was preaching to the people at Barnes, and she had seen the looks on the people's faces, too. He was being so careful not to tell the people what he planned to do. But many of them thought they knew.

And she knew. Had she not helped to mold him?

Yes, she did know.

His time was coming ... soon!

* * *

At John Thomas Barrow's place, John and his beautiful young wife Mary spent much of the afternoon at the dining table with an old deck of cards, happily at play.

She was winning, as usual, and thoroughly enjoying every minute of it.

So was he.

Among other matters, they talked about doing some visiting tomorrow — with Newitt Harris, whose wife (John's widowed mother) was away visiting a daughter in Sussex; or with Mary's mother Rebecca Vaughan, who was really counting on it; or, ideally, with both.

In the cabins, Barrow's few slaves, including reliable Aunt Easter and the younger and less reliable Lucy and Moses, had little to do, and so didn't.

* * *

The invalid Captain Newitt Harris, well attended in his wife's absence by his Ben and Aaron and Aaron's wife Aunt Edie, was hoping for at least a couple of visitors tomorrow — his especially precious daughter Charlotte Elizabeth, whose marriage to the good Doctor Robert Musgrave had made her father extremely happy because it made her extremely happy, and that baby of hers!

Newitt, for all of his cantankerous and crotchety ways in old age, always felt a special joy and contentment in his grandson's presence.

For some of the afternoon, the slow-moving but sharp-witted and feisty old man exchanged memories with the comparably old and outspoken Aaron — about the time they went off together to see some action in the war against the British, the second war against the damned British. They hadn't seen much action, but had seen some of the world beyond Southampton.

* * *

Bill Bryant

At Levi Waller's place, ordinarily so busy but today so quiet, Levi and his two young sons finally returned from their trip to the river, to fish. The catfish were going to taste good at supper.

Smiling, Levi's wife was waiting at the front door of the main house, her little daughter at her side, holding a doll.

* * *

Further along the Barrow Road toward the Jerusalem Road, the widow Rebecca Vaughan and her niece Anne Eliza Vaughan spent most of the day, or so it seemed, discussing Anne Eliza's wedding plans.

The lovely Anne Eliza — esteemed, in the biased opinion of some, as the finest beauty of Southampton — wanted every little detail of her wedding to be absolutely perfect, and memorable, of course. And there were so many details!

Rebecca was enjoying herself. She loved the romance of it all.

Alerted by a gunshot at the end of the long lane leading to the house, the women were on the front steps in time to welcome home Rebecca's sons George and Arthur, returning from an unproductive but pleasant hunting expedition, their shotguns cradled in their arms.

* * *

In the living room of James Rochelle's home in Jerusalem, young James Henry sprawled on the floor listening raptly to his older sister Martha — Mattie to most folks — reading from a big and richly illustrated book about King Arthur, and Camelot, and the Knights of the Round Table.

James Henry relished every word, every picture. Someday, he knew, he would be able to read that book himself. In the meantime, he was thankful for an older sister who happily indulged him.

Mattie, folks agreed, was a girl of some promise, the sort of girl who would probably marry well.

* * *

Sitting against the trunk of a great oak at Thomaston, young George Henry blissfully whiled away the afternoon with a new book, about botany.

* * *

Sitting in the middle of a boat in the middle of the Nottoway River near Monroe, fishing, little Billy Mahone wasn't catching anything.

But it was fun.

Neither was his father having any luck, nor the poor white man who lived not far away and had built the boat in which they were all wasting away the remaining hot daylight hours.

It was such fun.

*Tomorrow Jerusalem: The Story of Nat Turner
and the Southampton Slave Insurrection*

* * *

CABIN POND

With the lowering Sun still blindly shining, the cratered Moon began rising at 5:10, unnoticed by the seven slaves - soon to be free men - gathered at the secret place.

The men talked much about the route they would follow, weighing (again) the arguments for and against going this way or that, trying (again) to choose among the many roads and traces and paths lacing toward Jerusalem - reckoning (again) just where and how quickly and with how much effort and risk they could recruit new soldiers and obtain the shotguns and fowling guns and pistols and gunpowder and ammunition, the swords and knives and axes, the horses and mules, the food and drink necessary to wage war, and win.

So much guesswork!

Even now, at this late date!

This talking about it had begun in February (not to mention Nat's more than three years of thinking about it), and was no less challenging, and frustrating, today than it had been on all of the previous occasions. There seemed to be no easy answers, and no end to the details requiring their attention.

But today, the talking was more concentrated, more focused, more serious - deadly serious, because this time, they knew, the talking would lead directly to action.

"How many miles to Jerusalem - Anybody know?" Henry asked around the campfire, its embers slowly cooling.

"'Bout 20 miles," Sam reckoned, "as the crow flies."

Nat smiled. "You ever seen a crow fly straight?" he reminded them, waving away a brief sudden storm of tiny flyin' insects.

"Only seven o' us," the nervous scared Jack reminded them, again.

"Seven now," Nat assured him, again, not needing this distraction now. "But tomorrow at this time - in Jerusalem," he promised all of them, again, "we be hundreds! - An' soon thousands! ... I'm tellin' you, my brothers: Trust the Spirit! - God will add soldiers to our army as we follow the path He will make clear to us, as we advance ... even if we do have to change directions every now an' then ... Have faith!" the Preacher, the General exhorted them.

Easy enough, he knew, for him to understand, and say. No matter how hard he had tried, since February, to explain it to them, to educate them, he knew that not one of them would ever, could ever see as he saw, know as he knew, believe as he believed, devoutly.

"I don' know," Jack muttered. "I jus' don' know."

"You don' have to know nothin'!" Hark exclaimed. "You jus' listen to what Nat an' ol' Hark say - We knows!"

Jack slowly shook his head, but said no more. Instead, he wandered off to the water's edge, to stare into the woods across the pond.

The others noted his behavior, and the problem it represented.

Nat, too, now wandered off, to be alone.

No one thought it odd.

*

Bill Bryant

The men knew that the farm nearest Cabin Pond belonged not to Joseph Travis but to Giles Reese, who owned not only Cabin Pond itself but also, of course, Cherry — which, Nat insisted, was not why they would bypass the Reese place. They would bypass it, he told them, because Reese was a powerful man with two big and mean bulldogs.

The men accepted his explanation, but knew better.

Otherwise, they had agreed — as a rule — they would strike at every farm along whatever route they traveled — sparing no man, woman or child, leaving no witnesses, letting no white person escape to spread an alarm — making certain that when the whites did finally learn what was happening, they would be utterly confused, bewildered, fearful, terrified.

Only when the army of liberation had gained the strategic advantage and had conquered Jerusalem — establishing a place where the more numerous slaves and free blacks of upper Southampton and elsewhere could rally — only then would the women and children be spared, as well as any men who offered no resistance.

Until then, there must be no survivors!

In fact, in his own mind Nat intended his army to make various exceptions to these simple rules of combat. But he did not intend to disclose them until the time came, along this or that roadway, to announce and explain each change in the plan. Surely, certain places needed to be struck, and certain planters deserved it. But some needed or deserved it less than others, some not at all, and Nat was more sensitive to the exceptions than his followers could hope to be.

In the final analysis, he reasoned, he, better than all of them combined, knew the county and its people. He expected his men to trust his judgement.

The General must know best.

*

Nat wandered back into the clearing, carrying a collection of twigs to renew and sustain the fire.

"Pass the brandy," Nelson asked Hark. "Nat, you sure it ain' bes' we jus' skedaddle off to the Dismal Swamp?"

"Not doin' this," Nat said, masking his annoyance, "to conquer a swamp!"

"I mean, jus' for now," Nelson said, "'til we be stronger — Men be flockin' to us there, 'stead o' ... "

"No," Nat said, tired of hearing an idea he had long ago rejected, because it made no sense to him. "Not doin' this jus' to run into the swamp an' become bandits — Not doin' this," he said, for the final time, "to burn down the white folks' houses, or take their money, or their women ... Why we doin' this?"

"To make our people free," Nelson soberly replied. "Don' worry none 'bout me, Nat — I be doin' my part o' the work tomorrow."

"I know," Nat said, without a doubt.

"An' I," said Will, with lethal passion, "be doin' my part!"

"Ol' Will," said Sam, who knew his friend well, "he jus' itchin' to kill some white folks!"

"Ol' will," said Will, with a grin, "be doin' more than killin' 'em — I be openin' 'em up like pigs at the slaughter!"

"Speakin' o' killin'," Henry said, "we gonna visit the widow Harris once we done with Mastuh Salathiel?"

Tomorrow Jerusalem: The Story of Nat Turner and the Southampton Slave Insurrection

"Yes," Nat answered, "and no," he added, puzzling everyone but Hark.

"What you mean?" Sam asked.

"What Nat means," Hark said, "is that her man Joe say he come with us — if we leaves his white people alone."

"But we agreed," Sam protested. "We spare nobody!"

"We leave 'em be," Nat said. "We need Joe more than we need the blood o' his people."

"Pass the brandy," Will asked Nelson. "When we be startin'?"

* * *

SOUTHAMPTON COUNTY

As the Sun set and the Moon rose higher, candlelight and lamplight as well as bright moonlight illuminated the lives of the people finishing their meals, doing the late chores, knitting, sewing, reading, chatting, praying, settling in for the hot night.

Throughout Southampton, an almost perfect peace and quiet prevailed.

The memory of the strange Sun was still vivid and disturbing, but gradually fading in its urgency — a thing to be discussed and debated and dealt with some other day, for countless days to come.

Someday, perhaps, someone would sensibly explain the phenomenon of the 13th, as something other than an announcement of the coming of the Day of Judgement.

In the meantime, life must go on, no matter what.

Good heavens, everyone knows that much, at least!

* * *

With her children asleep, Cherry stood for a long time at the cabin door, occasionally staring at the Moon, constantly wondering.

Finally, she went to bed, to try to sleep.

God's will be done.

* * *

Guided by lamplight, Sally said good night to Putnam and Joel, then crossed the hall, checked on little Joe in his crib, put out the lamp and set it on the table, then got into bed alongside Joseph, who was asleep.

Sally missed her dear Thomas, of course, but she was more than well satisfied with her dear Joseph.

A good man.

* * *

Bill Bryant

Catherine Whitehead and her daughters Harriet and Margaret put away their knitting and rose to go to bed. Caty's other three daughters, and the baby, were already asleep, or soon would be.

Dick Whitehead remained seated as he wished his mother and sisters pleasant dreams, then returned to reading his Bible.

A good book.

* * *

Nathaniel's Easter and Charlotte required a stern reprimand following yet another squabble, but tranquility was soon restored to the Francis place, where the cabins were quiet.

In the modest but adequate main house (to which the master planned to build an addition in the near future), Lavinia said good night to her mother-in-law, checked on her sleeping young nephews, then went to the embrace of Nathaniel.

He gently placed his hand on her enormous belly – and the baby kicked – and he was delighted, and so was she.

Nathaniel had been doing some serious thinking about George's sermon, and about Dick's, and about the strange Sun. None of his thinking changed his firm opinion of the practicality and necessity of slavery, mind you. But he did now wonder if he should attempt some sort of reconciliation with Nat – if Nat would allow it, which he probably wouldn't. Still, Nathaniel could see no profit in tilting lances with Nat, or making him any madder than he was. Nat might be only a slave, but he did have considerable influence among many of the neighborhood slaves (including some of his own), and even some white people listened whenever Nat Turner talked. If Nat really wanted to, he could cause Nathaniel a heap o' trouble, in a lot o' ways, and Nathaniel knew it. So, naturally, he wondered.

To bed, to sleep, Nathaniel and Lavinia went.

All things considered, Nathaniel Francis was quite content with his life. The farm was beginning to prosper, the cotton and tobacco crops were going to be abundant, his health was good, and Lavinia was in his arms.

A good woman.

* * *

Standing at the door to one of the cabins at Nathaniel's place, a troubled old woman shook her head as she decided to go to bed.

She could not understand it. Her son Sam had promised he would be home long before now, and still no sign of him. It wasn't like Sam, who was usually more reliable than this.

A good boy.

* * *

In the moonlit shadows along the Bellfield Road south of the Nottoway, upriver from Jerusalem, Doctor Simon Blunt returned home, finally, from a visit to a patient.

*Tomorrow Jerusalem: The Story of Nat Turner
and the Southampton Slave Insurrection*

Simon Jr. helped the gouty old doctor down from the carriage, then led the horse and carriage away.

Simon Sr. slowly walked over toward the slave quarters, listening for the late-night sounds of conversation ... hearing only the silence of well-deserved sleep.

Good people.

* * *

In his bed at home above the Nottoway, Jeremiah Cobb drifted toward untroubled sleep, happily thinking of the past week's election results and already dreaming of the day later this year when he would become a member of Virginia's House of Delegates.

A good dream.

* * *

The love and labor of this day were done.
The struggle would continue tomorrow.

* * * * *

10 p.m.
CABIN POND

On the ground around the glowing embers of the dying fire, the seven men sat motionless, in thought.

Then, with the Moon reaching just about its highest point in the sky, Nat rose to his feet, and the others arose ... Jack most slowly.

Nat extended his hands left and right, and all of their hands were soon linked in a chain around the fire ... Jack's least strongly.

"No more prayin'," Nat said. "No more to talk about ... It's time – Praise be to God! – Amen!"

"Amen!" said the others, including Jack ... weakly.

Their hands parted.

One by one, during the evening, Nat had taken each man aside, privately, to strengthen every man's commitment and courage, confidence and faith. Only with Jack had it really been necessary. Only with Jack had it failed.

Now, one by one, at a purposeful but unhurried pace, the General led them from the clearing onto the path, followed by Hark, Jack, Henry, Sam, Nelson and Will.

Hark would be second in command. If anything, God forbid, happened to Nat, the others would obey Hark.

Jack was Hark's problem.

Henry, Sam and Nelson would be fearless fighters, and leaders – generals, someday.

Will would be a warrior – the one among them, Nat knew, whom the white people would fear the most, if the white people only knew.

Will, far more than any of the others, perhaps more than all of the others combined, was determined to do unto the white people what they had been doing unto the black people for so long – too long – much too long! Will, if only Will, would put the fear o' God into the enemy.

* * *

11 p.m.
JOSEPH TRAVIS Place

Now, they were nine, being joined by Joseph's Austin and the boy Moses, who wouldn't be of any service as a soldier but could help with the horses and mules.

The younger boy Samuel observed the gathering at a distance, wondering what was going on.

The men idled in the shadows near the kitchen house and the cider press, several of them enjoying the cider. Jack sat off to the side, fretting.

The drinking did not bother Nat. These men were drinking men. And if the brandy and the cider made them bolder, better fighters, if drinking helped to give them an extra courage neither he nor the Spirit could provide, then so be it.

So he let them enjoy themselves, quietly, and waited with them, patiently, until he could be absolutely sure that the family was sleeping soundly, until he could be absolutely confident that the men were truly ready to translate their brave words into brave deeds, until . . .

! ! !

2 a.m.
MONDAY
August 22nd

At the front door, Nat stood with a hatchet, Hark with a broadaxe.

"Windows be latched, too," Hark reported in a whisper. "Massuh jus' don' trust other folks' niggers – Nat, you wan' me to put this axe to the door?"

"No – Too much noise. You wake up the whole neighborhood ... Fetch me the ladder."

Hark handed the axe to Will, and went for the ladder.

Quickly returning, Hark leaned the ladder against the side of the house, under the small open window to the upper hallway. Nat handed the hatchet over to Austin, then climbed up, and with some difficulty squeezed himself into the house.

Soon, the downstairs door opened.

Hark and Will entered, the two of them and Nat soon exiting with four shotguns, three muskets and a small quantity of gunpowder.

Nat again held the hatchet.

Will still held the axe.

Tomorrow Jerusalem: The Story of Nat Turner and the Southampton Slave Insurrection

Nelson spoke: "We knows you don' 'specially wants to, Nat, but you's the leader - You's the Gen'ral ... You should strike the first blow."

Nat braced himself, and re-entered the house, closely followed by Hark and Will and Nelson, up the stairs.

Hark and Nelson stationed themselves at the door to the boys' room as Nat and Will entered the master's bedroom.

Nat knew what must be done, but his hand shook at the thought of it.

He raised the hatchet, hesitated - then struck at Joseph Travis, the blow glancing off Joseph's head but stunning him awake.

"Sally!" the master cried out.

Will swiftly raised his axe, and swiftly brought it down - then raised his axe again, and brought it down again - and Joseph and Sally Travis were dead - just like that. It was so simple, really.

Within seconds, across the hall, Putnam Moore and Joel Westbrook likewise passed from the here and now into eternity.

While Hark and Will and Nelson hurried downstairs, to let the others know it had happened, the insurrection had begun, Nat lingered - to kill little Joe, now awake but quiet in his crib.

Nat reached down and picked up the baby. In the faint moonlight, little Joe looked up and smiled. Nat returned him to the crib, stepped back, slowly turned his head toward the bloodied bed, then left the room, rubbing his eyes, erasing the tears.

It was done, and he must not regret it.

*

For another hour, with the Moon gradually lowering in the sky, the men - insurgents now, soldiers now, leaders of the army which would liberate all of the slaves of America - remained at the Travis place.

In vaguely military fashion some of the men who wore hats decorated them with turkey feathers and most of the men adorned their waists and shoulders with strips of red fabric torn from the interior of the master's fancy carriage. As the army increased in number, they agreed, strips of bloodied sheets would serve the purpose.

At Nat's direction, the soldiers practiced some of the most basic military drills he had seen.

From time to time, some of the men visited the cider press, but it did not bother Nat.

Their mood was right.

Finally, with Nat and Hark riding the master's mules, Will and Nelson riding the master's horses, followed afoot by the others, the group started down the lane toward the road.

And the instant they left, a small shadow cautiously entered the house ... and soon quickly left it.

Senseless with fright, the boy Samuel ran into a cotton field toward the woods, and disappeared into the night.

*

Scarcely onto the road, the group halted.

Bill Bryant

Hark had asked about the baby, and Nat told him, and Will objected - and Nat could not afford to argue, not with Will, not now.
"Nits do make lice," the General muttered. "Will ... You an' Nelson."
Will and Nelson rode off toward the house.

*

Within only a few minutes, barely enough time to do what they went to do, Will and Nelson returned, Will claiming he had taken the baby by its heels and smashed the baby's brains against the downstairs brick fireplace.
Sickened, Nat said nothing.
Wordlessly, the group again began to move.
Not a one of them had ever killed another human being, until tonight. Now, already, all of them were involved in the killing of five white people. And many more blacks would soon become involved in the killing of many more white people.
Some must die, to make others free.
It was as simple as that.

Southeasterly a quarter of a mile

SALATHIEL FRANCIS Place

With the others standing around the corner of the small house, well out of sight, Nathaniel's Sam and Will stood at the door.
Will knocked, loudly, with deeply felt urgency.
"Who is it?" Salathiel sleepily demanded to know, at this ungodly hour. "Wha' do you want?"
"Massuh Salathiel, this be Sam! Your brother Nathaniel, suh, he as' me to bring you this here note - He say it mos' important, suh!"
Salathiel unbolted the door and opened it.
Will reached out and grabbed Nathaniel's younger brother and pulled him outside, and the three men grappled, Salathiel yelling out: "Red! - Get me my gun! - Hurry, man - for God's ... "
As Will finally brought his axe in action, Red Nelson dashed out of the house, ran a short distance, then paused, to see whatever he could see. At the flash and roar of a shotgun, he winced in pain, then ran away.
And the group moved forward, unworried about Red, quickly forgetting him.

Southeasterly a half of a mile

WIDOW HARRIS Place

As the group proceeded silently through the farmyard, the widow's man Joe joined the army.
The widow and her daughters and grandchildren slept undisturbed.

*Tomorrow Jerusalem: The Story of Nat Turner
and the Southampton Slave Insurrection*

And when morning came, the children would walk to school, as usual — thanks to Joe — no thanks to Will, who grumbled more than once to Nat about the need to kill, without exception.
But the second exception was made.
Nat had decided, and Nat was in command.
Forward!

Southeasterly a mile

PIETY REESE Place

The door was unlocked.
Will and Joe entered.
In a moment, a boy's voice could be heard in the darkness: "Who is there?"
And suddenly, the boy could speak no more. Nor could his mother.
Piety's overseer James Barmer, awakened in another room, tried in the confusion to flee, but could not, and called for help, but none came. And when Will with his axe and Joe with his grubbing hoe were satisfied that the crumpled form on the floor was lifeless, they left the house.
Barmer had no difficulty pretending to be dead, and wished he was.

Southerly three miles

WILEY FRANCIS Place

Wiley Francis didn't know why his slaves were so agitated and apprehensive, but they definitely were troubled by somethin', and they had let him know it.
His men claimed not to know just what was happening in the neighborhood, or what was supposed to be happening, but said that a lot of other local blacks had been very restive yesterday. The men thought they should let the master know — somethin'.
Francis trusted them, which explained why he and half a dozen of his men now stood on or near the porch of the house at the head of the lane, only 15 yards from the gate at the road, waiting, for somethin' — Francis armed with a shotgun, his men with hoes and scythes.
"I can' believe there really is any trouble," Francis assured them. "But if there is, here is where we'll find it."
Another slave, carrying a shotgun, appeared at the front of the house — almost breathless. "I's here, massuh."
"You sure my wife an' daughters are well hidden?"
"Yassuh! — They be good an' safe in the woods."
"Well done," the master said.
"But they sure wishes you was with 'em."
"No! I'll not ... Shush!"
Whoever the would-be troublemakers were, they were now in the roadway, in moonlit silhouette, halting.
Francis, to be on the safe side, assumed the worst. "Here I am, boys!" he called out. "I will not go from my home to be killed!"

Bill Bryant

Will responded: "We jus' wan' somethin' to drink, massuh — some brandy, or some water. We won' be botherin' you none — Please, massuh!"

Wiley's man with the shotgun moved toward the gate. "You boys cross that fenceline, it'll be the last thing you do! — Now be gone! Ain' nothin' here — not for you!"

Nat, counting the shadows near the house, whispered to Hark: "The ol' man ain' worth killin'. There'll be time for takin' him — an' his people — later. Let's move on."

Thus, without another word, the group in the road departed, at a leisurely pace.

"I do not like the looks o' this," Francis said. "Go fetch my family!"

"Yassuh," said the gun-toting slave, promptly moving to do it.

"We," said the master, "are gettin' out o' here — all o' us — Tell Mary to come here, right now!" he shouted at the departing slave.

"Yassuh!"

Francis thought it best to send the mulatto girl Mary directly to the farm of Howell Harris and his wife, Wiley's daughter, with some sort of message ... Better safe than sorry.

The crisis here seemed to have passed, for now.

The trouble-makers were gone ... God knows where.

Northeasterly four miles

5:30 a.m.
ELIZABETH TURNER Place

A light rain began falling while the nine insurgent slaves made their way to the Turner place, where life was already stirring by the time they arrived, in early dawnlight, thirsty, in Nat's old neighborhood.

Elizabeth's overseer Hartwell Peebles was at the still along the lane when Henry, Sam and Austin arrived ahead of the others. Austin aimed his musket and fired, and Peebles fell dead.

Soon, all of the insurgents were moving up the lane.

Someone inside the main house opened the front door, then quickly shut and bolted it. Will dismounted, went to the door, and broke it open with his axe.

Inside a back room, Will and Nat located Elizabeth and her neighbor Sarah Newsome, standing clutching one another, terrified.

Their terror was brief.

As Will applied his axe to the widow Turner, Nat grabbed the other woman's arm and with his sword struck at her — once, twice — each blow glancing off.

Will finished the job.

*

Nat found his mother hard at work inside the kitchen house, unaware that it had started.

He told her.

*Tomorrow Jerusalem: The Story of Nat Turner
and the Southampton Slave Insurrection*

Initially speechless but not surprised, really, frightened for him but believing devoutly in his mission, of course, Nancy held her son in her arms, but only briefly, for time was precious. "I be prayin' for you," she promised him. "I be prayin' for all you boys!"
"Jus' you wait here – We be back soon!" he promised her.
"I be waitin'."
He gave her a tight hug, kissed her on the cheek, then turned and walked away – refusing to stop and look back. He would see her again, he promised himself.

*

While Nat was with Nancy, the other insurgents refreshed themselves with Turner brandy and visited the cabins, to recruit.
And the army now numbered 15.
Considering his options, Nat decided to send six men on foot in one direction, under the command of Hark, while he and eight other mounted men headed in another direction – knowing exactly where, if not exactly when, they would all be together again.
As the groups separated, the widow Harris' Joe was happily adjusting his new suit of clothes – Hartwell Peebles' Sunday-go-to-meetin' best.
Nat did not look back, to see if Nancy was watching.
She was ... proudly.

* * * * *

JOHN WILLIAMS Place

With his horse saddled and eager to go, Choctaw Williams stood at the foot of the front steps saying goodbye to his wife, standing in the doorway with the baby in her arms.
"I'll be comin' straight home when school is over," he told her.
"I do envy your pupils. They get to spend so much more time with you than I do."
"But they don't enjoy it half as much! – When are you leavin' to go visit Lavinia?"
"As soon as I can get rid o' you – Go!"
"Your wish is my command!"
He stepped up and leaned over and kissed his baby on the forehead, gently, then kissed his wife on the lips, and shared a happy smile with her.
As he pulled himself up onto the saddle, she took the baby's hand and began waving goodbye.
He turned the horse toward the road, and began the ride to work, calling to his darling: "I love you!"
He did not hear her reply.

*

Bill Bryant

    Someday, he had often promised her, they would be able to afford a nice new carriage – well, maybe not new, but certainly very nice – so she would not have to walk so far to get to wherever she wanted to go.
    Of course, a carriage in any condition would cost money, more than he could afford at his current salary. But Nathaniel, a great believer in education, was talking about starting a school at his place, with Choctaw as the teacher – at a better wage. If Nathaniel's dream became a reality, the teacher's wife might soon be riding around in a nice new (or very nice second-hand) carriage – and the teacher would be working closer to home.
    He missed her already.

* * * * *

GROUP 1

Northeasterly several hundred yards

HENRY BRYANT Place

    Henry Bryant and his wife Sally and their child and Sally's mother were at home when Hark and his men stormed in.
    The white people were dead when the black people left.

GROUP 2

Easterly a mile

CATHERINE WHITEHEAD Place

    Downstairs in the main house, standing next to a big tub of soapy water on a table, Caty Whitehead was cheerfully bathing the baby of the family, with two of Caty's own daughters as well as her mother standing nearby. Four generations thus enjoyed the morning routine.
    Upstairs, Caty's other three daughters were getting dressed, the first important decision of the day being made when, after much discussion and debate, Margaret opted for a light-colored dress and Harriet opted for a dark one.
    Some distance away along the winding lane leading up to the house, Caty's son Dick, having fed the pigs, joined several of his slaves working in a cotton patch.

*

    The mounted insurgents rode into the lane, halting at the scene of labor.
    Dick turned to one of his slaves. "What do you suppose this means?"

*Tomorrow Jerusalem: The Story of Nat Turner
and the Southampton Slave Insurrection*

"I don' know, massuh," the puzzled slave replied, beginning to sense fear, in himself and in the young master.

Will spoke: "Dick! ... Come over here!"

More than wary now, noting the weapons the men were carrying, but not daring to ignore the challenge, or run, Caty's boy obeyed and with as much authority as he could muster walked over to the split-rail fence along the lane.

And there, near the cedar tree in whose shade he liked to sit and read his Bible — there, with his own people just standing by and watching, dumbfounded, helpless — there, asking again and again why they were killing him even as the blacks in the lane shouted at Will to kill him, kill him — there ... Richard Whitehead was summoned to the feet of his Creator, bewildered, unprepared.

*

Through an upstairs window, Caty's old Hubbard witnessed the distant horror in the field.

Immediately, Hubbard began shouting for everybody to hide — quickly — now, hurry — running into the girls' bedroom, telling Harriet to get herself under the mattress on the big bed, herding Margaret and the other sister into a closet space between the chimneys — then running downstairs, breathless, shouting.

Seven of the insurgents entered the house, Nat, along with Moses steadying the horses and mules, remaining in the farmyard.

*

As the work began inside, Nat saw a girl run from the back of the house, and the General gave chase — twice lunging with his sword, to strike a fatal blow — twice missing — giving up the chase only when he realized she was a servant girl.

At the Travis place and at the Turner place and again here, he had failed to make the final awful leap from being one sort of person to being another sort, to serve the cause — had failed, again, to prove that he, too, could slay an enemy.

Questioning himself, Nat walked back toward the house, demanding to know what he lacked, to be fully the leader these men needed, and expected.

*

One by one, the insurgents came out of the house, with captives — soon slain.

In time, Will emerged, dragging behind him Caty Whitehead, struggling and sobbing.

Wailing at the sight of the accumulated bodies, released from Will's grip, Caty kneeled on the ground among them, and bravely pleaded with Will: "I do not wish to live without my children!"

Will decapitated Caty.

Bill Bryant

Suddenly, Margaret ran from the house, fleeing toward a field of corn. But the General chased after her, caught up with her, and struck at her repeatedly with his sword without striking her, then in a blinding rage cast aside the sword and grabbed a nearby fence rail — and hit her with it, and killed her — and stepped back ... stunned to see what he had done, in the sight of his men.

Yet even as the warrior blood within him surged, the person he had been was sickened.

He did what needed to be done, and would do it again, if necessary.

But he would not necessarily enjoy it.

*

More numerous now, Nat's group assembled in the farmyard.

Two of Caty's men had joined. Now two more stepped forward.

"Preacher Nat," said one, "here be another fightin' preacher for the army — a good Methodist! — An' this other man, he say he be comin' along, too!"

Nat, tightly gripping the hilt of his sword, welcomed them.

The insurgents moved back down the lane, past Dick's body at the edge of the abandoned cotton patch, toward the road where the General's forces would be united, then divided again.

Seven lifeless bodies remained behind beneath the early-morning Sun ... yet only seven.

* * *

Hubbard lifted the mattress — and there she was, terrified, but alive.

"Miss Harriet! Thank God, you are saved!" He helped the girl onto her feet. "We don' be stayin' here, child — Come along with me, to the woods!"

He led her downstairs, out the door, past the bodies, dear God, into the woods.

* * *

7:30 a.m.

In the roadway at the end of the lane leading to Caty's place, Nat's group and Hark's group met and merged, immediately engaging in a spirited exchange of experiences, of conquests.

Most of the insurrectionaries were now mounted. All of them were now armed, though with a crude assortment of guns (with limited ammunition and gunpowder), knives and sharp-edged farm tools, and at least one sword, though dull.

Nat watched as Hark finished talking with two men who had come walking down the road, cradling shotguns.

Hark approached, followed by the men.

Tomorrow Jerusalem: The Story of Nat Turner and the Southampton Slave Insurrection

"This here's Joe, an' Nat," Hark said. "Say they been coon-huntin' with ol' massuh's guns — Say they got better game to hunt now!"

"Praise the Lord — Welcome, brothers!" Nat said, then: "Hark, how many men you count?"

"I counts 24 — an' no sign o' the whites bein' warned."

"They'll know soon enough — You take half the men over to Mistuh Doyle's an' the Harris place. I'll take the others to Mistuh Porter's. We'll meet at Nathaniel's — From here on," he said commandingly to Hark and the other generals nearby, "we put the best men in the front," now raising his voice to all of his soldiers, "an' we moves faster! We strikes harder!"

The men cheered.

* * * * *

8 a.m.
NATHANIEL FRANCIS Place

Apprehensively, Lavinia and her mother-in-law stood at the door of the house as Nathaniel approached, leading by the hand a very scared, badly scratched and thoroughly exhausted black boy — Joseph's boy Samuel.

"I don' know what to make of it," the baffled Nathaniel tried to explain, satisfactorily, to the women. "Accordin' to the boy, there's been some kind o' trouble at Joseph's place. The boy's in such a state I can' get any facts from him — an' I don' think he really knows what he's talkin' about. But I'm gonna ride over there, to see for myself that everything's all right — Now, don' worry yourselves, ladies — I'm sure there's nothin' to this."

"Do be careful, Nathaniel," Lavinia said, as her little nephews appeared from nowhere, attracted by the flurry of excitement.

"Y'all be watchful," Nathaniel instructed them, mounting his horse. "Take care o' Samuel — an' try to keep an eye on the other boys, too," he said with a glance at his nephews. "An' tell Henry when you see him," he added, thinking it best that his overseer and stiller Henry Doyle be told, somethin'.

Riding away at a hard gallop, Nathaniel strained to remain convinced that he was doing the right thing, assuming the best, which a quick trip to Joseph's would confirm, rather than assuming the worst, which required him to be with his family, to protect them — but from what?

When he heard Samuel's frantic declaration that "folks had killed all the white folks," Nathaniel could only smile in disbelief, of course, and tell the boy he didn't know what he was talking about — an' not to repeat such talk to the womenfolk. But now, with the boy's words echoing relentlessly, he could only frown. He had to be right, doing this — Why, if because o' him not bein' there anything should happen to Lavinia, or ...

*

No sooner had Nathaniel's dust begun to settle than his mother, knowing her boy was truly worried, made up her mind.

Bill Bryant

"I must go over there, too," she said, removing her apron and handing it to Lavinia. "If anything has happened to Sally an' the children, I ... "

"I understand. We'll be all right - Please be careful!" Lavinia called out as the older woman headed toward the bypath through the woods, making as straight a line as possible to Sally's, walking as fast as she could, wanting to run.

* * * * *

GROUP 1

Westerly a mile

TRAJAN DOYLE Place

On their way to the mill, to work well together, as usual, Trajan and his man Hugh were interrupted by the arrival of General Hark and his men.

Even as the master was being overwhelmed, Hugh ran toward the house.

Slamming open the front door, never pausing, not saying a single word to explain his bizarre behavior, he grabbed up the baby playing on the floor and grabbed the master's wife by the arm and while she begged for an explanation he carried the baby and led the mother out the back door, into the thicket overgrowing the old graveyard nearby.

The insurgents soon arrived in the farmyard, searched through the house and the outbuildings, found no one, then paused to refresh themselves.

GROUP 2

Northerly a mile

RICHARD PORTER Place

The white people had all gone, but had left behind their guns - and their black people, among whom Henry had much influence.

"Jacob here," said Henry, indicating one of the four new recruits, "he say a mulatto girl name o' Mary done brought Mastuh Porter a message - from Wiley Francis! Jacob say that gal be warnin' other white folks, too!"

Nat, seeing the task becoming harder, the danger greater, the prospect of battle more real, tried not to frown too hard, too visibly. He had known this moment would come, but knowing it did not lessen its impact, when it came.

Jacob reported: "Porters all wen' skedaddlin' jus' as y'all come up - jus' took to the swamp! Sweet Jesus, it was a sight to behold, yassuh! ... So now, Preacher Nat - General Nat - we is your people! Me an' Moses here, an' Aaron an' Daniel, we been prayin' with you for years, an' now we be ridin' with you on the road to glory!"

*Tomorrow Jerusalem: The Story of Nat Turner
and the Southampton Slave Insurrection*

"Hallelujah, brothers!" Nat exclaimed. "But to ride with us, you be needin' horses - Go mount up," he told them. Then: "Will!"

"Here, Nat!"

"We got to ride harder, faster - Take the men an' go to Nathaniel's," he ordered, turning his mule in a different direction.

"Where you goin'?"

"To find the others, hurry 'em along - Try to keep the men away from the stills. Can' get but so much courage that way - The men've got to be sober enough to fight!"

"I'll do what I can, Nat," Will promised. "But this a powerful hot day, an' mighty hard work ... How we gonna find you?"

"Don' try - We'll find you! If we don' meet up at Nathaniel's place, you know where to go next - Now move 'em out!"

Prodding his mule in a southwesterly direction, away from Jerusalem, soon Nat was alone with his troubled thoughts. A battle could come at any time, his forces were divided, and their General was advancing into the countryside - alone, with his troubled thoughts, and recent memories - Damn the white man for making him do this!

* * *

GROUP 1

Northerly a hundred yards

HOWELL HARRIS Place

Now carrying Trajan Doyle's pocketbook in his own pocket, to keep his own money and important papers in, Hark was more than frustrated, he was downright angered, to learn that Howell Harris and his wife had fled only a few minutes earlier - warned by a mulatto girl, name o' Mary.

Hark was angry at Howell, he was angry at Mary - he was angry at his men, for lingerin' so long at Trajan's - he was angry at himself, for lettin' 'em.

So he decided to give chase to Howell, in the direction indicated by the master's people, even if it meant retracing the group's previous course, which it did.

* * *

GROUP 2

Northerly a mile

NATHANIEL FRANCIS Place

While his eight-year-old brother Samuel lurked among tall weeds not very far away, three-year-old John Brown fearlessly approached the insurgents now reining their horses near the main house.

"Can I ride on horse?" the boy asked.

Bill Bryant

Will answered him, Will's way.
Witnessing his brother's beheading, Samuel screamed, and ran ... and soon shared his brother's fate.

*

Having seen the menacing blacks riding up the lane, Henry Doyle was inside the house trying to warn Lavinia when Red Nelson entered the upstairs room, gasping for breath as he grasped the situation here.
"I simply cannot believe it!" Lavinia said, in defiance of the overseer's general alarm – in defiance of what Joseph's boy had been babbling, 'bout folks killin' folks – in defiance – now panic at the unplayful screams and ungodly noises coming from outside. "It cannot be true!"
"It be the truth, Miss Lavinia!" Red exclaimed. "They done already killed Massuh Salathiel – You got to hide! Now!"
"Do as he says, Lavinia," Doyle said.
"Up there!" Red said, pointing to the darkened cuddyhole where the family's dirty clothes were collected for washday, just over the front doorway.
As quickly as the burden of her unborn baby allowed, Lavinia concealed herself, with Red's help, among the dirty clothes.
Doyle raced down the stairs and out the door, shot down the very instant he emerged from the house, falling mortally wounded at the foot of the steps, beginning to groan as with excruciating slowness he passed away.
Lavinia, hearing him so near, fainted.
Thus did Will and Jack discover only Red in the upstairs room, standing near the cuddyhole.
"You again!" said Will, readying his axe.
"I's on your side now, Will," Red had sense enough to say. "Ol' Red, he be ridin' with y'all now!"
"Where Massuh Nathaniel?" Will demanded, unconvinced.
"Not here," Red guessed.
"Where Miss Lavinia?" Will demanded.
"Don' rightly know – But I helps you find her!"
While Will searched the closet and Jack checked under the bed and under the mattress and Red thoroughly rummaged through the dirty clothes, there was no hint of life or motion within the cuddyhole, except within Lavinia.
"She not here," Red announced. "I bet she hidin' in the garden – out in the tall cabbage."
Will scowled, still doubtful of Red's true loyalty but disposed to believe him when Red said, more convincingly: "No suh, she sure ain' here!"
"Le's go," Will growled.

*

Following a fruitless search of the garden, General Will began the chore of reassembling his scattered troops.

*Tomorrow Jerusalem: The Story of Nat Turner
and the Southampton Slave Insurrection*

As he did so, a woman clutching a baby suddenly appeared in the lane near the house — just standing there, befuddled by the strangely busy scene in the farmyard, and at the cider press.

Several of the men went to her.

And soon, the beloved wife of Choctaw Williams and their precious baby were no more.

*

Nathaniel's Sam and Will had influence among Nathaniel's other people.

Dred and another man came forward, followed slowly by the older boys Nathan, Tom and Davy.

"Dred," Sam asked, "what you plannin' to do?"

Dred grinned. "Plannin' to make a trip into Jerusalem ... Them three boys ain' too happy 'bout the idea, though."

"Make 'em come," Sam said. "More men be ridin' with us, more fearsome we be! Jus' put 'em toward the rear, with Jack, an' keep a close watch on 'em!"

"Le's go!" Will shouted, for all to hear.

*

Finally, with nearly all of Nathaniel's men and boys now more or less willingly serving as soldiers in the army of liberation, Will — outwardly the model of a confident commanding officer, inwardly desperate for some sign of Nat or of Hark and the others — led his column down the lane.

The mid-morning Sun had blazed away what little relief the light rain had brought, and the day promised to become ever more scorchingly hot, the work ever harder.

And Jerusalem was still many miles away.

* * *

In the lingering dust of the departing riders, the dazed Lavinia came out of the house, stumbling over Henry Doyle's mercifully lifeless body.

In the farmyard, Charlotte and Easter were squabbling again, this time disputing the possession of Lavinia's wedding dress, Charlotte brandishing a knife.

Seeing Lavinia, Charlotte let go of the dress, and redirected the knife. "I thought you was dead! — If you not dead, you soon be!"

Easter dropped the dress onto the ground, then stepped between Lavinia and Charlotte, declaring: "You not gonna kill my mistress! She been real kind to me! Touch her if you dare, an' I will kill you!"

Charlotte moved slightly forward.

Easter stood firm.

"Where," Lavinia asked, "are those men?"

"They gone," Charlotte said. "But they be back for dinner — Done already killed the chickens!"

Charlotte again advanced.

Bill Bryant

    Easter stood firm.
    Charlotte thought about it, turned, and ran down the lane.

* * * * *

BENJAMIN BLUNT Place

    At the fence in front of the house, a mounted white man excitedly told his story, then jabbed his heels into his lathered horse's flanks and rode away.
    The white man and woman standing at the fence glanced at the four black men gathered at the well, then ran into the house.
    "Ah," said one of the black men, with great self-satisfaction, "didn't I say there would be a war? - I told you so!"
    The men congratulated one another - and the prophet in their midst - for living long enough to see this blessed day.

BENJAMIN EDWARDS Place

    At the hitching rail behind the house, Berry Newsom, Isham, Hardy and a free black woman were discussing the earliest reports, or rumors.
    "Well, if it do be true," Berry easily decided, "I gots to go find 'em! - I gots to be with 'em!"
    "We all gots to be with 'em!" Hardy said.
    "Fools!" the woman proclaimed. "You all be fools! - Berry Newsom, you be the biggest fool! - You a free man! You ain' got no sense mixin' in this!"
    "Woman!" snapped Isham. "Shut your mouth! - You already got your freedom! - This shoulda happened a long time ago! We been punished long enough! ... Le's stop talkin', an' go!"
    The woman frowned and shook her head as the three men hurried off to borrow some horses from the master.

CROSS KEYS

    With a rider galloping away into the distance, kicking up a fierce storm of dust, the owner of the general mercantile store tried to explain the hastily conveyed garbled message to several other white men who had come running over when they saw the hullaballoo.
    "The British?!" the merchant incredibly repeated. "I don' know whether to believe it or not - But somethin' bad is happenin'. I'm goin' over to the schoolhouse ... Somethin' very bad ... I'm gonna recommend the children be sent home - The British?!"

JERUSALEM

    Amid the frenzied concern of the white men and women crowded near the front counter of his store, postmaster Thomas Trezevant shakily

*Tomorrow Jerusalem: The Story of Nat Turner
and the Southampton Slave Insurrection*

scribbled a note, most closely watched by Edward Butts, the deputy sheriff of Southampton, and the young but strong and experienced horseman Thomas Jones.

Such a short and simple note, really ... Such a monumental labor!

"No need waitin' for more information," Trezevant muttered, urgently trying to shape the letters into legible words, to make the words into a coherent - and credible - message. "We know for a fact that there's an uprisin' an' that several families have been murdered - God knows how many people may be dead already! - We need help!"

"A lot o' help," said Butts. "If what we're hearin' is true, this could be a general risin'!"

"Could be," Trezevant grimly said, attempting his signature - forcing the pen to perform the familiar routine, finishing, finally! - "Thomas!" he said with calm authority now, pushing his way through the crowd toward the door as he tried to fold the note neatly, almost crumpling it, then handing it to the young horseman as they reached the street - where many more men and women and children were anxiously gathered, even as many more were anxiously arriving, mostly from south of the Nottoway.

"Tommy," the postmaster said as Jones smoothly mounted his horse, "we are all dependin' on you, son - Ride as hard as you can! - Godspeed! - Go!!!"

Immediately, without a word, Thomas Jones went - as fast as his beloved and pampered but powerful and obedient horse would allow - carrying the brief astonishing message addressed to the Governor of the Commonwealth of Virginia ... in Richmond ... some 70 miles away ... as the crow flies.

* * * * *

GROUP 2

Northerly a mile

PETER EDWARDS Place

Congregated to the side of the main house in the wonderful shade of ancient oaks, Will counted 20 men now, including five new faces.

Apart from the insurgents stood other slaves of the prosperous master, in varying aspects of amazement.

Standing alone at the rear of the house, near the brick steps leading down to the basement, Peter's overseer old Jeff duly noted the five familiar faces in their new identity as rebels.

Will was hot and thirsty and furious. "Ol' Jeff over there done warned the family! - I say we should kill him!"

"Leave him be!" said Nelson, no less hot and thirsty but less furious with his brother-in-law. If he let Will kill Jeff, his sister would never forgive him. "Nat say we supposed to be killin' white people - not our own! ... 'Sides, he can' do us no more harm now."

Joe, formerly the property of the widow Harris, asked the question to which all of the men wanted, needed, deserved an answer: "Where is Nat?"

"Nat be comin' along any minute now," Nelson said firmly, wondering, "an' Hark, too - You gots to have faith ... like Nat say."

Bill Bryant

From a cabin along the orchard lane, Nathaniel's Sam emerged, having made a brief visit just long enough to say hello, and possibly goodbye forever, to his dear mother - who, knowing that her dear son must do what he must do, tried only weakly to talk him out of it, then hugged him tight enough to squeeze the breath out of him, then sent him on his way, with her prayers.

Rejoining the ranks, mounting his horse, Sam said: "Time to go! - Still no sign o' Nat? - or Hark?"

Northeasterly three quarters of a mile

JOHN THOMAS BARROW Place

Having learned the basic truth but none of the circumstances of the killings even before reaching the Travis place, Nathaniel Francis had gone no further - and had dispatched the first trustworthy slave he could find on a mission to warn certain people, including John Barrow.

Barrow was more puzzled than alarmed as he thanked the messenger and watched him leave.

A curious message indeed - somethin' about the British comin'!

No sooner had the black man left than a white man arrived, neighbor Drewry Bittle, with a much more rational and infinitely more threatening report - The slaves're risin'!

John asked a personal favor of Drewry, who, naturally but with very little enthusiasm, agreed to do it.

Then, while Drewry hastened back along the lane to position himself to give John some advance warning, John positioned himself to put up a fight if need be, fetching his shotgun and rifle and pistol - even while preparing to flee on a moment's notice, exhorting his wife Mary to get ready, quickly, please.

Mary, ever mindful of her beauty and not disposed to go somewhere visiting wearing an ordinary workdress, was not in that great a hurry. She insisted on changing into something more appropriate. Besides, she called out from the bedroom to the front steps: "We should wait for my brother George - Y'all are goin' fox-huntin', remember? - Shouldn't we wait?"

"No!" John shouted at her, not for the first time inconvenienced by Mary's sweet vanity, but for the first time endangered by it. "For God's sake, Mary!"

"But if we ... "

"We are goin' to Newitt's - an' that's final! - Please, Mary!"

*

By the time Drewry Bittle saw Will and his men charging along the road, the blacks were almost on top of him.

There being no time even to think much less worry about warning John, the good neighbor did the next best thing and ran, pursued by several of the blacks.

Reaching swampland, Drewry stopped to remove his shoes and cast them aside, then waded and stumbled into the swamp, beyond the reach of the horses and guns of his pursuers.

Tomorrow Jerusalem: The Story of Nat Turner and the Southampton Slave Insurrection

"Never mind!" one of the blacks shouted to him from the water's edge. "We get you yet!"
"Not today!" replied the gasping voice from within the swamp.

*

By the time John saw Will and his men charging up the lane, the blacks were only 30 yards away.
"Run, Mary! – Run for your life!" he begged his wife now standing shocked at his side.
She hesitated, and then, just as her husband squeezed the trigger of the shotgun, she grabbed his arm and deflected his aim – and then and only then, finally, she ran, for her life.
And there on the front steps of his home, Captain John Thomas Barrow made his stand!
As the rapidly dismounting insurgents stormed toward him, Barrow fired his rifle to no apparent effect, then fired his pistol to no apparent effect – then shattered the stock of the rifle against the heads of his assailants.
The blacks forced Barrow through the doorway, battled him into the hallway, struggled with him into a side room, pressing him against the wall, toward an open window, straining to control the man enough to kill him.
Outside, an insurgent with a razor reached inside, and ... cut the man's throat!
Thus did the desperate combat finally end, leaving the black men staggered, gasping, stunned by the ferocity of the man.
The courage of the man!
The late John Thomas Barrow.

*

Even as the fighting within the house began, out in the farmyard the slave Lucy had grabbed hold of the frantic Mary, managing to control her for more than a minute – an agonizing eternity – while repeatedly screaming to the insurgents outside the house preoccupied with the drama inside: "Here she be! – I got her! Over here! ... Come get her!"
The men at the house did not respond.
But Aunt Easter did.
The old slave woman yanked Mary away from Lucy's grasp, shoved Lucy to the ground, then ran hand in hand with Mary toward the woods.

*

Will and the men who had fought Captain Barrow, together with the other men who had witnessed the fight, did honor to the fallen warrior, in an African way.
They wrapped his body in a bed-quilt and placed it in the middle of the floor of his bedchamber, and put a plug of chewing tobacco on his chest ... Then, one by one, all of the insurgents touched fingers to

Bill Bryant

the man's fatal wound and tasted his blood, to strengthen their courage, with his ... Alone among the victims of the insurrection, he was respected.
   Then, joined by the master's Moses, the insurgents departed this place ... with Nat and Hark and the others nowhere to be seen.

*

   Someone else, however, did appear in the roadway – cradling a shotgun.
   George Vaughan, Mary's brother, Rebecca's son, Anne Eliza's cousin, never knew what hit him.

Northwesterly a mile

NEWITT HARRIS Place

   With Newitt's wife off visiting in Sussex and his married daughters living hither and yon, if anyone was going to take good care of the feeble but stubborn old man, it would have to be his overseers and stillers, the brothers Ben and Aaron, and Aaron's wife Aunt Edie.
   Ben had heard the admittedly questionable but nonetheless disturbing rumor about the British while returning home this morning from a weekend visit with his wife. But Newitt vigorously shook his head and utterly refused to credit Ben's report, gruffly dismissing the pleas of Ben and Aaron and Aunt Edie.
   "I do not care what you have heard, Ben!" the old warhorse thundered. "I will say it again: The story you heard is ridiculous! It's, it's preposterous! The very idea!"
   "But massuh," Ben started to try again, "what if ... "
   "No!" Newitt roared, wanting to get up out of his chair and make a proper demonstration of defiance. "The British would not dare to set one foot on the soil o' Southampton County!"
   "But massuh ... "
   "It is only a rumor – An' I am not scared by rumors! – I was not scared when Aaron an' I went off to fight the British durin' the war, an' I shall not retreat now from a mere rumor – not one inch!"
   Ben braced himself. "Massuh Newitt ... You shall go!"
   And with that, Ben reached down and lifted up Captain Harris and draped the protesting old man over his shoulder and, followed closely by Aunt Edie tellin' the master jus' to stop his complainin', carried him out of the house into the nearby swamp, while Aaron went to alert Newitt's other people.

*

   Just in front of the gate at the head of the lane leading up to the Harris place, two roads – one approaching from the southwest, the other approaching from the southeast – converged to become the Barrow Road, the way to the road into Jerusalem.

*Tomorrow Jerusalem: The Story of Nat Turner
and the Southampton Slave Insurrection*

And as soon as Ben returned to the house, he could see the trouble comin'!

From the southwest - a speeding carriage, trailed by a thin line of dust.

From the southeast - a mass of horsemen riding hard, raising a stormcloud of dust.

The carriage had the racing advantage, and Ben ran to meet it.

In the carriage were Newitt's daughter Charlotte Elizabeth and her baby boy and her husband's 10-year-old brother George Musgrave. George had been sent home from school with a report - silly, it seemed to Charlotte Elizabeth - that the British were coming, but then she had been told by a slave that the slaves were risin', that she should seek safety at her father's place - sensible advice, it seemed to Charlotte Elizabeth, so she immediately obeyed it.

So here she and the young ones were, unwittingly riding straight into the center of the insurrectional storm!

Met by Ben, who hurried the carriage into the farmyard, she received not a word of advice but a set of strict orders - to go into the house, fast, closing the door behind them, then to run down the center hallway, out the back door, to the fence at the edge of the cornfield, then ...

"But where is my father?" Charlotte Elizabeth pleaded.

"He be all right," Ben assured her. "Y'all jus' get on over the fence, an' hide in the corn - I be comin' for you directly!"

"But where ... ?"

"Go!"

So, holding her baby to her bosom, with young George at her heels, the bewildered woman went - fast.

*

Will with his axe was the first to dismount, followed by several others with their guns, confronting Ben.

"Where your white people?" Will demanded to know. "An' who was that in the carriage?"

"Cap'n Harris an' his wife both gone," Ben said. "Miss Charlotte Elizabeth, she 'round here somewhere - Came tearin' through here lookin' for her daddy - I helps you find her!"

So together they entered the house, and together they searched throughout it, finding no one.

And in the hallway near the open back door, Will with his axe and the others with their guns again confronted Ben.

"Ain' got time for this foolishness!" Will fumed, brandishing his axe. "Now, where she be?"

"Maybe," Ben began, pausing, stalling long enough to brace himself just well enough to - bolt out the back door, running for the cornfield when the fowling gun spoke through the doorway and stung his back with birdshot, wincing but not slowing, clambering over the fence, into the corn.

Done with that problem, Will and the others soon exited the front door of the house, to discover another problem - the master's Aaron exhorting the other insurgents to quit, telling them bluntly that what they were trying to do was impossible and they had better return to their homes and just pray for the best. In plain language: "Y'all be makin' a big mistake! Y'all jus' better stop it right here an' now!"

"Shut your damn mouth!" Will roared. "Or I shut it for you!"
"I ain' 'fraid o' you, Will Francis!" Aaron shot back. "You men gotta listen to me! - My massuh done took me with him to Norfolk when we was fightin' 'gainst the British, an' I'm tellin' the truth ... "
"An' I'm tellin' you for the last time," Will began. "You ... "
"There's too many white folks for y'all to be fightin' 'em - too many! - I seen 'em with my own eyes!"
As Nathaniel's Will moved to solve this problem, Nathaniel's Sam intervened. "Jus' you back off an' be quiet," Sam sternly told the master's man. "Jus' you step aside."
Aaron backed off, and stepped aside, but not very far ... observing, quietly.
Sam turned his attention to the troops. "Rest your mounts, men! Check your guns! - Search the house for weapons an' powder! ... Nat an' Hark be comin' along soon - real soon!" he needed to believe and therefore promised the men.

* * *

Deep in the cornfield, the excitement and the heat overcame Charlotte Elizabeth. She fainted, her baby in her arms, the doctor's kid brother just sitting on the ground at her side, wide-eyed, unable to do anything about any of this.
However, soon Aunt Edie was at hand, reviving Charlotte Elizabeth and leading her with the baby and the boy toward the swamp, to locate the old man.
But the finding of Newitt Harris proved to be more difficult than the hiding of him, and soon they were back in the woods, lost.
Then, to make matters worse, the baby began to cry, fitfully at first but obviously building toward an ear-splitting outburst, a real wailing.
Charlotte Elizabeth tried to comfort her baby. "The poor thing is dyin' o' thirst!" she cried, patting the infant's head with her handkerchief.
"I hates to do this," Aunt Edie said - taking charge of the situation and stuffing the handkerchief into the baby's mouth. "But if they hears this chil' cryin', they catch us for sure - I go fin' some water."
"How? - Where? - Oh, Edie, don't leave us here alone!"
"Shush!"
"Please don't go!"
"I said shush!" The older, wiser woman harshly whispered, no less lovingly but now more urgently than she had quieted Charlotte Elizabeth as a child. "Ol' Edie be findin' that baby some water ... somewhere."

*

Remarkably, Aunt Edie soon returned carefully carrying in her hands a crude cup contrived with oak leaves, filled with rainwater painstakingly collected from the deep indentation of the hoofprint of a cow.
Remarkably, too, she had chanced to find Newitt Harris.

*Tomorrow Jerusalem: The Story of Nat Turner
and the Southampton Slave Insurrection*

And as soon as the baby was pacified, Aunt Edie led the master's kinfolk to him.

* * *

9:30 a.m.

Will and most of his men were mounted and ready to ride, Will puzzled that not only the white people but also the black people had deserted this place - even Aaron having slipped away, unnoticed.

Some but not all of the insurgents had helped themselves to brandy from the barrels now split and littering the farmyard - some but not all because of the nagging pleas of Sam, who kept reminding them: Nat is comin', and when he ...

Suddenly, a distant swarm of dust, approaching on the road from the southeast, settled all doubts.

And soon enough, Nat and Hark and 20 others rode into the lane toward the house, doubling the strength of the fighting force - with the road to Jerusalem apparently wide open - with many whites still quite unaware, surely, of what was happening - and with most other whites fleeing in disorderly terror from the path of the advancing army ... which might be any path.

And there in Newitt's farmyard, the groups merged.

(Their cheering and shouts of jubilation loudly penetrated the edge of the woods, where Ben and Aaron and the master's other men, armed with pitchforks and hoes, were standing guard, just out of sight. And the sounds of celebration reached well into the woods, where Aunt Edie was doing the best she could with Charlotte Elizabeth, the baby, the boy and Captain Harris, who now was calm and cooperative, and still unafraid, for himself.)

Surrounded by his soldiers, Nat explained his - and Hark's - delay. He had located Hark's group still searching for Howell Harris. Then, riding hard, they had arrived too late at the Francis place, and too late at the Edwards place, and too late at the Barrow place - so rapidly had Will's group been advancing.

Will, anxious to leave here, rushed through a description of what his group had experienced, making special mention, of course, of Captain Barrow, the great struggle, the tribute to the white man. "Like a demon, that man fought! ... We tasted his blood."

Nat nodded, appreciating the tribal honor. "I am truly sorry such a brave man had to die. Good thing we didn't meet up with him early on - An' bes' we pray there ain' no more John Barrows!"

"Amen," several bloodied men in the congregation murmured.

Henry spoke: "We goin' by Major Drewry's next? - Lot o' the men want to go by there. He make some mighty fine brandy."

"No!" Nat stated in no uncertain terms. "Been too much brandy already," he muttered, knowing that on this hot day, with these men, doing this work, there would be much more.

"Amen to that, too," Sam solidly agreed.

"From here on," Nat addressed the impatient assembly, "I want Will an' Hark an' our best armed men ridin' up front - From here on, we moves even faster! We strikes even harder! - We really puts the fear o' God in 'em!"

The men cheered.

Bill Bryant

Then onto the Barrow Road the army moved, Nat on his mule lagging behind as the best of his fighters charged forward.

Northeasterly three miles

LEVI WALLER Place

Levi was working at his still, a quarter of a mile away from the school near his house, when several local slaves arrived in a hurry to confirm the fact, not the rumor, that the Negroes, not the British, were killin' people – an' were at the Harris place, an' headin' this way.

Levi sent one of the men to fetch teacher William Crocker, and to alert the master's wife to make ready to flee.

Soon, midway the still and the school, near the crossroads, Levi encountered Crocker and most of his more than a dozen pupils.

"You understand the situation, William?"

"'Fraid so – Levi, your wife thinks you an' I should leave, but that she an' all o' the children should stay – She figures you an' I are the ones they want, an' surely they wouldn't harm the little ones."

"Can't take that chance," Levi decided. "Go to the house! Load the guns! – Then ... "

But it was already too late.

Much too late.

The sudden hard-charging arrival of the point of Nat's thrusting spear sent the white men and boys and girls running for their lives.

*

Levi fled toward the tall weeds next to the fence at the blacksmith shop just as his blacksmith Davy came upon the scene.

Davy, seeing his master running, started running in a different direction, pointing and yelling frantically: "Here goes the ol' fox! – This way!"

The distraction succeeded, several of the insurgents giving chase to the phantom fox while the others rode by.

Davy then ran to the tall weeds, and helped the shaken Levi into the plum orchard, and up into the leafy branches of a tree, to observe what was happening.

*

Twelve-year-old Clarinda Jones tried to persuade 10-year-old sister Lucinda to run toward the tall weeds. But Lucinda fled instead into the kitchen house, and climbed up into the chimney, so Clarinda hid outside in a dark corner space between the kitchen and the chimney.

It did not take long for one of the insurgents to find Lucinda, to pull her screaming from the chimney, to slay her.

Clarinda, doing well to control her panic, waited for the man to leave.

Tomorrow Jerusalem: The Story of Nat Turner and the Southampton Slave Insurrection

*

Hiding behind a tree, William Crocker waited until it seemed safe, then fled toward a cornfield, unpursued.

But his gold watch fell out of his pocket, and, thinking it unwise to leave behind a clue to his direction, he went back to get it – thereby attracting the attention of an insurgent, who with sword in hand pursued the white man toward the cornfield, got almost close enough, then reined his horse, cast aside his sword, pulled out his pistol, and began to aim.

But the insurgent was distracted by a white girl crossing the nearby lane, so he turned to pursue her – firing his weapon at her as she scrambled over a fence, into tall weeds.

There, slightly wounded with buckshot, Clarinda did not panic, but remained quiet and motionless, trying not even to breathe, as the insurgent came near – nearer – very near, his horse munching on the weeds concealing her ... until, finally, he went away.

*

Inside the main house, one of Levi's men killed Levi's wife with a slashing razor, and the insurgents began ransacking the place, looking for victims and for valuables.

Levi's little daughter Martha, concealed under the apron of her black nanny, betrayed herself, emerging from hiding to protest the breaking of the furniture, and threatening to tell her daddy.

The nanny begged the men to spare the child, but they pushed her aside.

And one of the insurgents seized Martha, took her outside, and slammed her to death upon the ground.

*

When it was all over, Levi Waller and his two sons and William Crocker and a few of the schoolchildren had managed to escape. But not Levi's wife and not his daughter, nor at least 10 of William's pupils.

When it was all over, two of Levi's people had joined the army. Yellow Davy changed into a suit of Levi's clothes. Albert headed for the still.

When it was all over, Nathaniel's Sam sat upon the back steps, surveying the carnage, and wept.

And when it was all over, Nat arrived.

*

Clarinda, hiding now in the crawlspace under an old workshop, as calmly as possible practiced her numbers as the attackers departed.

Bill Bryant

She counted higher than 40 ... easily.

Southeasterly three miles

WILLIAM WILLIAMS Place

William Williams was working with the young brothers Miles and Henry Johnson out in the fodder field, some distance from the neat and comfortable cottage he now shared with his recent bride.

So his bride was at home alone when the hardest riders among the insurgents arrived at the doorstep, one of them immediately giving her a choice – either to die right then and there, or to die alongside her husband.

She chose the latter, waited until the riders had started off on their angry search, then ran, away from the house and toward the woods, as fast as she could.

But one of the blacks, glancing back, saw her, turned his horse around, gave chase, and, finally, overtook her. Then, with distant gunfire echoing, he made her sit behind him on the horse ... and transported her to the field where the echo had begun.

There, amid the three bodies, the insurgent told her to dismount.

She did as she was told, then got down on the ground alongside her man, and was shot to death.

*

Briefly resting his men near the cottage, once he himself had arrived, Nat reckoned the strength of his army at approximately 50 now – adding the men who had heard he was approaching and made the effort to join him, subtracting the men who had imbibed too much brandy and fallen by the wayside.

Still, there were many white people, even this near to Jerusalem, who didn't have the faintest idea of what was happening.

Still, there was no hint of resistance.

* * * *

LEVI WALLER Place

"Incredible," said Captain Arthur Middleton, as the stunned commander of the Southampton County militia and a hastily organized group of 20 men rode so slowly through the scene of slaughter. "Horrible," he said, thinking of his wife and children, at home.

"Captain Middleton!" one of the men called out. "There's a little girl over here – badly wounded!"

"Put her in the shade of a tree! There isn't anything else we can do for her now, there isn't time ... My God, this is ... "

"We must find 'em!" declared Captain Alexander Peete. "An' stop 'em!"

*Tomorrow Jerusalem: The Story of Nat Turner
and the Southampton Slave Insurrection*

Captain Middleton made up his mind. "I am goin' home, to take care o' my own family — Some o' you other men may wish to do the same, now that we realize what we're dealin' with."

"Your concern is understandable," said Captain James Bryant, "but isn't it more important now to ...

"I am goin' home — Most o' you men are unmarried — Go with Captain Peete an' Captain Bryant an' find these murderers! ... I must go home!"

Middleton and two other men then rode away in one direction.

Captains Peete and Bryant and 16 other men rode away in another direction — southeasterly along the Barrow Road.

* * * * *

Southeasterly a mile and a half

JACOB WILLIAMS Place

At about 11 o'clock, William's uncle Jacob had been puzzled but not alarmed when he chanced to see his man Nelson near the main house, wearing his, Jacob's, best clothes. But the master had better things to do than to deal with eccentric Nelson, so he went off into the woods to measure some timber.

At about noon, Nelson tried to entice overseer Caswell Worrell from a field, where he was supervising some slaves, up to the main house. Caswell started for the house, but noting whose clothes Nelson was wearing and remembering Nelson's recent strange prophecy, soon reconsidered the situation carefully — and fled.

Just in time.

At noon, the insurgents began arriving.

Jacob and Caswell were off in the woods somewhere, but other white people were at Jacob's place, and at Caswell's a few hundred yards away, all quite unsuspecting.

In the corn crib next to the lane near the road, James Bell's overseer Edwin Drewry and Bell's man Stephen were waiting for Jacob to return.

"I sure do hope Mister Williams gets back here soon," Drewry said. "We got to get this corn loaded, an' — Lord ... who is that comin'?"

Too late, Drewry tried to run.

In a fury of dust and rage, the insurgents shot, then disemboweled, Bell's overseer ... then forced Bell's man Stephen to come along with them.

*

Jacob Williams was not at home, but his wife and their three children were, and died.

*

145

Bill Bryant

Caswell Worrell was not at home, but his wife and their two children were, and died.

*

When Jacob finally did emerge from the woods, unnoticed, he had just enough time to comprehend the meaning of the bodies in the farmyard and the guns in the hands of the blacks who seemed to be everywhere — just enough time to dash, unnoticed, into a cornfield.

There, he crouched, observing the insurgents raiding the kitchen house and eating their noontime meal, hearing Nelson shouting somethin' about havin' "the ol' fox" now.

He waited for them to leave.

Southeasterly a quarter of a mile

REBECCA VAUGHAN Place

Rebecca's son George had been sent to John Thomas Barrow's to fetch her dear daughter Mary, with instructions to return promptly not only with Mary, but also with several men who planned to do some fox-hunting — after being properly fed, of course, by the always hospitable widow Vaughan.

Rebecca's other son Arthur happened to be walking in the lane well away from the house, with Rebecca's overseer, when the leading insurgents galloped into the lane.

Shots were fired, and the two white men fell dead.

*

Rebecca was on the back porch preparing the beverages, and the lovely soon-to-be-wed Anne Eliza was upstairs, when the women happily heard the gunshots.

Rebecca went upstairs, to hurry Anne Eliza along.

"I think our hunters have arrived," the widow said, "though I didn't expect 'em quite so soon."

"Not too soon for me," Anne Eliza said. "I am starvin' to death!"

Then, there was much talkative commotion just outside the house.

"What could that be?" Rebecca wondered, straightening the sheet on the bed, gently smiling despite the odd ruckus. Anne Eliza was less than a perfect housekeeper.

"I'll go an' see," her niece said, leaving the bedroom, proceeding down the stairs.

Then, there was a scream, and there was a gunshot — and Rebecca hurried to the open upstairs hallway window, and she saw — "Oh, no," she whimpered.

Will spoke: "Come on down, Miss Rebecca ... Make it easy on yourself!"

"Please," she said, understanding what must soon happen, "allow me to pray!"

*Tomorrow Jerusalem: The Story of Nat Turner
and the Southampton Slave Insurrection*

"Bes' be brief!" Will told her. "Don' take too long!"

She got down on her knees, and started praying ... and continued praying, ignoring the shouted curses and threats from down below ... and took too long.

Then, she heard men stampeding up the stairs ... And there at the window, on her knees in prayer, Rebecca Vaughan met the axe.

Southeasterly two miles

Along the BARROW ROAD

Riding all together slowly now in the glaring hot sunlight of early afternoon, enabling the stragglers and the more heavily intoxicated men to catch up, if they could, Nat counted more than 60 men.

The new recruits, Nat noted, did not include a single one of the supposedly influential Nelson's fellow slaves at Jacob's place – only Bell's visiting man Stephen, who clearly did not want any part of this.

"Not much gunpowder," Hark reported, riding up to Nat and Will and Henry. "An' we's mighty short on ammunition."

"Use sand! Use gravel!" Nat declared. "Serve the same purpose ... There'll be plenty o' ammunition – an' guns an' gunpowder – in Jerusalem!"

"I still don' understan'," Will grumbled, "why we didn't go on up to ol' man Gray's place."

"Got my reasons," Nat replied, still debating the decision. The ol' man himself deserved no special charity on this day, but his son, well ... Thomas did merit some consideration, even on this day. "Nothin' to be gained by goin' on up there – not with Jerusalem so near!"

"More white folks," Henry said, "be livin' jus' up ahead."

"We pass 'em by," Nat calmly said, not questioning now a decision made some time ago.

"Why?" Will asked with scarcely concealed anger.

"'Cause they jus' po' white folks," Nat firmly explained. "Think no better o' themselves than they do o' us – I said," he quickly added, stifling Will's next protest, "we pass 'em by – We are goin' to Jerusalem!"

Finally, with his well mounted if weakly armed force massed behind him, Nat increased the pace – but not too much, to enable the mass to remain intact.

Finally, passing by several lanes leading to the homes of poor whites, Nat could see the ending of the Barrow Road meeting the main road into Jerusalem – only four miles away.

Finally ...

Northeasterly three quarters of a mile

JAMES PARKER Place

With the army halted near the front gate of the very long lane leading up to the especially prosperous Parker place, Nat kept staring toward Jerusalem even as he heatedly discussed with his generals what to do next.

"We should ride!" Nat declared.

"But some o' the men," Hark argued, "have kinfolk here - an' think we can recruit some o' Parker's people."

"Nat," Nelson said, "we's powerful hot an' tired an' thirsty - an' we needs more men!"

Nat could not argue with that, and yet: "Jerusalem ... "

"Nat," Hark said, sensing the leader weakening, "we won' be long up at the house," he promised.

Nor could Nat afford to spend the rest of the afternoon idling here discussing the matter, so: "I want some o' the men to stay here with me, jus' in case - Y'all go - but don' be long!"

*

Seven men remained with the General as the army advanced rapidly along the narrow lightly curving lane, gradually disappearing among the weeds and bushes and trees lining the path.

Dismounting, Nat stood in the middle of the road and gazed intensely toward Jerusalem - and saw a lone rider entering the road from another Parker lane a few hundred yards away, toward town - his eyes keen enough to see that the rider, galloping hard, was a woman, carrying somethin'.

Nat waited.
And waited.
And waited.

Until finally: "I'm goin' up to the house," he announced, mounting his mule. "Preacher," he told the former property of Caty Whitehead, "you in charge here!"

* * * * *

JERUSALEM

The town was in total turmoil.

The streets and alleys and yards were teeming with hundreds of agitated and extremely fearful people, most of them white, very few of them able-bodied, armed men.

There was precious little time for explanation, or argumentation, when James Parker finally located, then forcefully confronted Edward Butts near the north end of the bridge.

"An' then," the planter said to the deputy sheriff, "my wife remembered she had forgotten the baby! - So she had to ride back to get the child, an' barely got away - I'm tellin' you: They're at my place right now! - Send every man you've got available, an' you can stop 'em!"

Butts tried to make Parker understand: "Most o' the men are already lookin' for 'em - You got to appreciate the situation here, Mister Parker! - There mus' be upwards o' 400 women an' children here - an' damn few men to protect 'em - jus' a handful o' militiamen who've managed to report for duty!"

Tomorrow Jerusalem: The Story of Nat Turner and the Southampton Slave Insurrection

"If you don't send 'em out there – now! – there's gonna to be a massacre here – soon!"

"All right!" Butts yielded. "All right! ... God help us!"

* * * * *

PARKER'S Gate

Riding even harder after discovering the new evidence at Rebecca Vaughan's, Captain Peete and Captain Bryant and their men – including the darkly grieving John Vaughan, Anne Eliza's daddy – slowed the pace as they turned onto the Jerusalem Road, warily, nervously looking ahead, slowing ...

The whites saw the blacks at the gate before the blacks saw them – and the whites charged, firing their weapons and scattering the blacks.

The gunfire made Hartie Joyner's new colt friskier than usual, and Captain Bryant's horse started becoming skittish.

Pausing only long enough to reload their guns, the men proceeded with great caution, and grim resolve, into the lane.

PARKER'S Home

Nat's worst fears had been realized when he reached the farmyard.

Having ransacked the house, the men had rolled several barrels of Parker's brandy into the yard, poured the contents into tubs, sweetened the brandy with sugar, then freely indulged themselves – not all of them, but too many – too freely.

So more time had to be lost while Nat tried to restore a sense of order to the army, reminding his other generals of their neglected duties, waking up some of the groggy soldiers, stirring his men into action.

Once, he thought he might've heard the distant sound of gunfire, but amid the noise of the farmyard he couldn't be sure.

When the troops – including not even one of Parker's people – were finally reassembled, Nat and Hark led them slowly into the lane.

PARKER'S Gate

With no one in sight and no sound or sign of disturbance anywhere, the handful of men sent out from Jerusalem dismounted.

"They've got to come this way," one of them reasoned aloud. "Here is where we'll meet 'em!"

PARKER'S Lane

At a distance of 150 yards

The opposing forces found one another.

Bill Bryant

Both groups slowed almost to a halt, then began fanning out into the large adjacent cotton field, forming crude lines of battle.

Captain Peete said to his men: "Hold your fire 'til we're at 30 paces!"

General Nat said to his men: "Be brave, men! ... Forward!"

Both forces advanced, ever so slowly, the whites becoming ever more aware of the number of blacks approaching them.

PARKER'S Field

At a distance of 100 yards

By odd chance, the colt being ridden by Hartie Joyner recognized among the insurgents' horses its own dear mother – and bolted forward, causing Hartie to fire his gun aimlessly as helplessly he charged, alone, toward the enemy.

Both sides watched in brief amazement.

In the confusion and indecision, with the battle prematurely beginning – and the impressive number of the blacks now painfully apparent – several of the whites began to turn back.

Nat seized the fleeting moment of opportunity.

"Fire!" the General shouted. "An' God-damn them!! – Rush!!!"

And most of his men charged, and many of them fired.

PARKER'S Gate

Hearing the echoing report of a single gunshot a half a mile or so away, the militiamen had tensed.

Hearing the serious splattering of gunfire, the militiamen mounted their horses as fast as they could – and rode hard to the sound of the guns.

PARKER'S Field

At a distance of 50 yards

Seven of the whites were now in full retreat, and Hartie was plunging into the midst of the insurgents, his colt peppered with buckshot.

Captain Peete and Captain Bryant and the other eight men held their ground, and fired their weapons – and suddenly Bryant's horse bolted, becoming wildly unmanageable, bucking the helpless militiaman across the cotton field, away from the action.

Peete and the others now also began retreating into the field, but slowly, clumsily reloading their weapons as the blacks returned fire as fast as they could finish reloading, advancing in disarray, slowly – but advancing.

Maddened, John Vaughan picked a likely target and during the fierce exchange once, twice, thrice shot a horse out from under his elusive target — and once, twice, thrice Hark found himself a new mount, once with Nat's timely assistance.

Two of the whites had fallen to the ground, though only stunned. Several of the blacks had been killed and several others wounded, one of them, Nathaniel's Dred, dreadfully.

Retreating some 200 yards from the loosely advancing blacks, the whites disappeared over the crest of a small hill.

Reaching the crest of the hill, the blacks discovered the whites not only halted and reloading, but also re-enforced and preparing to counter-charge ... And at the sight of them, the rebels leading the advance reversed course, triggering a panic among the rebels following them.

The battle in Parker's cotton field was at an end.

*

Nat rallied some 20 or so men to him — including all of his generals — and with undiminished resolve led them toward a private path he knew, a shortcut to the Cypress Bridge.

They would cross the Nottoway downriver at the Cypress Bridge, Nat told his men as soon as it seemed safe to halt and rest, and then they would advance upon Jerusalem from the east, recruiting along the way — perhaps even joining forces with other groups of armed slaves inspired by word of the insurrection.

Have faith, the Preacher exhorted them, the cause no less holy.

* * * * *

JERUSALEM

The mounted man hollerin' as loud as he could as he charged across the bridge was a black man — claiming to belong to James Bell, claiming there had been some sort of battle out at Parker's place, claiming a victory for the whites — and claiming he had seen it only because he had been forced to accompany the rebels, at gunpoint.

At gunpoint, Stephen was escorted to the empty jail.

There would be time later for sorting out the details of his story.

CYPRESS BRIDGE

One of the white men guarding the bridge thought he saw some movement among the bushes near the south end of the bridge, but it was brief.

There weren't many men at the north end of the bridge, but they were well armed and felt secure behind the overturned wagon serving as a barricade.

To be even more on the safe side, the men had removed some of the bridge's crossplanks, to impede cavalry.

Bill Bryant

Near MONROE

Downriver, several rowboats congregated near the middle of the Nottoway, under the merciless Sun.
Colonel Mahone, not knowing the direction the trouble might be coming from, solved his problem for the time being simply by putting his people in the safest place he could think of – in position to flee to either shore – while he went to Jerusalem to serve with the militia.
Thus, Billy Mahone, and the others, baked, for the time being.

BILLY KITCHEN Place

In front of a crude "fort" in the woods, contrived with hewn bushes and tree limbs and old timbers, within which the master's white and black people were very closely huddled, Billy Kitchen finished his conversation with his main man.
"I mus' go," Billy said. "They'll need all the men they can muster. 'Sides, we've done about as much here as we can."
"You jus' be on your way, Cap'n Kitchen," the slave said. "Our people be doin' jus' fine – Don' you worry none!"

JOHN IVEY Place

At the front of his small house, John Ivey and ol' John made it clear to one another.
"If I don' come back, John ... "
"You be comin' back, massuh."
"But if I don' come back, you're a free man, an' the place is all yours – That paper I wrote for you will make it right with the law."
"You comin' back!"

GATES COUNTY

Many Southamptonians were among the hundreds of folks attending the camp meeting down in North Carolina, sharing in the rejoiceful singing of a favorite hymn when a man rode into the encampment at full speed, shouting, trying to get their attention, shouting louder, until ...
Finally, with the faithful murmuring against this rude interruption of the sacred service, he made his hellish announcement: "The Negroes are in a state o' insurrection in Southampton County, an' are killin' every white person from the cradle up – an' are comin' this way!"
Oh so briefly, there was perfect silence.
Then, perfect terror.
And the camp meeting ended ... in perfect chaos.

*Tomorrow Jerusalem: The Story of Nat Turner
and the Southampton Slave Insurrection*

MURFREESBORO

A large crowd quickly gathered around Levi Waller, standing next to his exhausted, frothing horse.
Having located his two sons, Levi and William Crocker had found horses and ridden to Cross Keys, Levi then obtaining a fresh mount and riding hard down into North Carolina, to spread the alarm.
Repeatedly pointing northward, constantly gesturing frantically, speaking almost incoherently at times but sensibly enough, he provided the North Carolinians with the first eyewitness confirmation of the awful but not credible rumors they had been receiving — about the British!

SOUTHAMPTON COUNTY

As the afternoon progressed, throughout the county thousands of people were fleeing, in every direction.
Growing streams of refugees poured into Jerusalem, into Cross Keys, into Murfreesboro, and toward hastily fortified places like Pate's Hill and Thomas Ridley's.
Many people fled into hiding, in the woods and swamps.
Some people, mostly north of the Nottoway and in the southeastern area of Southampton, were staying right where they were, either in continuing ignorance of the insurrection or in uncompromising defiance of it, or at least until the danger became immediate and obvious.
Many people were searching — individual whites looking to find loved ones, individual blacks wanting to join the insurgents, white patrols hunting for some sign of the murderers, the army of liberation seeking new recruits. Along separate paths leading nowhere, the free blacks Will Artist and Berry Newsom and Thomas Haithcock and others, free and slave, tried to locate the army.
Some people, white and black, were busily warning other people.
Gradually, control of most of lower Southampton passed into the hands of the slaves remaining at home.

* * * * *

Heading eastward from Parker's field, discovering the fortification of the Cypress Bridge, Nat turned his men to the southwest.
Men who had been waiting for an opportunity to escape the army had done so, most now trying to return home hoping that neither their absence nor their participation in the day's events had been noticed, several now helping to spread the alarm among the whites.
Even subtracting these, the army's strength again began to grow, adding not only a few of the men who had been scattered at Parker's field but located the army and rejoined it, but also a few new recruits who had heard about the risin' and managed to find the army, to join up.
More than 30 strong, Nat reckoned, the men now with him were either proven fighters or eager to prove it — still an effective force, perhaps more effective now. Encouraged, Nat sent several of the men

Bill Bryant

riding toward the home neighborhood, to tell the insurgents returning there to be ready to link up with him again in a few days.

The new recruits were only trickling in, while the army moved, finding it mostly by chance, yet they convinced the General, again, that a great many more men were willing and waiting to join – if only he could sustain the army long enough to enable them to join.

And perhaps, Nat repeatedly reminded himself and his men, the Spirit had been speaking to others like him, and perhaps, he prayed aloud with his men, the Sign had been understood elsewhere – and he and his men were now a part of some much greater enterprise – a general insurrection – a risin' everywhere ... perhaps.

Faith!

Southwesterly

SUGARS BRYANT Place

Just before the insurgents came, Sugars went, warned of the impending visit by neighbor James Gurley, who at a safe distance was riding ahead of the blacks and alerting the places being approached.

Halting here only briefly, Nat again consulted his memory of this part of the county, and then again consulted his other generals, all agreeing on their next destination, some two miles away.

Southwesterly

THOMASTON

As soon as James Gurley delivered his message, he rode away.

As soon as the widow Elizabeth Thomas got the message, she wasted no time collecting her children – George and Judy and Lucy – and telling her man Sam to fetch the carriage.

And as soon as Sam hurriedly led the horse and carriage around to the front of the house, the white people climbed aboard, Elizabeth taking the reins, telling Sam to take care of the place, then telling the horse to "Git!"

*

And at the very moment the carriage passed through the front gate, the insurgents arrived along the path entering the rear of Thomaston, charging toward the house – Elizabeth's white stiller seeing them just in time to leap over the well near the still shed and scurry into the bushes.

Nat, told by Sam that the white folks had skedaddled, rested his men at the still shed, only briefly but long enough to compel Sam and his son Leonard and several other Thomas slaves to mount up and prepare to ride.

Sam whispered to Leonard to lag behind and slip away from the group at the earliest opportunity, return home and tell his mama where his

*Tomorrow Jerusalem: The Story of Nat Turner
and the Southampton Slave Insurrection*

daddy had hidden the keys to the place, so she could take care of things until he, too, returned. Leonard understood.
The insurgents departed, riding hard.

Southwesterly

Glancing over her shoulder at the ominous dust cloud in the distance, Elizabeth realized that the insurgents were not only trailing and rapidly gaining on them, but also would soon overtake them — so she yanked hard on the reins and parked the carriage on the side of the road, and told the children to follow her, quickly now, toward the small bridge across the nearby creek.
And very soon the insurgents rode past the abandoned carriage and thundered across the bridge under which Elizabeth and her children were tightly huddled.

Southwesterly

At a considerable distance across open fields, James Gurley could see the blacks unknowingly pursuing a wagonload of white women and children.
His own horse too tired to go much further, Gurley pointed out the problem to neighbor Pitt Thomas.
And Major Pitt Thomas addressed the problem by racing his horse across the fields and daring to interpose his well armed self between the blacks and the whites — briefly retarding the progress of the former, until the latter could unknowingly escape onto another path.
Then, being brave but not stupid, Pitt made good his own escape.

Southwesterly

At the Spencer place, and at the Blow place, and at all of the other places the insurgents raided, all of the white people were gone.
With his generals surrounding him, and with the Sun in decline, Nat proposed their next destination: "Buckhorn?"
All agreed, and off the army rode.
And as it did, Leonard, lagging behind, slipped away.

* * * * *

WALNUT HILL

When, early in the afternoon, bachelor Harry Vaughan learned about the insurrection, he had assembled his slaves, and told them: "Now, y'all are at liberty to do as you like — Y'all can stay here, or y'all can go with the rebels ... I, for one, am stayin'."
The decision was made.

Bill Bryant

When, late in the afternoon, word reached the whites still at home along the Bellfield Road that the insurrectionaries were heading this way, no one at Walnut Hill budged.
Not Harry.
Not his people.
And the rebels rode past the gate.

SIMON BLUNT Place

Hearing of the uprising, Doctor Blunt had assembled his slaves.
With his family and his overseer Shadrach Futrell at his side, Blunt, speaking in his natural fatherly way - loving but stern - stated what he understood to be the facts of the situation, the facts being few, the situation being very muddled. He said he did not doubt the ultimate outcome of the risin' and the consequences for the men who participated in it.
Finally, he told his own people to make their own choice: "You can either stay here, an' help defend me an' my family - an' this place we share ... or you can go with the rebels - It's up to you!"
Thus, by the time word reached the doctor's place that the insurgents were heading in this general direction, the issue had long since been decided.
One slave who heard the doctor's blunt appraisal of the situation, and chose to stay, was a neighbor's man visiting his wife.

* * * * *

Northerly

BUCKHORN Quarters

The insurgents had ridden in a more or less straight line from the southeastern area of the county to the northwestern, unopposed, crossing the Jerusalem Road, crossing the Barrow Road, turning left onto the Bellfield Road, passing by Walnut Hill as quickly as they were passing by every other place along the way, making for this place.
Fewer than 20 hours and more than 30 miles after striking the first blows, the bone-tired, hot, thirsty, hungry army encamped, at sunset, on the edge of a swamp amid the cabins of one of several slave quarters belonging to the wealthy Thomas Ridley.
Further up the Bellfield Road (not far from Levi Waller's place over on the Barrow Road), Major Ridley's home - venerable Bonnie Dune - was itself an armed encampment, civilian soldiery encircling the white women and children of the neighborhood.

*

*Tomorrow Jerusalem: The Story of Nat Turner
and the Southampton Slave Insurrection*

As night began to cloak Southampton County, with a full Moon high up above, Nat sat down on the ground with his generals, to nibble at, or devour, the food provided by some of Ridley's slaves.

"Sentries posted?" Nat asked.

"Yes," Nelson answered. "How many o' Massuh Ridley's people have agreed to join us?"

"Four," Sam answered.

Nat added: "An' Curtis an' Stephen over there are gonna ride some mules down to Newsom's an' Allen's quarters, to recruit. I told 'em the whites are much too scared to give 'em any trouble — How many men we got?"

"'Bout 40," Hark guessed. "Stragglers an' new men still comin' in, one by one — I ain' seen Sam or any o' those others from Thomaston for quite a spell. Where do you suppose ... "

"Not here!" Will angrily observed. "Nat, where we goin' in the mornin'?"

"Doctor Blunt's," Nat replied. "I figure he an' his family are up at Major Ridley's — but his slaves're prob'ly still at home, an' there's plenty o' 'em. I figure some'll join us ... Now, everybody try to get some sleep. It's been a long, long day — an' tomorrow ain' gonna be no shorter!"

*

Sleep, such as it was, was too soon interrupted, Nat awakening to a scene of general confusion punctuated by a gunshot blast into the night, then another.

"Stop!" the General ordered, complaining: "Can' be shootin' at every shadow!"

"Settle down!" Nelson shouted all around him. "You men," he barked at a few, "dismount!" Then to Nat he reported: "The boys're mighty nervous! — One o' the sentries say he thought the whites were attackin'!"

"Not likely at night," Nat said. "But better safe than sorry — Send out a patrol."

*

But when the patrol returned from finding nothing, its sudden unannounced arrival sent another streak of panic coursing through the encampment.

And when the new fever of fear had subsided, there were fewer soldiers than before. It was impossible to reckon how many, with so much comin' an' goin' in the middle o' the night.

* * * * *

Bill Bryant

3 a.m.
TUESDAY
August 23rd
GOVERNOR'S MANSION in RICHMOND

Upstairs, illuminated by the moonlight and occasionally cooled by a slight breeze entering silently through the open window, John Floyd was sleeping, droplets of perspiration on his forehead.

A lamplight appeared in the open doorway, and an old black man approached the bed, with respectful urgency.

"Massuh Floyd?" he softly asked, getting no response. "Massuh Floyd!"

"Uh," the Governor grunted.

The black man poked the white man's shoulder. "Massuh Floyd, suh, please wake up!"

"Wha' ... Uh," His Excellency grumbled, unready to wake up.

It was no time to stand on ceremony.

"John!" the slave declared.

"Wha' - what is it?" John Floyd demanded to know, knowing enough already to sit up and pay attention.

"Massuh Floyd, the Mayor downstairs, suh - He say he gots to see you - He say it mos' important, suh!"

"It had better be! - What time is it?"

*

Downstairs at his desk, in the light from two bright lamps, the Governor sat, adjusted his spectacles, then unfolded a battered sheet of paper.

Standing anxiously at the Governor's side was Joseph Tate, the Mayor of the capital city of Virginia.

Tate spoke: "Accordin' to the fellow who brought this from Petersburg, the courier from Jerusalem rode two horses to death carryin' this message."

"Chicken-scratch," the Governor muttered. "Didn't anybody ever teach penmanship to this ... this Tre- ... Who is this man?"

"Trezevant - Thomas Trezevant, the postmaster - The people in Petersburg managed to track down someone who could authenticate the signature."

"'Insurrection' ... 'several families killed' ... 'considerable force required' ... My God," the Governor whispered.

"It might be the start of a general uprisin'!"

"It might be anything! ... Rode two horses to death ... But for the time being, we must assume that it is somethin'!"

"What shall we do, Your Excellency?" asked the Mayor.

"Pray," John Floyd softly responded.

"Amen to that," said the old black man standing in shadows.

The master looked at his faithful manservant. "Do make us some coffee, please ... An' awaken my son ... He might jus' learn somethin' from this!"

The Governor removed his spectacles, and rubbed his eyes.

John Floyd had been a young man when Gabriel Prosser made his attempt at insurrection, that potential great tragedy so miraculously averted, by Providential rain and flood. And the name and fame of

*Tomorrow Jerusalem: The Story of Nat Turner
and the Southampton Slave Insurrection*

Prosser — and, of course, Vesey — were ever near the mainstream of his political, and personal, thoughts. Now, down in Southampton, a new passage in Virginia history was being written, no doubt inspired by some new Prosser, some new prophet. And he, John Floyd, was Governor — so, yes, this would indeed be an excellent educational experience for his son John Buchanan Floyd ... Now, where to begin?

The Mayor just stood there, outwardly composed but naturally nervous.

Joseph Tate was ready to act on his own initiative, to organize the defense of the City of Richmond. But a sense of tradition as well as common sense disposed him to wait, patiently, for leadership from the commander in chief of the armed forces of the Commonwealth of Virginia.

* * * * *

Northwesterly

SIMON BLUNT Place

Only the baby had slept well this strange night, all of the others in the hot main house, as well as all of the others stuffed inside the sweltering kitchen house, having slept little, or not a single second.

All night, ever since it became known that the insurgents had encamped only a mile or so away, a constant watch had been maintained here, awaiting an attack which could come at any moment.

Through much of the night, a bonfire dancing in a distant field continually shattered into tiny fragments upon the front windowpanes of the main house, and of the kitchen house.

Once, twice, the people at the doctor's place had heard remote noises of an obvious uproar coming from the direction of the Buckhorn Quarters. But each time, silence eventually returned.

On the front steps of the house stood Shadrach Futrell, the overseer cradling a shotgun, a pistol tucked inside his belt.

At the open front windows of the two downstairs rooms flanking the central hallway were two young, nervous, rapidly maturing neighborhood boys, armed with shotguns.

The solid double front doors in the hallway were solidly cross-bolted by a heavy beam.

At the three open dormer windows upstairs were Doctor Blunt, at the center window, 15-year-old Simon Jr. and neighbor Drewry Fitzhugh, armed with the only other guns available.

Also upstairs were the doctor's wife and the master's girl Mary, the women taking turns, from time to time, checking on the baby sleeping on the floor at the far end of the master bedroom. The women knew what they were there to do.

*

Again, the doctor's wife walked quietly from the blissful darkness of the bedroom to the bare shadow of the man sitting in the chair facing the front of his property.

Bill Bryant

"Simon ... I do wish you would reconsider," she tried one final time.
"No, my darlin'," he said, again, with stubborn sweetness. "I will not, I cannot abandon my home - our home. Jus' can' do it ... I'm tellin' you not to fret. Believe me: If they come here, we can handle 'em - 'specially with our own people and Drewry's people waitin' for 'em - Trust me, my darlin'," he said with a gentle smile. "You ladies know what your job is. Jus' worry 'bout reloadin' the guns."
"But ... "
"But if they do come, like I said earlier, give the baby to Mary - Mary!"
"Yes, massuh, I hears you - I takes the baby an' runs!"
"Straight to the woods - An' you wait there 'til it's over, you hear?"
"Yes, massuh."
"Are you satisfied now?" the husband asked his wife, knowing she would have to be.
"As satisfied as I can hope to be, my dear," she said, shaking her head but patting his shoulder, gently. "I'm sure you know what's best."
"Now," Simon Sr. said, in the spirit of command, "let's have some quiet - An' remember, men: Be particular in your aim - Wait 'til they come close."
"How close?" Simon Jr. asked.
"Real close," Simon Sr. said. "Real, real close ... until you can see the whites o' their eyes," he remembered.
The silence survived only a few seconds.
"Doctor Blunt!" the overseer called out in a harsh loud whisper. "I ... I think ... I think I see ... Here they come!"

*

Just before the break of day, the insurgents - now numbering only 20 or so but including the bravest - arrived at the front gate, some 80 yards away from the main house, and the kitchen house.
Finding the gate padlocked and chained, Nat said: "Break it down!"
Will put his axe to work, and quickly the lane was open.
Slowly, with Hark leading, the insurgents moved up the lane, seeing no sign of life in, or near, the house.
Arriving in the yard, the procession slowed almost to a halt.
Hark aimed his gun toward the house, and - to ask whether anyone happened to be at home - squeezed the trigger ...

! ! !

Immediately, Simon Jr. returned fire, and so did Shadrach, and the other guns inside the house began to speak, and the doctor's wife began helping to reload as fast as she could - even as Mary, with the baby, ran!

!

*Tomorrow Jerusalem: The Story of Nat Turner
and the Southampton Slave Insurrection*

In shock – and seeing the great Hark tumbling from his horse – some of the insurgents fired toward the house and the unseen enemy, and most of them, including Nat, began trying to turn their mounts away from the house, toward the lane or the cotton fields flanking the lane.

!

Following another barrage of gunfire from the house, suddenly Blunt's people and Fitzhugh's people – armed with hoes and scythes and pitchforks – erupted out of the kitchen house.
Shocking the insurgents again!

!

Captain Barrow's Moses was not ready to leave.
Seeing someone running from the back of the house, Moses dismounted, and gave chase.
Blunt's Mary reached the garden and quickly hid the baby, then turned to confront her pursuer.
And Blunt's man Ben arrived on the scene, brandishing a pitchfork, menacing the rebel into a corner of the garden fence, telling him: "God-damn you, I have got you now!"
Moses surrendered.

*

Some of the insurgents fled in no particular direction except away from the place.
But a dozen or so managed to stick with Nat, and these he brought to a brief halt as soon as they reached the road, out of range of the enemy's guns.
Will was in a rage. "Niggers be fightin' us! – Our own people! – An' where is Hark? – We needs Hark!"
"He'll catch up to us, if he can," Nat said, with a prayer. "He knows what the plan is – We must turn to the north!"
"Niggers be fightin' us!"

*

One of the insurgents had been killed, several others wounded and captured.
One of the prisoners, found struggling to crawl away in a cotton field, was Hark, very badly wounded.

* * * * *

161

Bill Bryant

MURFREESBORO

At the break of day, the streets of the small town were thickly crowded with parked wagons and carriages and tethered horses and mules, the whole place packed with refugees - upwards of a thousand of them - most still trying to get some sleep.

JERUSALEM

At sunrise, the first warming rays touched more than a thousand restless, and unrested, people.

CROSS KEYS

By dawn, the wild fears of the previous day had eased somewhat. Overnight, more than 200 armed men had formed a wide circle of protection around the crossroads, vigilantly standing guard.
Within the circle, more than 1,400 refugees congregated.
All wondering where the rebels were now.

* * * * *

Northwesterly

NEWITT HARRIS Place

Behind the main house, a mounted patrol of hostile militiamen from neighboring Greensville County confronted Newitt's Ben, who had sense enough to be very scared, and was therefore very nervous.
"Ya-ya-yassuh, they b-been here, ye-yesterday - B-but ... "
"You mighty nervous, boy!" one of the troopers said. "I say you must be one o' the bandits!"
"N-n-no-no, massuh! - I swear! - I ... "
Seeing several of the whites raising their guns, Ben now had sense enough to run, heading toward a nearby dependency, rounding the corner of the building even as he heard the guns fire and felt the buckshot burning into his flesh - an' he just kept on runnin'!
Wounded now by both sides in this infernal uncivil war!!
The militiamen, more or less satisfied with the results of their first light skirmish, decided this was just as good a place as any to rest their horses.
Most of the militiamen dismounted.

*

*Tomorrow Jerusalem: The Story of Nat Turner
and the Southampton Slave Insurrection*

    The Sun now just high enough in the eastern sky to begin baking the soul, again, the insurgents reined their horses and mules as they arrived amid a swirl of dust at Newitt's front gate, again.
    Newitt's Aaron happened to be there, and Aaron let it be known in no uncertain terms: "The Devil hisself is up at the house, boys – enough whites to eat y'all up!"
    Will growled: "You jus' get out o' our way, ol' man!"
    Aaron got out o' their way, jus' stepped back a little ... an' then some more, an' then, as the insurgents rested and began discussing their situation, the ol' man jus' slipped away, up to the house, to let it be known there, too, in no uncertain terms!

!

    And very soon thereafter, the Greensville militiamen came charging from the farmyard.
    Immediately, the insurgents retreated into the nearby woods.
    And there, in a brief but fierce exchange of gunfire, Will and most of Nat's few other remaining soldiers fell into eternity, dead, or mortally wounded.

*

    Only two managed to stick with Nat as he rode his mule toward a nearby swamp and dismounted, and shooed the mule away, and waded into the swamp, not stopping until all were too breathless to continue – not until the echoing of the guns had ceased.
    When the danger had apparently passed and it seemed safe to leave the swamp, Nat spoke firmly to his men – Richard Porter's Jacob and Edwin Turner's Nat – concluding: "You know what to do. Try to find my generals – Tell 'em," Nat said, unwilling to tell these two too much, even though it had become common knowledge among the insurgents that the generals had started out from somewhere near Cabin Pond, "jus' tell 'em to rally at the place where we had supper on Sunday – Now go! ... An' be careful ... I'm relyin' on you boys!"
    They promptly went.
    And Nat, searching for his mule, was alone.
    Either it was all over, finished an' done, or the whole countryside soon would be bathed in the blood of the general insurrection he, Nat Turner, had started.
    He found the mule, and mounted it.
    Yet obedient to the Spirit, Nat hoped an' prayed for the best.
    The Preacher still had the faith!
    The General was not ready to concede defeat!!

Bill Bryant

The Search

Bill Bryant

*Tomorrow Jerusalem: The Story of Nat Turner
and the Southampton Slave Insurrection*

Early Morning
TUESDAY
August 23rd
VIRGINIA CAPITOL in RICHMOND

    All of the windows were wide open, to invite the occasional welcome breeze, but the crowded conference room was uncomfortably warm.
    Seated around the massive oaken table, searching for answers to questions so rarely asked, were Governor Floyd, Mayor Tate, Captain Randolph Harrison of the Richmond Light Dragoons and assorted other functionaries of state and local government and the state militia. Standing were other men necessary to the task at hand, plus the Governor's son, John Buchanan Floyd.
    On the table were coffee cups and water glasses, ashtrays, various official documents, a large unfolded map of Virginia and, conspicuously at the center of the mess, the small unfolded message from Jerusalem.
    There had been no subsequent communication from the area of the uprising, merely the vague alarming rumors beginning to ripple through the capital city - mostly echoes from along the path young Thomas Jones had traveled.
    But the absence of any further word from Jerusalem was among the least of John Floyd's worries at this moment. Quite aside from the formidable logistics of mobilizing an appropriate response to what might be happening in Southampton, there was another problem, more pressing. The gentlemen who had designed the new Constitution of the Commonwealth of Virginia included most of the finest minds in the whole state, indeed some of the finest minds in the whole nation, but the product of their collective genius had certain gross defects - and one of these now aroused the wrath of the Governor.
    Floyd finished reading a recently delivered note, and exploded.
    "Well, that settles it! At last! - That wretched Constitution - I never did like it! Damned foolish, in an emergency like this, for my hands to be tied while we look all over town for a single other member of the Governor's Council to give me advice which I am free to ignore! Foolish! ... Where were we?"
    "The Lieutenant Governor, sir," said Tate.
    "Yes, well, he is back in town, he concurs - So let's get on with it ... Monumental stupidity!" the Governor growled. "Mister Tate, please continue."
    "I am satisfied with the arrangements being made to assure the security of Richmond," the Mayor reported. "Most of the people still haven't heard the news, but everyone will know by nightfall - and we'll be ready by then. Street patrols are being strengthened, barricades will be erected at the bridges, and all of the entrances to the city will be guarded - soon."
    "Good, good," the Governor said.
    One of the state functionaries leaned forward. "A dispatch rider is already on the road to Chesterfield, to alert the overseers of the coal-mining crews - and another rider is headed toward Stafford, to the stone quarries."
    "Wherever," the Governor emphasized, "there are large concentrations of the blacks, we must be very watchful. That includes the great plantations, especially along the James River."
    "And," added one of the local functionaries, "the public works projects."

Bill Bryant

"Yes, yes," the Governor remembered. "Make a note of it ... Speaking as a doctor, gentlemen, there is no way of determining just how grave the situation in Southampton actually is, or where the contagion may spread."

Tate had to report it: "There is already a rumor circulating that an army of 800 blacks has forced 300 whites into full retreat."

"Poppycock!" Captain Harrison declared. "I simply cannot imagine the men of Southampton retreating from a gang of field hands — whatever the numbers may be!"

"I agree," Floyd said, "that it is probably nonsense — But speaking now as a brigadier general, I am impatient to be prepared for battle. Captain Harrison, how many of your Light Dragoons can be mustered effectively, and how soon?"

"At least 60, sir, and we can be ready to leave for Southampton by late this afternoon — no later than 5 o'clock, I reckon."

"Excellent," the Governor said. "And what about Captain Richardson?"

"He has already begun mustering the Lafayette Artillery," Harrison reported, "and arrangements are being made with the arsenal for the transfer of a thousand rifles to his custody."

One of the militia functionaries added: "The steamboat Norfolk is available to transport Captain Richardson and his men, and the rifles, to Smithfield."

"Every county in the state," Floyd grumbled, "will be asking for its share of the guns ... Richardson does understand that he has my complete authority to requisition whatever wagons and horses he may need, at Smithfield or anywhere else?"

"He understands," Harrison said, "though I very much doubt he will need any special authority."

"Better safe than sorry," Floyd said.

Another one of the militia functionaries spoke: "Four companies of infantry are being mustered in Petersburg. We're assuming that the Southampton militia are already in the field, and that the neighboring counties are also responding — including the North Carolinians, of course."

The Governor yawned and stretched. "Make certain that our instructions are clear: The militia of Southampton and Sussex are to concentrate on crushing the insurrection. The Nansemond, Isle of Wight and Surry militia are to guard along the perimeter, to prevent any of the rebels from escaping — And General Eppes is in command — full command ... With 3,000 men, he should be able to do the job, and do it well."

The Mayor was still nervous. "Should we not reconsider the idea of asking for assistance from Fortress Monroe?"

"Absolutely not," the Governor replied, with a trace of annoyance. "This is a matter for Virginia to handle, and Virginia can handle it, and will handle it. And that is what frightens me the most."

Captain Harrison spoke for all of the other men in the room: "What do you mean, sir?"

"I mean ... Do you men realize how many Virginians I could call to arms if I felt like it? Counting all of the cavalry, the artillery units, the grenadiers, riflemen and light infantry at my disposal, the grand total exceeds 100,000 — Thunderation! Ol' Andy Jackson himself would not dare to move against so powerful a force!"

Harrison leaned forward. "I ... We still do not understand ... sir."

Tomorrow Jerusalem: The Story of Nat Turner and the Southampton Slave Insurrection

John Floyd – the doctor, the brigadier general, the politician, the slavemaster, the Christian, the husband and father, the human being – had felt this speech building urgently within him ever since the terrible truth of the message from Jerusalem, and its troubling implications, had penetrated to the core of his most inner self ... "Gentlemen," he began, "I regard slavery as an evil, as a curse we have sadly inherited. My position is a matter of public record: I very strongly favor compensated emancipation, with transportation, ideally to Africa. And I shall not rest until I have done everything within my power, as a private citizen and as Governor, to move Virginia in that necessary direction ... "

"But, sir," the Mayor began.

"Let me finish ... Heretofore, my opposition to slavery has been motivated primarily by economic considerations. But now, we are confronted with the reality of an uprising, which not only challenges many of the fundamental assumptions of our previous thinking, but also will surely cloud our future judgement. Yes, we can deal with this. We must. We shall ... But in the final analysis, I fear the dreadful truth of what Governor Hamilton of South Carolina said in 1822, when he was serving as the prosecutor in Charleston, in the case against Denmark Vesey. He said – and I consulted my personal papers earlier this morning to be reminded of his exact words: 'There is nothing they are bad enough to do that we are not powerful enough to punish' ... Gentlemen, I fear this insurrection, I truly do. But I fear even more the punishment it may provoke – I fear it mightily. I am confident that General Eppes will get the job done. But I do not envy him his assignment ... There will be complications, and dangers, we cannot foresee."

No one spoke. Everyone knew what John Floyd meant.

Slowly, Captain Harrison stood. "I should be going now ... with your permission, Your Excellency."

Wearily, the Governor nodded.

In the Office of the RICHMOND ENQUIRER

Thomas Richie, the editor (a Democrat and a man of principle), was pleased with himself, as usual, when he heard the rhythmic mechanical rumbling signaling the beginning of the printing of today's edition, which readers would be enjoying by late morning.

"Did you get an opportunity to look at the poem?" Richie asked a colleague.

"No. I couldn't find it on your desk."

"Well now," Richie said, searching his cluttered desktop for the out-of-town newspaper which had provided the dramatic verse, "allow me to read some of it to you – It's here someplace."

"I can read it later. Besides ... "

"On a slow day," Richie persisted, "we need somethin' to catch the reader's eye, get his attention – and Poland always serves the purpose, yes, sir, it is here someplace – There seems to be no limit to American sympathy for the Poles and their latest revolution – It's got to be here!"

"I really don't have the time ... "

"Hold your horses, young fellow – Here it is! ... Listen to this!"

Bill Bryant

> 'Tis freedom that calls you,
>   Though dim be the sun
> The darkness around you dispelling,
> Though death-fires enshroud you,
>   And waste is begun,
> She to deeds of high worth compelling
> Points to every loved altar and dwelling,
> And demands from the sons
>   of the noble in fame
> If the hell-mark of slave must still
>   blacken their name ...

"And to this!" the editor continued.

> The call of each sword upon Liberty's aid
>   Shall be written in gore
>   on the steel of its blade!

"Lofty sentiments," the listener said. "But it's a pity that so much of the gore belongs to innocent Russian women and children."

"War is war, and poetry is poetry. Both fill space – and sell newspapers!"

"True enough, I suppose ... What did you finally decide to write regarding the phenomenon?"

"I kept it quite brief," Richie said, smiling, as usual, as the apprentice boy handed him an early copy of the new edition. "There really isn't a lot one can write about it. Besides, you had to be blind not to see it for yourself ... Ah, here it is."

> The singular appearance of the sun, owing to the vapors which load the atmosphere, has been noticed from New York to Savannah – *perhaps further*.

In the Office of the RICHMOND CONSTITUTIONAL WHIG

John Hampden Pleasants, the editor (a Whig and a man of principle), was in a great hurry to leave – the cause of his urgency indicated by the military uniform he was wearing.

Pleasants frowned as he hastily scanned the last-minute news item he had rushed to compose, unhappy to be reporting such a tragedy, of course, unhappy about the few reliable details available – unhappy, too, about the necessity of dashing down to Southampton County, of all places, to help put down a slave uprising, of all things! He liked excitement as much as any man, but this would be an adventure no sane man would seek.

The editor finished his quick review. Nothing he could add or subtract now would lessen the impact of this item, or quell the fears it would arouse.

"It's not much," Pleasants said to a colleague, "but it's all we've got – and at least we can still squeeze it onto the front page – Hard to believe, and yet ... I'll start sending dispatches from Jerusalem as soon as I can – assuming I can find the time. I'll do my best."

"Stroke o' good fortune, you bein' in the Dragoons – I doubt if the other newspapers know about this yet."

Tomorrow Jerusalem: The Story of Nat Turner and the Southampton Slave Insurrection

"We shall see how much 'good fortune' is worth. Remember: I am going there as a soldier. If I survive, I shall be an editor - Here - Take this to the typesetter. He's waiting for it - I'll be in touch."
"John ... Do be careful."
"I shall - Don't worry about me, or about this 'situation' ... Trust me! The very sight of the Light Dragoons will put the rebels to flight!"
"Godspeed, my friend!"
As the citizen-soldier departed, his colleague paused long enough to read the item - to see for himself, in writing, the fatal truth, beginning ...

> Disagreeable rumors having reached this city of an insurrection of the slaves in Southampton, with loss of life ...

* * * * *

SOUTHAMPTON

With the first faint light of day, in a totally improvised and uncoordinated exercise, dozens of mounted civilian patrols began probing the extensive area known to have been visited by the insurgents, uncertainly seeking the nameless, faceless, uncountable blacks who, at one time or another or constantly during the day, seemed to be just about everywhere south of the Nottoway.
North of the river, the militiamen were mustering in Jerusalem.
And as the insurgents had discovered at Newitt's place, armed whites from the neighboring counties were beginning to respond.
All of the whites were ignorant of the facts of the situation, except for one indisputable brutal fact - the many killings of Monday.
Here and there in the sky above lower Southampton, buzzards in great numbers congregated, to land and feast.
Some of the military expeditions, reaching the places where whites had been slain, quickly became burial details, with little or no regard to the niceties of Christian ceremony. Everywhere, the task was gruesome.
Particularly at Levi Waller's school.
In strictly military terms, it was, all things considered, a quiet day.

Near the BUCKHORN QUARTERS

John Clark Turner was in the patrol which encountered Thomas Ridley's Curtis and Stephen, riding their master's mules.
"I know you," Turner said to the men. "Where are y'all goin'?"
"Home, Massuh Turner," Curtis replied.
"Yassuh, we jus' goin' home," Stephen confirmed.
"But you are goin' in the wrong direction," Turner observed.
The hands of Major Ridley's slaves were tied behind their backs, assuring their eventual delivery to the proper authorities in Jerusalem.

Bill Bryant

Near the LEVI WALLER Place

Riding slowly along the edge of a swamp, a patrol chanced to see a little girl, soaking wet and filthy dirty and badly mosquito-bitten, cowering behind an old cypress stump. One of the men recognized her.
"Clarinda!"
He dismounted and waded into the shallow swampwater and went to the girl, kneeling to embrace her, noticing the bloodstains on her dress. She clutched him desperately, and cried.
"It's all right now," he said softly. "You're safe now, Clarinda ... We thought you were at the school!"
"I was."
"But we thought ... How did you manage to escape?"
"The Lord helped me."
"Yes ... Yes, o' course, my dear ... Come with me now. I'll take you to your father."

Near JERUSALEM

Toward sunset, Captains Arthur Middleton, Alexander Peete and James Bryant mounted their horses and prepared to ride.
In the field in front of the officers - surrounded by anxious townspeople and refugees - upwards of a hundred other mounted militiamen awaited the command to move out.
Enough to do the job, Middleton reckoned. Besides, he assumed, the militia of the neighboring counties certainly must be heading toward Southampton by now, or soon would be, for a fact. Plus, the postmaster's message to the Governor had probably been delivered by now, he hoped, he prayed.

SIMON BLUNT Place

In late afternoon, a friendly slave had reported the rumor that some of the insurrectionists who had been repulsed and scattered in this morning's action had reassembled, and were vowing to return. So the state of martial alert, never much relaxed during the day, was fully restored - and word of the renewed threat was immediately communicated to Jerusalem.
Thus, at sunset, Captain Peete and 10 militiamen arrived as re-enforcements, to spend a sleepless night among the nervous shadows.
In the main house, in a downstairs room well guarded, the doctor's special patient - Hark, he said his name was, Hark Moore - remained in very critical condition, but receiving the best care available.
On the floor of the front rooms upstairs, shattered glass and splintered wood testified to the recent violence.
Atop the bookshelf, the clock was still ticking, and tocking, despite the buckshot imbedded in it.
The night would seem to last forever.

Tomorrow Jerusalem: The Story of Nat Turner and the Southampton Slave Insurrection

PETER EDWARDS Place

In the bright moonlight, Peter Edwards detected movement in the crawlspace under the front of the house. He raised and cocked and aimed his shotgun, then called out to whoever was under there to come out from under there, right now — this instant!

Slowly, Nathaniel's Sam emerged, and Edwards marched him around to the rear of the house, and into the basement.

Standing at the door of her cabin, Sam's mother watched, and wept.

THOMAS HAITHCOCK Place

Pausing occasionally to rest his mule, and himself, Nat had cautiously made his way across the countryside in as straight a line as possible, avoiding the open fields and major roadways, trying to keep well out of sight and range of anyone who might recognize or challenge him — or, not knowing or caring who he was, might take a shot at him.

Past sunset, he made one stop en route to Cabin Pond.

Thomas Haithcock was sitting in lamplight at the table, dreading the future, when he and his wife and two stepdaughters heard the clomping just outside the cabin, and soon the knocking, a soft but urgent rapping, on the cabin door.

Haithcock slowly rose and went to the door, then, pausing for a deep breath, opened it.

"Thomas, I ... "

"Get inside," Haithcock said, anxious to close the door.

"Thomas," Nat said, quickly stepping inside, "I ... "

"Nat — God knows, it's good to see you still in one piece — But you ain' safe here, Nat — You ain' safe anywhere!"

"It has gone badly, but ... "

"I knows all about it," Haithcock said, truly surprised and pleased to see Nat again and truly eager to hear all about it, but anxious to end this visit as soon as possible. "Some o' your men done come by here earlier, to leave off some o' what they took from the white folks — Nat, I tried to join up with you, me an' a couple o' boys — Berry Newsom tried, too, an' Will Artist an' four boys done took off after you — But none o' us could find you, an' ... Oh, Nat, you jus' ain' safe here ... Jus' a matter o' time 'til the white men be comin' for me!"

Nat tried to find the words. "It ain' over yet," he said, believing it.

"Nat ... "

"Come tomorrow an' the next day, we'll rally at Cabin Pond — Tell the men you see, tell 'em to rally at Cabin Pond. It ain' over yet!"

Haithcock wanted to believe it. "Sure, Nat ... I tells 'em."

Nat offered his hand to his friend, and his friend took it, and their handshake was firm and confident, but with a certain unavoidable finality to it.

"Thomas ... I be goin' now."

"Nat ... You take care."

"You, too ... You jus' wait an' see, ol' friend — Someday, soon, we be ridin' into Jerusalem, together!"

The door quickly opened, and quickly closed.

Bill Bryant

CABIN POND

Too weary for words to describe, Nat finally stopped pacing back and forth across the small clearing, and collapsed onto the ground, to try to sleep.

Too weary to think sensibly about how he might have done it all differently during the past two days, or the past 10 days, or the past six months – or the past three years, ever since he began knowing his mission ...

Too weary to worry about where Hark and Henry and Nelson and Sam and Will and all of the others might be, or about how many of his men – perhaps with new recruits, perhaps many new recruits – might soon be rallying to him, here, to try again ...

Too weary to weep for little Joe, or for Sally or Joseph, or for anyone else ...

Too weary to dream about being where he really wanted to be right now, with Cherry and the children – whom he knew he must not go anywhere near, absolutely not ...

Too weary to fear what the whites might do to his wife, because of what he had done, or to his mother ...

So weary ...

Now armed only with his sword and with his Bible – and with his shaken but unbroken faith that the Spirit had not misled him and that the Sign had in fact appeared – Nat struggled into restless sleep.

* * * * *

WEDNESDAY
August 24th
SOUTHAMPTON

Before the Sun rose, the temper and the tragedy of this hot day, and of the several hotter days to come, had been ordained by the cruel logic and chaos of the situation.

The contagion of raw fear and panic which had swept throughout Southampton on Monday and Tuesday had now spread throughout southeastern Virginia and northeastern North Carolina, and beyond.

Countless thousands of white people had fled to more defendable locations.

Bridges were barricaded – not only to discourage the approach of insurgent slaves, but also to apprehend any white traders or other poor whites who might be spies for the rebels.

Confronted with the unthinkable truth of the reports from lower Southampton, as well as plausible rumors of servile disturbances elsewhere – not to mention that in such an excited climate it could be happening anywhere and everywhere – the men of the region looked first to the safety of their own people. Then, grimly, they turned their attention, and their weapons, and their anger, toward lower Southampton – to assert, in no uncertain terms, the full authority – and the full power – of the white man's law.

Much if not most of what was about to happen would be done not by the men of Southampton, who themselves were not blameless, but by the

Tomorrow Jerusalem: The Story of Nat Turner and the Southampton Slave Insurrection

men rushing from other places to the supposed assistance of Southampton.

In addition to the organized soldiery, among whom discipline and the rules of civilized war would not seem quite so important in this particular situation, numerous civilians began entering the county, individually and in small groups. Many of them meant to be helpful. But many others, some drunk, some sober, had no nobler purpose than to kill some niggers.

The white people, and the black people, did not know that the insurrection was already over, that the rebel army had been scattered, that no real threat now existed.

To many whites, such knowledge would not have mattered.

Thus, for many blacks, the war was only just beginning.

Near the ELIZABETH TURNER Place

Howell Harris, who thanks to the slave girl Mary had fled with his family just in time to avoid being a victim of the insurrection, was sleeping fitfully on the ground among the other civilians on this patrol, when something awakened him.

Harris reached for his pistol, cocking it as he aimed at the shadow moving stealthily near the horses — and fired.

The shadow collapsed. And all of the suddenly wide-awake whites converged on it, to learn who had been shot, dead.

The shadow had been a slave, preparing as quietly as possible to saddle a horse, as the master had told him to do.

SIMON BLUNT Place

At about the same time the insurgents had arrived the previous morning, a sentry shouted an alarm, and one of the militiamen fired at a shadow, and he hit it.

The shadow had been a neighbor's slave, who had been visiting his wife at the doctor's place when the trouble erupted on Monday and had chosen to remain here for the time being, for safety.

SOMEWHERE in SOUTHAMPTON

Except for the fact that this was Southampton County, Shepherd Lee did not have the slightest idea of where he was as he finished relieving himself in the woods, then began trying in the darkness to find his way back to the unlit camp of the visiting militiamen.

A sentry spotted the incoming shadow, and immediately fired at it.

Lee was not dead, not yet anyway, but one of his legs had been very badly wounded by the blast. Following some discussion among his comrades, the decision was made not to amputate, not yet anyway.

Some of the men did their best to make Lee comfortable.

Others saddled, then mounted their horses and rode off into the night, in several directions, seeking a doctor ... somewhere in this dark wilderness.

Bill Bryant

EVERYWHERE in SOUTHAMPTON

   White or black, young or old, awake or asleep, all of the people were as one in fearfully awaiting the dawning of the new day.
   And more than one person thought again, or dreamt again, about the ominous Sun of the 13th - the Sign all had seen, or should have seen.

* * *

Near FORTRESS MONROE
In the JAMES RIVER
Aboard the Steamboat HAMPTON

   In the cramped lamplit cabin of the captain, Lieutenant Lee stood off to the side as Colonel James House and Lieutenant Colonel William Worth, United States Army, leaned over the map spread out on the small table.
   House, the commanding officer of Fortress Monroe, had a problem, for which little of his extensive military training and experience had prepared him.
   With a gentle knock, the steamboat's captain appeared at the cabin door, to announce: "Gentlemen, a longboat has come alongside - from the Natchez."
   "Thank you, sir," House said. "Come with us, Lee."
   "Yes, sir!" the lieutenant replied, eager to please always - but especially now.

*

   In the distance, outlined against a pastel dawn, the old three-masted 18-gun sloop of war USS Natchez bristled with uncommon activity for so early in the day. Nearby, the sloop Warren presented a similar scene.
   On the topdeck of the steamboat, increasingly crowded with embarking troops, a council of war began - House and Worth exchanging information with Commodore Jesse Duncan Elliott, the commanding officer of the Natchez. Elliott was one of the Navy's senior officers, and one of its most controversial. As the second in command to Oliver Hazard Perry during the Battle of Lake Erie in the War of 1812, Elliott had either performed his duties with distinction, or not. The continuing debate about his performance had divided the Navy's officer corps into pro-Perry and pro-Elliott factions - none of which now seemed to matter.
   Off to the side, but close at hand, stood Lee.
   "A stage-coach passenger from Jerusalem brought the report to Norfolk," said House, "and Mayor Holt and the City Council decided to send Captain Capron of the Norfolk Independent Volunteers to me - The man barged right into my quarters and woke me up!"
   "I had the same experience," Elliott said. "In fact, the man who woke me up was the stage-coach passenger - a Mister Gray. He painted

Tomorrow Jerusalem: The Story of Nat Turner and the Southampton Slave Insurrection

a rather bleak picture of the situation in Southampton. It sounded implausible – but I had to believe him. He seemed like a highly respectable man. I understand that the Norfolk Independent Volunteers are on their way to Southampton – probably some men from Portsmouth, too – and that Commodore Warrington at the Gosport Navy Yard is now making arrangements for a substantial quantity of muskets, pistols and swords to be transported to Southampton."

"So we understand, as well," House said. "We also assume that local militia are being mobilized -- and that the Governor has been notified, and is reacting. As the Army's contribution, we have mustered three companies of infantry, with an artillery piece. Fortunately, the Hampton was available."

"Colonel House," Commodore Elliott said, stiffening his posture and saluting, "the Navy is at your service."

"Sir," Colonel House replied, saluting, "your cooperation is appreciated in this great emergency."

"To your three companies of infantry," Elliott reckoned, "I add a detachment of sailors and marines from the Natchez and the Warren, enough to bring our total strength to 300 or so. I shall personally command our men."

"Excellent," House said. "And Lieutenant Colonel Worth will be in command of our men. Combined, we should have a good effect. I do not care to make a greater commitment of forces at this time – just in case this disturbance in Southampton is part of a general insurrection."

Lieutenant Lee, sensing his moment of opportunity, stepped forward. "Colonel, I ... "

"Yes?!" House said abruptly. Then, knowing the answer to his own question, he patiently asked it: "What do you want, Lee?"

"Sir," Lee said, mustering his nerve, "I again request permission to go with the expedition, sir!"

"I again deny it. I said you could come this far, but no further."

"Sir, I ... "

"No," House said. "This will be a combat mission, and you are an engineer, Lee. Your job is to help build my fort – Understood?"

"But ... "

"Gentlemen!" the Colonel said, ending the skirmish by simply ignoring it. "May Providence decree an early termination to this unhappy affair – Lee!"

"Sir!

"Go below and fetch the map."

Lee promptly went below.

"An overly eager young man," House observed to Worth and Elliott. "Reminds me of myself, at that age – a bit too aggressive for the circumstances. He has been at Monroe only two weeks, and he wants to go to war – But Bobby comes from a fine family, and he will make a good soldier, someday – Gentlemen, I shall be praying for the swift and safe completion of your work – God!" he confessed. "How I have dreaded this day, for years!"

* * * * *

177

Bill Bryant

CROSS KEYS

Their impending arrival had been announced in advance by a courier, to avoid alarming the mass of refugees who soon after daybreak pressed tightly along both sides of the Jerusalem Road, anxiously looking southward - erupting into cheers of rejoicing and deliverance when the Hertford County militiamen, approximately a hundred strong, finally did arrive, Colonel Elisha Sharpe riding proudly ahead of the column of North Carolinians.
Here was the proof of power.
Law and order would be restored - soon.
Justice would be done!

*

Soon after dismounting, Elisha Sharpe dealt with his first tactical problem: Richard Porter and a wagon loaded with the chained insurgent slaves Jacob, Moses, Aaron and the boy Daniel.
Porter explained his own personal problem. "They actually had the nerve to come back home - well, that was their second mistake! Colonel, I have managed to bring 'em this far safely, but without a proper escort I doubt if they'll live to see the inside o' the jail in Jerusalem - an' they ain' worth a penny to me dead! ... May I place them in your custody, sir?"
"Well," Sharpe said, annoyed by the distraction, "very well, Mister Porter. My boys'll see that your property is delivered to Jerusalem."
"Safely ... Colonel."
"Safely," Sharpe grumbled.

SOMEWHERE in SOUTHAMPTON

Peacefully hoeing in his little garden near his cabin near the road - well away from the scene of the troubles and glad of it - the free black man was not concerned when the white men came galloping along, nor when the hard-riding men suddenly reined their horses, nor when one of the men asked, reasonably enough: "Is this Southampton County?"
"Yes, suh," the black man replied, beginning to aim his hoe. "You have just crossed the line, by yonder tree."
Enough said, the Richmond men shot the Southampton man, dead.

PETER EDWARDS Place

The five who had bravely left home early on Monday morning to ride with the army of liberation quietly returned home early on Wednesday morning, encouraged by the apparent absence of all of the white folks to believe that maybe - just maybe - their own absence had not been noted by any of the white folks.
But old Jeff and the other black men who had remained at home grabbed hoes and pitch-forks, and surrounded the five, detaining them

Tomorrow Jerusalem: The Story of Nat Turner and the Southampton Slave Insurrection

until a passing patrol of white neighbors could be summoned up the lane to the yard of the house.
And there the neighbors summarily executed the five.

Near PATE'S HILL

Delicate young Lavinia Francis, feeling more pregnant than ever and therefore more resolved, would not quit — would not even think of it! She had come too far and survived too much to stop hoping now.
Hot and sweaty, dirty and wet, dead-tired and ruthlessly mosquito-bitten, and hungry, following a day and two nights of hiding in the swamp, she slogged through the knee-deep water at the swamp's edge, along the tree-shrouded roadway, when suddenly she thought she heard the sound of horsemen approaching, so quickly she crouched behind a cypress and waited, watching. Whoever — or whatever — may be coming, it would be better than being at Pate's Hill!
Eventually, this whole long nightmare must end.
A witness to killing, herself (and her baby) barely saved from the rebels, then rescued from Charlotte by Easter, at the beginning of this ordeal, Lavinia had taken her keys from the pocket of her workdress and hung them on the wall, then had placed a large cheese in the pocket, and then, closely accompanied by Red Nelson, had started for the Travis place ... There, she climbed onto the gate-post and, seeing two strange men at the house, fainted. The men chanced to see her collapse, went to her, and revived her by pouring water on her face. One of the men then put her behind him on his horse, and transported her to supposed safety at Pate's Hill. There, among the scores of thoroughly frightened and easily excitable refugees, mostly women and children and old men, Lavinia found Nathaniel's mother, which was a huge relief. But otherwise, the place was noisy and crowded and weakly defended — and tense. And when a runaway flock of sheep came storming along the nearby road Monday night, pure panic reigned, compelling the refugees into the swamp ... And here, Lavinia had chosen to stay.
The horsemen came into view, and were white, and there, the third man in the column, was "Nathaniel!!!"
Lavinia rose and sloshed onto the embankment and ran to him as he instantly reined his horse and dismounted, and they embraced as though their lives depended on it.
"They told me you were dead!" Nathaniel said. "So instead o' goin' home ... "
"I went to Joseph an' Sally's — It's so horrible!"
"I know," he said, trying to comfort her. "I know."
"Nathaniel — Charlotte tried to kill me, but Easter ... "

CATHERINE WHITEHEAD Place

Amid the savaged bodies in the yard, the detachment of Hertford militiamen, accompanied by several Southampton men familiar with the countryside, remained in the saddle.
Already, their fury had added a black man to the collection of corpses.

Bill Bryant

Now, another black man approached, prodded forward by the rifle of a dismounted militiaman.

The leader of the patrol pointed his pistol at the dead slave as he said to the new suspect: "That one fessed up to bein' one o' the bandits – what you got to say for yourself, boy?"

"I's a preacher, massuh," the Methodist said with all of the servile charm at his command. "I don' have nothin' to do with them murderin' niggers!"

"He's a liar!" declared one of the Southampton men. "I saw him at Parker's place – In fact, he seemed to be the leader o' that group we met at the gate!"

"No, massuh – They done forced me to ride with 'em – An' they treated me awful rough, too – No, massuh! – No ..."

He fell alongside Caty Whitehead.

*

The solid volley of gunfire rolled across the cotton field to the ears of another detachment of Hertford militiamen, who had just about completed their own action – in which some of the men absolutely refused to participate.

A dismounted militiaman walked away from the three bodies and the wild-eyed black boy standing nearby, and approached the mounted officer.

"How much?" asked Colonel Elisha Sharpe.

"'Bout $23, all in silver – an' this fine gold watch."

"Let me see the watch."

The militiaman handed the watch up to the Colonel, then asked: "Sir, what'll we do with the boy?"

"We'll take him into Jerusalem. He might be tellin' the truth – An' as for them," the Colonel said with a nod toward the three bodies, "I'd say this was a slap on the wrist, considerin' what we saw up at the house ... Nice watch."

"What should we do with the money?"

"Distribute it among the men. I shall keep the watch – How 'bout it, boys?" the Colonel asked all of his men. "We've come a long way, on a dangerous mission – We might as well be paid for our troubles, eh?"

Some of the men laughed at the remark, but others didn't.

Some of the men shared in the money, but others didn't.

Some of the men were as proud as ever to be riding with Elisha Sharpe.

But others were now shocked and ashamed, and began planning an action of their own.

JACOB WILLIAMS Place

The fugitive Nelson, reportedly one of the leaders of the insurrection, was spotted in his master's orchard – but got away.

The searchers continued to hunt him.

Tomorrow Jerusalem: The Story of Nat Turner and the Southampton Slave Insurrection

SIMON BLUNT Place

The patient Hark — now said to be one of the leaders of the insurrection — remained in critical condition.
The defenders remained on alert.

JERUSALEM

In the emptied store now busily serving as military headquarters, General Richard Eppes was still whisking the dust of the long ride off his uniform even as he began his conference with the sheriff, Clements Rochelle, and his deputy, Edward Butts, and Captain Arthur Middleton. Nearby stood Collin Kitchen, special deputy in charge of the suddenly crowded and soon to be overcrowded jail.

Proper introductions having been made, the General began with an apologetic explanation: "Gentlemen, I know I do not look well. Truth is, I've been feeling ill lately, and this new exertion does not make me feel any better — However," he said, standing fully erect and adjusting the sword at his side, "we have work to do. So let's begin!"

Middleton began: "Sir, Colonel Sharpe is expected to arrive within the hour, to report on the progress of the Hertford militia. His courier made a point of saying that the use of Southampton men as guides has been especially helpful."

"Let us make it a matter of policy," the General instructed. "Sheriff, can you assist with that? There will be many patrols of men totally unfamiliar with Southampton. We shall require dozens of your men."

"Certainly, General."

"Captain Middleton, I want an efficient system of couriers established — immediately — between here and Richmond, Murfreesboro, Norfolk, Smithfield and Suffolk, for the time being."

"Certainly," Middleton said.

"How many prisoners in your custody, Mister Kitchen?"

"Twelve in the jail, at last count, sir, an' more due to arrive soon — an' no tellin' how many down at Cross Keys, or at other places — Plus, there's the wounded prisoner out at Doctor Blunt's — one o' the leaders — name o' Hark."

"I was told about him," the General said, curious to meet the man who could survive such wounds as he had been told about. "The rest of 'em, so I understand, have been scattered to the four winds — Is that correct?"

"Apparently," Middleton said, unwilling to be definite, knowing full well that in the vastness of Southampton in the current climate of fear and confusion, almost anything seemed possible, even a resurgence of the insurrection. "But we will find all of 'em!"

"Yes, we shall," the General said, with authority. "Gentlemen, it does seem to me, from the reports I have received en route to Jerusalem, that 20 resolute and well armed men could have quelled this uprising at any time. And it does seem to me that the worst of the storm has passed. Still, there is much to worry about, and much to be done. From what I've been told — and from what I saw while en route — the situation in lower Southampton is ... "

Bill Bryant

Suddenly, the undivided attention of the men inside headquarters shifted to the demanding sound of a great gust of excitement among the townspeople and the refugees along the Main Street, announcing the arrival of a troop of cavalry.

Moving to the doorway, trailed by the others, the General easily recognized the uniforms. "The Richmond Light Dragoons," he informed the others. "Excellent! The sooner we replace the irregular forces with regular troops, the better!"

One of the Dragoons immediately dismounted, handed the reins to a comrade, and walked toward the headquarters, focusing on the General, whom he saluted.

"Sir, Captain Harrison presents his compliments."

"My compliments to the Captain."

"Sir, I am John Hampden Pleasants. I ... "

"Any kin to James Pleasants, our former governor?"

"My father, sir."

"And a good friend of mine — Then you must be the Pleasants who edits the Whig."

"Yes, sir."

"You were about to say?"

"Sir, when I can be spared from my military duties, I would appreciate very much an opportunity to share some of your information — for my readers."

"Yes, that can be arranged — But do see me later, Pleasants. I am rather busy at the moment."

"Yes, sir — One question, sir."

"What is it?"

"There had to be a leader ... Who was he?"

The General turned to the Southampton men, who glanced at one another before Rochelle answered: "Apparently, it was the work of a slave named Nat Turner."

The editor had to ask at least one more question: "Had anyone ever heard of him ... before this?"

"Well," Rochelle began, glancing at the other Southampton men, uncomfortable with the answer, "yes — although he seemed to be a Negro of good character ... until this."

"And what," the General needed to asked, needed to know, "has become of this Nat Turner?"

"God only knows," Rochelle said.

CROSS KEYS

Throughout Tuesday and Wednesday, the shattered peace and stability of lower Southampton in some ways became worse, the war changing course and complexion. In scores and scores of incidents, isolated yet of a pattern, slave and free black men and women who happened to be at the wrong place at the wrong time became the new crop of victims of the insurrection.

As word circulated regarding what the patrols were discovering at the places visited by the insurgents — as one white family after another began learning of the horrible deaths of kinfolk and friends and neighbors — as the rising number of women and children and even little babies among the dead had its inevitable, maddening effect — the mood of the whites became ugly in the extreme, virtually erasing

*Tomorrow Jerusalem: The Story of Nat Turner
and the Southampton Slave Insurrection*

the line between the ideal quest for law and order, with justice, and the primal craving for revenge.

The conflicting emotions aroused among the whites were perhaps nowhere more vividly demonstrated on this day than in late afternoon amid the swirling chaos at Cross Keys.

Nathaniel Francis, his Lavinia now safely with her kinfolk in Northampton, was in the grimmest of moods as he marched toward the storehouse now crowded with blacks collected by various patrols.

By now, he knew that six close members of his own family had been killed – and upwards of 30 other kinfolk.

By now, he knew that some of his own slaves had prominently participated in the killing.

By now – and this made the whole situation even more incomprehensible and infuriating – he also knew the identity of the author of the massacre, and it ate at him. He and Salathiel both had tried to warn Sally – and more than once, too – yet both of them had failed to act on their fears, both had hesitated to force the issue, and now Salathiel and Sally and so many others were dead, and he would have to live with that knowledge forever, and with the guilt of having chanced to survive.

Thusly, Nathaniel entered the dimly lit storehouse, searching for certain familiar faces, the work of judge and jury already done.

He identified his Easter.

He went to her, and embraced her, and she embraced him, both in tears. Then, he gently escorted her outside the storehouse, and there told her to wait for him, saying it loudly, his tone and manner making it perfectly clear to all witnessing the scene that anyone who so much as touched a hair of Easter's head would pay for it dearly.

Renewing his search inside, he identified his Charlotte.

He went to her, roughly grabbed her by the arm as she tried to resist him, led her outside – calling for some rope and promptly getting it as master and slave passed hurriedly among the people – then tied the alternately pleading and defiant Charlotte to an oak tree at roadside, stepped back as he pulled out his pistol, cocked it, aimed, fired ... and walked away.

Whatever the girl had done, the witnesses reckoned, it must have been very bad indeed. And many of the men, eager for any opportunity to vent their own rage and frustration, readied their guns, then joined in the act of execution – their punishing gunfire riddling the girl's body, and mortally wounding the tree.

Nathaniel had made an example of Charlotte.

Now, if only he could get his hands on Nat!

CABIN POND

Toward sunset, sitting against a tree, his Bible and his sword and his hat on the ground beside him, his arms resting on his knees, Nat stared across the pond ... sighed ... then closed his eyes and lowered his head, slowly.

Quickly, his head jerked upward, his eyes wide open, at the alarming sound of a horse neighing – not threateningly near, but too near to be ignored.

Rising, grabbing Bible and sword and hat, he went into the woods toward the source of the sound – and soon spotted them – several of

Bill Bryant

them, he couldn't tell how many, white men, riding slowly through the woods, obviously searching ... gradually moving away.

Nat returned to where he had been sitting, and sat down again, holding his Bible and his sword and his hat, resting his arms on his knees, staring across the pond ... thinking hard, again.

No one had rallied to him at Cabin Pond, yet.

No one.

But some of his men did know that he was here at the secret place, or at least that he was somewhere near Cabin Pond - and any one of them might have been captured, might have been tortured, might have told the white men - and there, just now, he had seen the white men searching, near.

It was only a matter of time until they found him, here.

But, with the night falling, they would not be finding him here or anywhere else today.

So, he decided, placing his sword and his hat on the ground, he would stay right here for now, praying that some of his men might yet rally to him, praying that tomorrow would somehow be better than today ... though he could not now imagine how.

Where were his men?!

NATHANIEL FRANCIS Place

At sunset, as Nathaniel rode into the yard, his girl Easter behind him on the horse, his man Dred approached - a sight to behold.

"Massuh Francis," the man said, weakly but with a brave attempt at his best smile, "good day to you, suh - You got any chores you want ol' Dred to be doin' for you?"

The master, at a loss for words, stared at the slave - at the tattered and bloodied sleeve where his left arm used to be.

Finally, Nathaniel found the words: "You ... jus' sit down on the ground, there ... an' wait."

Dred obeyed, and thus began his final journey into Jerusalem.

* * * * *

**THURSDAY
August 25th
JERUSALEM**

The initial reports of the violence in the countryside had enkindled within the conscience of the ailing General a flaming rage, to which subsequent reports constantly added fuel. John Eppes, a good man, began to take this offense personally.

Being also a reasonable man, he had initially assumed that his very presence and authority here - and the presence and authority of the regular forces in the countryside - would quickly put an end to the irrational (not to mention illegal, uneconomical, immoral) brutalities being inflicted on the rightly frightened black people of Southampton, above as well as below the Nottoway.

He had hoped and prayed for the best.

And he was wrong.

*Tomorrow Jerusalem: The Story of Nat Turner
and the Southampton Slave Insurrection*

Now, in military headquarters, alertly observed by John Hampden Pleasants, Lieutenant Colonel William Worth, Commodore Jesse Duncan Elliott and a variety of other federal and state soldiers and local militiamen and civilians standing near the center of the steadily growing blaze of righteous indignation, the General at first refused to believe his ears when the courier from Cross Keys breathlessly finished describing what he himself had seen, early this morning.

"Within an hour of his capture?" the General specified.

"Yes, sir," the courier affirmed.

"And he offered no resistance?"

"None, sir."

"And he was securely in custody?"

"Yes, sir."

"And they simply executed him?"

"Yes, sir."

"And piked his head?"

"Yes, sir."

"Damnation! – Hellfire! – We cannot tolerate this sort of thing!"

"Not to mention ... "

"Please do not!" the General commanded. "Once was enough! – Dear God, what has happened to law and order?" the General demanded to know, begged to know, and resolved to know. "Not to mention common human decency! ... You are dismissed, young man – with my gratitude for your candor. Go, and refresh yourself."

"Thank you, sir – General, sir, I very much regret havin' to bring you such information."

"You did your duty. The blame attaches to the message, not to the messenger. Begone!"

"Yes, sir – Thank you, sir!"

The General, visibly straining to control his persisting anger, returned to his conversation with the recently arrived federal officers. "Gentlemen, I trust that you can understand my situation. The presence of you and your men is deeply appreciated, but also quite unnecessary. The Richmond Light Dragoons are in the field, the Lafayette Artillery arrived this morning, cavalry troops from Norfolk and Portsmouth and Prince George are combing the countryside, all of the militia units in Southampton and the neighboring counties have been mustered. Gentlemen, I now have more than 3,000 men under my command, either already here or heading in this direction – not to mention the North Carolinians ... I think it reasonable to hope that tranquility will soon be restored, and I have so informed Governor Floyd – In fact, I have also informed him that I intend to send our own regular infantry and artillery troops home beginning tomorrow, if the situation permits. So ... as you can plainly see, we do not require your generous offer of assistance."

"We are as relieved as you seem to be, sir," Lieutenant Colonel Worth said, with a mixture of genuine sincerity and genuine regret.

"General," Commodore Elliott said, "I trust that you would have no objection if Colonel Worth and I made a personal inspection of the scene of the uprising?"

"No objection whatsoever," the General said. "What about your troops?"

"We shall limit their movements," Lieutenant Colonel Worth said, then asked: "The beheading at Cross Keys was not an isolated incident?"

Pausing, to compose himself, the General finally answered: "I deeply regret to say ... No, it was not ... God-damn them!"

Bill Bryant

Along the JERUSALEM ROAD

In a tribal display, the clamoring mob of vengeful white men erected what all agreed would be a useful signpost at the intersection where the Barrow Road met the Jerusalem Road, firmly planting the post in a hole dug deep and tightly packed, to make it stay.

The head atop the pole was meant as a reminder and as a warning to all who would come this way.

He had been a slave - Richard Porter's Henry - a leader of the risin'.

BRANCH'S BRIDGE

Among the white men at the barricade, only one posed a threat to the black boy being escorted to safety while several of the white men forcibly restrained Choctaw Williams, who was furious.

"The man's a lunatic!" said one observer. "Wants to kill every nigger he sees!"

"Can' say that I blame him," said another, "considerin' what they did to his wife an' child."

"But that boy was jus' bringin' us a message - an' at some risk, I might add."

"Still, considerin' what they did at Waller's school ... "

Along the BARROW ROAD

He had given them a good chase, and at least a brief final struggle.

Now, in appearance but not in spirit broken, his hands tied behind his back, Nelson the property of Jacob Williams walked down the middle of the road between the slowly riding columns of Norfolk Independent Volunteers.

Whites and blacks came to the roadside to watch the passing procession.

Many of them recognized the prisoner.

Some of the blacks spoke of him as "the General" - General Nelson - which pleased him very much.

SOMEWHERE in SOUTHAMPTON

Thirty-five hours after being shot, Shepherd Lee died, in the middle of nowhere.

No doctor could have saved his life, said the doctor who arrived too late to try.

*Tomorrow Jerusalem: The Story of Nat Turner
and the Southampton Slave Insurrection*

SOMEWHERE in SOUTHAMPTON

Having waited as long as he dared to wait at Cabin Pond, Nat left, as the Sun was setting, to find a better place to hide.
He had such a place in mind, but did not go directly to it. Hunger forced him to make a detour to the abandoned Travis place, to raid the kitchen house.
Then, in the moonlit night, he went to his new hiding place.
And there, employing his sword to carve out a shallow hole beneath a carefully rearranged pile of old fence rails, he created the crudest of caves, and concealed himself, and ate.
He hid not in the deep woods or in a swamp, where they expected him to be.
He would not make it so easy for them.
He hid where he knew they would never think to look — well within his own neighborhood ... in the middle of a field.

* * * * *

**FRIDAY
August 26th
SIMON BLUNT Place**

The patient would live, the doctor confidently assured Lieutenant Colonel Worth and Commodore Elliott following their close inspection of the still weak but also still impressive Hark.
Standing in front of the house, with Simon Jr. standing guard at the front door, Simon Sr. allowed as how his patient's exceptional physique and the man's powerful will to live had contributed greatly to the healing process.
"There is only so much a doctor can know," Blunt said, "and therefore only so much a doctor can do. Sometimes, the patient is the real doctor ... Hark has been a very good patient."
"He is a superb specimen," Worth said, "one of the most perfectly framed men I've ever seen — a regular black Apollo!"
"Indeed," Blunt said. "The description is apt."
"A lucky man, too," Worth said, "to be wounded at the house of a doctor."
Blunt shook his head. "In this case, the definition of 'luck' is debatable. I have merely helped to save him for the hangman."
"Your son," Elliott observed, "seems like a fine young man. We were told in Jerusalem that he performed with distinction during the fray. You must be very proud of him."
"I am."
"Doctor," Elliott thought out loud, "your son said something to me earlier about wanting to see something of the world beyond Southampton. He expressed an interest in the military profession — It can be a good life, you know, sir, an honorable life."
"I concur," Worth said. "The lad shows great promise."
"Well ... "
"I have some influence in the Navy," Elliott said, "which I enjoy using."

"We shall see," Blunt said, seeing both sides of the coming argument.

VICKSVILLE

Through the small crossroads community now crowded with refugees, past the front of John Denegre's store, the column of mounted Navy marines rode in proud triumphal review.

The captain riding at the head of the column held high his battle sword - impaled on its gleaming shaft a trophy of war ... a black man's head.

CROSS KEYS

Whether or not one wanted to hear it, and many did not, there it was - from inside the back room of the storehouse, the pitiably pleading painful screaming of a black woman, interrupted only by the voice of a white man demanding to know the truth, until the screaming ended ... finally.

Whether one happened to see it, and some did, there it was - at the opened door to the back room of the storehouse, a broom sweeping out the blood.

EVERYWHERE in SOUTHAMPTON

Except in their very midst, the white people searched for the leader of the insurrection, whose name was now on everyone's lips.

Many hundreds of mounted men and many hundreds of men afoot combed through the woods and swamps of Southampton, seeking him - even as countless other white people throughout southeastern Virginia and northeastern North Carolina looked for him.

Yet few of the men searching in Southampton, and none of the men searching elsewhere, had the slightest idea of what this Nat Turner looked like, or where he might be - assuming he was still alive and had not fled to the Great Dismal Swamp, where you could just forget about ever finding him.

In fact, he could be anywhere, which meant that almost any black man, unaccompanied by a white man, might be Nat Turner - or perhaps one of the other rebels - or maybe a sympathizer - or, as was usually the case, an innocent victim of blind reason.

CROSS KEYS

It had to end, Captain Pitt Thomas decided.

So he braved the mob and stepped between it and the three black men lined up against the outside back wall of the storehouse.

"Stop right there!" he commanded the mob. "Stop right there, I say! - We must end this senseless killing!"

The mob pressed closer, angrily grumbling as one.

*Tomorrow Jerusalem: The Story of Nat Turner
and the Southampton Slave Insurrection*

"Stop! - Think! - What crimes have these men done, do you know? - Well, do you?"

The mob inched closer.

"If you want these men," Captain Pitt Thomas declared, summoning all of his considerable moral authority as an eminently well respected citizen and veteran of war, "you will have to go through me!"

Since he put it that way, the mob stopped advancing, pausing to think about it as one, then slowly began retreating, bitterly muttering.

JERUSALEM

It had to end, lawyer William Parker decided.

Standing on the top step of the porch of the jail, flanked left and right along the front of the building by Clement Rochelle and Edward Butts and a thin line of nervous civilian guards, Parker confronted the blood-lusting mob.

A voice from the mob called out: "Step aside, Mister Parker! We intend no harm to you an' these other men - But we do demand all o' your prisoners!"

"We will not step aside!" Parker replied, determined to make a stand, but also desperate to reason with them. "Friends and neighbors, listen to me! - A terrible thing has happened, to all of us, and all of us are grieving ... "

"Step aside, sir!" the voice insisted.

"No! - We are all confounded by this tragedy, we are all enraged - But we must not forget who we are - civilized people - citizens of a nation dedicated to respect for the law and respect for civil authority - We ... "

"Tell that to those murderers in there!" the voice growled - to the mob's roaring approval.

"It is for the court to decide who among them is guilty - and who might be innocent!" the lawyer pleaded. "Citizens! Virginia is watching us! - The whole nation is watching us! - And we are demonstrating no more respect for human life than did the slaves on their evil rampage! - Dear friends, we must be stronger than the terrible passions of the moment! We must show the world that even in our profound grief and outrage we are still responsible, law-abiding people! And now, more than ever, we must ... "

"We demand justice!" the voice cried out. "Now!"

"Now!!!" the mob roared, with such conviction that the guards inched back against the jail.

"No!!!" Parker replied, the soaring power of his own conviction - daring to oppose them even now - stunning the mob, momentarily, long enough. "Not now, but soon! Yes, we shall make the guilty pay for their crimes - in fair and open trials at which the facts can be determined, and sober judgements made, by the able, honest, judicious men to whom we entrust the difficulty duty of justice - Men of Southampton! A hundred years from now, people will be looking at what has happened here - judging the Negroes - judging us ... Our own descendants - our own blood - will be living with the legacy we are creating for them now, here ... Let them be proud of us, for doing the right thing, when it mattered most ... Please," he asked politely.

189

Bill Bryant

The mob, overwhelmed by the sheer weight of the lawyer's argumentation but not entirely persuaded by it, retreated ... for the time being.

Collin Kitchen inserted the heavy key into the massive lock, turned it, and opened the door.

Parker entered, to consult with several of his clients.

SOMEWHERE in SOUTHAMPTON

In the twilight splintering through the pile of old fence rails in the middle of the field, Nat patiently applied the dull blade of his sword to a sturdy stick, making a second notch.

A thousand questions assailed him.

A thousand answers eluded him.

What if ...

* * * * *

**SATURDAY
August 28th
JERUSALEM**

At headquarters, Richard Eppes proclaimed that he had reached the limit of his endurance of the lawlessness in the countryside.

"Butchery is what it is!" the General thundered, wanting to crush the sheet of paper in his hand and hurl it at everyone in the crowded room. "The situation is intolerable! ... Intolerable!!! ... And I will not tolerate it! – Am I understood?"

No one dared to speak.

The General thrust the sheet of paper toward them, like a sword – which he intended it to be. "I want this proclamation posted and publicly read from one end of this county to the other! I want no one to misunderstand what I'm saying: This slaughtering of the blacks must end! – And I shall use every soldier and every weapon at my command to make it end! – And, by God, I have the authority to do it!"

No one dared to move.

"Well? – What are you waiting for? – Here!"

Timidly, a militiaman stepped forward, and reached out, and took the sheet of paper – then quickly headed for the back room, where men recruited for their penmanship were waiting to begin the labor of producing copies of the carefully composed document.

His bitter mission accomplished, Richard Eppes stalked out of headquarters.

Witnesses to this latest remarkable scene, John Hampden Pleasants and Jesse Duncan Elliott also had seen for themselves, or had at least glimpsed, the deeply troubling situation in the countryside, and in town. They understood, perfectly, the General's anguish, and his resolve.

"A necessary action," Pleasants said. "My patrol has been to several of the homes visited by the rebels, and I have been sickened by what I have seen – But these retaliations are hardly inferior in barbarity to the atrocities committed by the blacks – I swear, I have never seen such a spirit of vindictive ferocity!"

"I am told," Elliott said, "that somewhere between 55 and 60 white people were killed on Monday – Have you heard any reckoning of how many blacks might have been killed, so far?"

Pleasants briefly pondered the unanswerable question. "At a minimum, based on more or less reliable reports, anywhere from 25 to 40 – but probably more – many more ... This morning, my patrol encountered a man who claimed that he had personally killed between 10 and 15 – Said he was certain of their guilt – And when we challenged him, he defended himself by claiming he had risked his life to protect a black woman he believed to be innocent ... but others killed her."

"Deplorable," Elliott said. "War makes beasts of men ... Another uprising, I fear, would invite the total destruction of the whole black population where it occurs."

"I must agree ... The situation below the Nottoway is beyond description. Virtually every farm deserted – except for the slaves ... Whites crammed into Cross Keys and the other safe places ... Patrols everywhere, searching – or hunting ... Have you been to the jail?"

"No, though I've been meaning to. I'm told that it's filled to overflowing. How many prisoners are there?"

"Approximately 50 ... One of the rebels – Marmakduke, the one who killed the Vaughan girl – died of his wounds this morning. I observed him yesterday, and I must say: Considering the magnanimity with which he bore his sufferings, he might have been a hero."

"I have heard that some of them died quite bravely – One militiaman told me of several rebels who even in their death agonies seemed almost happy, saying God had a hand in what happened here."

Both men thought about it.

"Ironic, isn't it?" Pleasants asked.

"What is?"

"At this very moment, sir, the slaves are effectively in control of most of Southampton County!"

"Indeed ... And that is not the only irony," Elliott duly noted.

"Really?"

"Indeed ... At this very moment, sir, the military authority established here to quell the blacks is being employed to quell the whites!"

EVERYWHERE in SOUTHAMPTON

By God, he did have the authority!

By day's end, the General's proclamation was being posted and publicly read from one end of the county to the other, its message most emphatically clear.

From the General to the people:

> He will not specify all the instances that he is bound to believe have occurred, but pass in silence what has happened, with the expression of his deepest sorrow that any necessity should be supposed to have existed to justify a single act of atrocity. But he feels himself bound to declare, and hereby announces to the troops and civilians, that no excuse will be allowed for any similar acts of

violence after the promulgation of this order — and further to declare, in the most explicit terms, that any who may attempt the repetition of such an act shall be punished, if necessary, by the rigors of the articles of war ... This course of proceeding dignifies the rebel and the assassin with the sanctity of martyrdom, and confounds the difference that morality and religion make between the ruffian and the brave and honorable.

SOMEWHERE in SOUTHAMPTON

Only a week ago, he was perhaps the most fortunate and most privileged slave in Southampton County, blessed with talents and liberties unimagined by most other slaves — safe and secure, with a loving mother and a good wife and two wonderful children, a roof over his head and plenty to eat.
Now, he was here.
Only a week ago, he enjoyed perhaps the most extensive reputation of any man, white or black, in Southampton — a "fame" which many men, white and black, would envy — a good name, basically.
Now, he knew for a fact without the tiniest piece of proof, his reputation reached far beyond Southampton.
Only a week ago, he and his closest friends and confederates were planning for the final meeting at Cabin Pond and dreaming of storming into Jerusalem, to free the whole people held in bondage.
Now, he put another notch in the stick.
What if ...

* * * * *

SUNDAY
August 29th
SOUTHAMPTON

A few of the churches, in the safest places, conducted crowded services of worship, beseeching God's mercy and compassion for the living and the dead ... praying for the restoration of peace.
No one went to pray at Turner's Meeting House, to which, the living noted, a majority of Monday's dead had belonged.

* * *

Throughout the county, in fact, peace was restored on this day — not by the grace of God, but by the order of the General.
Throughout the day, the numerous military patrols shared the roadways with streams of civilians returning home.
Throughout the day, the white people and the black people began the uneasy task of rebuilding their battered lives, together.

Tomorrow Jerusalem: The Story of Nat Turner and the Southampton Slave Insurrection

In the Courthouse at JERUSALEM

Still attired in their Sunday best, the men who gathered in the courtroom in mid-afternoon fully appreciated the gravity of their situation, and therefore had not questioned the early-morning summons to be here, of all places.

The man presiding over this meeting was Jeremiah Cobb, who as chief among the county's 10 magistrates would also be presiding over many of the trials — truly extraordinary trials — now scheduled to begin on Wednesday in the Court of Oyer and Terminer. The magistrates, at least five of whom would judge each case, were among the county's most distinguished citizens, including several who had served as delegates to the celebrated Constitutional Convention of 1829.

Today, Cobb did not summon any of the other magistrates. They already knew what to expect, and what would be expected of them.

Cobb did summon the clerk of the court, James Rochelle; the sheriff, Clements Rochelle; the deputy sheriff, Edward Butts; the special deputy, Collin Kitchen; the special prosecutor, Meriwether Broadnax of Greensville County; the appointed defense attorneys, William Parker, James Strange French and Thomas Gray; and, of course, the General, Richard Eppes.

Broadnax, who had been asked to come here to prosecute all of the cases, no matter how long the process lasted, posed the first question: "How many cases do you anticipate?"

"Impossible to say," Cobb said. "Several dozen. Each of the prisoners must have a preliminary hearing conducted by two magistrates, to separate the blacks who are demonstrably innocent from the ones who are possibly or probably guilty. It is a time-consuming process — Have I more or less answered your question?"

"More or less," Broadnax smiled.

"Consistent with the letter and the spirit of the General's decree," Cobb specified, "we have strictly forbidden the use of threats or violence or promises of mercy, to obtain information from the prisoners. I should remind you that in capital cases the Court of Oyer and Terminer has jurisdiction only over slaves, not over free blacks — or, God forbid, any whites who may have been involved — They'll be held for trial in the Superior Court — Now then, Mister Parker, Mister French, Mister Gray: We shall continue to endeavor to assign cases to you evenly, at $10 per case. As you know," Cobb added, suspecting Gray might not know, "you have the same right as the Commonwealth in summoning witnesses."

Parker had a question: "Are we agreed on the common pleading?"

"Yes," Cobb said. "The magistrates concur that for the sake of justice, as well as appearances, pleas of not guilty will be entered in all cases — I need not remind you, gentlemen: Many eyes will be watching what we do." He glanced at Parker. "History will be watching us."

"Jeremiah," the General said.

"Richard?"

"The transcripts."

"Oh, yes — Governor Floyd has requested copies of the court transcripts, for immediate review."

"All o' the transcripts?" the clerk of the court asked, hearing this for the first time.

"Yes — except, of course, when the defendant is discharged without trial."

Bill Bryant

"But why?" the clerk politely persisted.

Cobb was patient. He had called this meeting for precisely this reason, to deal with the trivial as well as the substantial details of the drama soon to be enacted in this courtroom – a drama without exact precedent in local, state or national law, or life. He wanted, he needed each of these men to be comfortable in the role each would perform. So: "Gubernatorial review is routine in any case where the defendant is found guilty and sentenced to hang, but is recommended to the Governor for a commutation of sentence – transportation out of Virginia. Why does the Governor want all of the transcripts? I assume that he wants to be sure that we are acting properly, in all cases, with time to intervene if he thinks we have erred, somehow. It is an unusual request. But then, this whole nightmare is most unusual."

"To say the least," Broadnax said. "Are the prisoners being cooperative?"

"Mister Rochelle," Cobb said to the sheriff, "I defer that question to you."

"And I defer to Collin. He's been with 'em more than any of the rest of us."

"Well, sir," Kitchen began, "so far, yes, sir – although most o' 'em claim they were forced into goin' along, or say that Nat misled 'em – All o' 'em agree on one thing, sir."

"Yes?" Broadnax said, leaning forward.

"Nat was the one who inspired the risin'."

"And where," Broadnax inquired, of no one in particular, "is he?"

The local men squirmed in their seats, and so did the General in his, as the innocent question hung guiltily in the air.

Finally, the General failed to answer it: "God only knows."

* * *

Following the meeting, Cobb led several of the men over to the clerk's home, to review, with other men already waiting there, a copy of the final draft of a letter prepared by a special committee of Southampton citizens, addressed to the Honorable Andrew Jackson, the letter from the people to the President saying, in part:

> Most of the havoc has been confined to a limited section of our county, but so inhuman has been the butchery, so indiscriminate the carnage, that the tomahawk and scalping knife have now no horrors. Along the road traveled by our rebellious blacks, comprising a distance of something like 27 miles, no white soul now lives to tell how fiendlike was their purpose. In the bosom of almost every family, this enemy still exists. Our homes, those near the scenes of havoc, as well as others more remote, have all been deserted and our families gathered together and guarded at public places in the county; and, still further, the excitement is so great that were the justices to pronounce a slave innocent, we fear a mob would be the consequence.

*Tomorrow Jerusalem: The Story of Nat Turner
and the Southampton Slave Insurrection*

SOMEWHERE in SOUTHAMPTON

Soon after the Sun set, after the last patrol passed in shadowy silence along the far edge of the field, ignoring him, he hurried into the woods to the nearby stream to quench his thirst and appease his hunger with what little remained of his meager provisions.

Before the insurrection, he had resolved never to second-guess any of the many decisions which led to it. But during the past week, he had been endlessly torturing himself with second-guessing every decision he had made.

The time had come, he thought, walking into the open field and stopping to stare at the stars, to start figuring out what he should do next, or try to do.

Before the insurrection, his decisions had been relatively well informed by a wide variety of sources. Now, he knew next to nothing about current conditions in Southampton - only that the white men must be searching for him everywhere - and, as he had seen during the day along the distant road, that the white women and children were returning home.

That last fact had pounded the last nail into the coffin of his fading hope that the war he had started was continuing.

The war was over.

Only the search was continuing, and it seemed to be relentless.

Still, he dared not go near his wife and children, or near his mother.

Still, he refused to consider heading for the Dismal Swamp.

Soon, he knew, he must forage for food, anything he could safely get - and for information, anything he could safely overhear.

In the meantime, of course, he must wait, and pray.

* * * * *

WEDNESDAY
August 31st
JERUSALEM

With the men of the Richmond Light Dragoons mostly mounted and preparing to depart, white women and girls moved among them, distributing packages of food for the journey home.

"If," the General remarked to John Hampden Pleasants as they stood in front of headquarters, "there are heroes - and heroines - in this sad story, there, sir, are some of them - the women of Southampton! Their hospitality and caring, in the midst of so much danger and hardship, have been truly exemplary. Just the other day ... "

"An outrage!" Captain Randolph Harrison angrily shouted as he stormed out of Vaughan's inn, waving a sheet of paper as he shoved aside the horses blocking his path and made straight for the General. "We have been here fewer than five days, protecting his neck, eating his bad food - Hellfire, we even took care of our own horses - and he has the unmitigated gall to - General, sir: The man wants $800! - $800! - It's an outrage! - It's ... It's ... "

"Profiteering!" the General proclaimed, grabbing the sheet of paper.

Pleasants quickly reached inside his tunic for his writing pad and pencil.

Bill Bryant

In the Courthouse

To oversimplify the complex, the basic challenge to the judicial authorities of Southampton County was to determine who did or saw or heard what or whom when and where.

Some of the prisoners in the overcrowded jail (or chained just outside the jail under special guard) were mere strays who had been rounded up in the great confusion, had survived the trip to Jerusalem, and clearly had nothing to do with the insurgents. These were being released to their masters.

Others had been or would be discharged following a preliminary hearing.

Most would go to trial in the Court of Oyer and Terminer.

The dozens of trials would construct incomplete and/or conflicting versions of what had really happened, with compelling testimony from dozens of witnesses white and black, free and slave. Most conspicuous among them: Levi Waller (still suffering from some mental derangement), Hark (still recovering from his wounds), the heroic John Thomas Barrow's widow Mary, Nathaniel Francis, Thomas Haithcock (himself a prisoner now), Jacob Williams, Caswell Worrell, Doctor Blunt's Frank and Shadrach Futrell, and Hubbard, property of the estate of the late Catherine Whitehead.

Among the defendants known or believed to have ridden with the rebels, only the boys and those who could somehow prove that they were forced to ride along could reasonably hope to avoid the hanging tree, could dream of being sold south.

Some of the defendants did not directly participate in the insurrection, but were suspected of related acts or manifestations of criminal intent.

All of the accused men and boys — and one girl — would be formally charged with "feloniously counseling, advising and conspiring with diverse other slaves to rebel and make insurrection, and taking the lives of diverse free white persons of the Commonwealth."

To make a long story short: On this day in the Court of Oyer and Terminer, these trials were conducted and concluded:

- DEFENDANT: Daniel (Property of Richard Porter)
  JUDGEMENT: Guilty — To hang September 5th
  COMPENSATION TO OWNER: $100

- DEFENDANT: Tom (Estate of Catherine Whitehead)
  JUDGEMENT: Discharged

* * * * *

THURSDAY
September 1st
In the Courthouse at JERUSALEM

On this day in the Court of Oyer and Terminer, these trials were conducted and concluded:

Tomorrow Jerusalem: The Story of Nat Turner and the Southampton Slave Insurrection

- DEFENDANT: Moses (Estate of John Barrow)
  JUDGEMENT: Guilty – To hang September 5th
  COMPENSATION TO OWNER: $400

- DEFENDANT: Jack (Estate of Catherine Whitehead)
  JUDGEMENT: Guilty – To hang September 12th
      Recommended – Commutation and Transportation
  COMPENSATION TO OWNER: $450

- DEFENDANT: Andrew (Estate of Catherine Whitehead)
  JUDGEMENT: Guilty – To hang September 12th
      Recommended – Commutation and Transportation
  COMPENSATION TO OWNER: $400

* * *

SOMEWHERE in SOUTHAMPTON

Emerging from his cave at sunset, soon after a patrol had passed in review – uncomfortably close enough that he could see their unfamiliar faces and hear their unfriendly voices – he stood and stretched his aching muscles, then kneeled and reached inside his hideaway to get his sword, then stood and began walking slowly toward the woods, welcoming every slight motion after another long hot day of waiting.

He had gone again to the abandoned Travis place, where the kitchen house and the cupboards were not entirely bare, but almost. Other people had been foraging there.

Food would be a problem, for which his longtime habit of fasting could be only a limited remedy.

The hiding – the waiting – posed a lesser challenge. In fact, now that the initial shock of defeat was easing, he was becoming better able to appreciate the dismay his unknown whereabouts must be causing among the whites, the fear – not to mention the satisfaction it must be giving to at least some of the blacks, the hope.

The whole truth be known, the ol' fox was actually beginning to enjoy this aspect of his otherwise miserable experience.

He had some power, still.

* * * * *

FRIDAY
September 2nd
In the Courthouse at JERUSALEM

For the first time in the clerk's record, "Nat" was identified as the "head of the insurrectionists" – identified in testimony offered by his dear old friend and boyhood playmate and tutor John Clark Turner, in the cases of the misdirected Curtis and Stephen.

On this day in the Court of Oyer and Terminer, these trials were conducted and concluded:

- DEFENDANT: Davy (Estate of Elizabeth Turner)
  JUDGEMENT: Guilty – To hang September 12th
  COMPENSATION TO OWNER: $450

- DEFENDANT: Curtis (Property of Thomas Ridley)
  JUDGEMENT: Guilty – To hang September 12th
  COMPENSATION TO OWNER: $400

- DEFENDANT: Stephen (Property of Thomas Ridley)
  JUDGEMENT: Guilty – To hang September 12th
  COMPENSATION TO OWNER: $450

- DEFENDANT: Isaac (Property of George Charlton)
  JUDGEMENT: Guilty – To hang September 20th
  Recommended – Commutation and Transportation
  COMPENSATION TO OWNER: $300

* * * * *

SATURDAY
September 3rd
In the Courthouse at JERUSALEM

On this particularly notable day in the jam-packed courtroom, the defendants included three of the so-called "generals" – Sam and Hark and Nelson. (The trial of another who had started out from Cabin Pond – Jack – was suspended to enable the ailing slave to be in attendance, later.)

If anyone needed additional evidence of Hark's guilt – and no one did – it was noted that when he was wounded and captured he had in his possession a pocketbook believed to have belonged to Trajan Doyle, a victim.

In the trial of Nelson, overseer Caswell Worrell caused a considerable stir in the courtroom when he confirmed what was already widely and reliably rumored – that Nelson, on August 18th, had actually "warned" Worrell that the white folks had better take care, that something might be happening soon – a "warning" which Worrell had dismissed, of course, considering the source of it and the fact that any conjurin' man was capable of telling such things to a white man.

On this day in the Court of Oyer and Terminer, these trials were conducted and concluded:

- DEFENDANT: Sam (Property of Nathaniel Francis)
  JUDGEMENT: Guilty – To hang September 9th
  COMPENSATION TO OWNER: $400

- DEFENDANT: Hark (Estate of Joseph Travis)
  JUDGEMENT: Guilty – To hang September 9th
  COMPENSATION TO OWNER: $450

- DEFENDANT: Nelson (Property of Jacob Williams)
  JUDGEMENT: Guilty – To hang September 9th
  COMPENSATION TO OWNER: $400

Tomorrow Jerusalem: The Story of Nat Turner and the Southampton Slave Insurrection

- DEFENDANT: Davy (Property of Levi Waller)
  JUDGEMENT: Guilty – To hang September 9th
  COMPENSATION TO OWNER: $300

- DEFENDANT: Nat (Property of Edwin Turner)
  JUDGEMENT: Guilty – To hang September 9th
  COMPENSATION TO OWNER: $450

* * *

GILES REESE Place

    By the time Giles Reese fully comprehended what had really happened on the 22nd of August, he had experienced a bewildering range of powerful emotions – from extreme gratitude, that he and his family had been spared, for some reason, to a strange guilt, as the reason became clear.
    Learning of the insurrection only when the insurgents were long gone from the neighborhood, Reese had decided to remain at home, with his family and his guns readily at hand, and await the news. His slaves, like most slaves (and free blacks) throughout Southampton, did their absolutely necessary chores and kept to themselves, awaiting the news.
    Learning of Nat's involvement, Reese had immediately and sternly questioned Cherry. But her expressions of surprise and ignorance convinced him of what he desperately wanted to believe, that she was blameless.
    And when the first group of white men came around, to get some answers, he managed to persuade them that his slave – yes, Nat's wife – knew nothing about her husband's plans or whereabouts.
    He did agree to the posting of armed men around his property, just in case Nat tried to contact Cherry. A similar precaution, he was told, was in effect at the late Elizabeth Turner's place, with Nancy as the bait.
    By the time the second group of white men came around, the whole situation was beyond Reese's control.
    Threatened by the lash, Cherry cried and trembled but repeated what she had told her master.
    The white men did not believe her.
    So they faced her against a tree and wrapped her arms around it and tied her wrists, then ripped her dress down the back, then gave her one final opportunity to tell the truth.
    But she would not change her story.
    Cherry could not and did not try to conceal the pain inflicted by the first lash, and by the second lash, and by the third lash – at which point Giles Reese intervened, moving protectively to Cherry's side.
    "Let me talk to her!" Reese both pleaded and insisted. "Cherry ... Listen closely to me, girl ... Considerin' what's happened, I cannot stop these men – You must tell 'em everything you know – anything you know ... Cherry?"
    "But ... But Nat trust me," she wept.

Bill Bryant

"It's over, Cherry – You hear me, girl? The uprisin', your relationship to Nat, your duty to Nat – It's all over! – An' it's jus' a matter o' time 'til Nat gets caught! – Cherry?"

"But Nat trust me!"

"He misled you, Cherry, an' he misled your people ... Now, listen to me good: Don' think o' Nat! – Think o' the children! – They need you now, more than ever."

"Nat," she began, her will to resist collapsing in defense of her babies, "he start talkin' 'bout it three years ago ... "

*

"Well?" inquired one of the men, as another returned to the group with the packet so well hidden and so reluctantly revealed by Cherry (now being tenderly escorted to her cabin by the master's wife). "What did you find?"

"Let's see ... Not much here – A rough map o' the county, I'd say – an' a list o' what appear to be 20 or so names – slaves, probably ... Here's a sheet with a lot o' numbers on it – 6,000 – 30,000 – 80,000 – an' peculiar symbols. Might as well be hieroglyphics ... All of it written in pokeberry juice, I'd say, or, or blood ... An' look here!"

He pointed to the tops of the several overlapping sheets, each marked in pokeberry juice, or, or blood – with a cross, and with a representation of the Sun, a black spot upon it.

"That damn Sun," muttered one of the men.

*

"Nat, he start talkin' 'bout it ... "

Three years ago! For three years, Cherry – not merely Reese's slave but also almost a member of his family – had known what Nat was planning to do.

Reese could understand Cherry's devotion to Nat, and her duty to Nat as wife to husband. He could even understand – though it might now be dangerous for him to say it in the presence of other white men – Cherry sharing Nat's intense wish to see his people free. And Nat's opinion had never been much of a secret.

But three years of knowing that Nat – or anybody else, for that matter – was planning to kill other people – white or black – made Cherry guilty, too, and Reese could not ignore it.

Cherry could hang for what she had done, or not done.

Or maybe some other solution might be found, to the problem she so uniquely represented.

Reese did like the girl, even now ... and was alive, because of her.

* * *

SOMEWHERE in SOUTHAMPTON

Welcoming the sunset, he closed his Bible, and began the slow and

*Tomorrow Jerusalem: The Story of Nat Turner
and the Southampton Slave Insurrection*

awkward process of liberating himself from his cave, his muscles aching in protest with every move.

In his feverishly overworked but unproductive mind, he could think of only one "plan" which had a ghost of a chance of succeeding.

It was simple: He would wait until the whites decided that he probably was not in Southampton but had fled to the Dismal Swamp, and relaxed their vigilance, then he would make contact with Cherry and Nancy, if he could, then figure out a way for all of them to escape into the Dismal Swamp. And there, perhaps, he could organize a new and better army among the escaped slaves, free blacks, poor whites and Indians who populated that impenetrable place. He could not forget the Spirit, of course.

It was so complex.

* * * * *

Office of the LIBERATOR
BOSTON, MASSACHUSETTS

William Lloyd Garrison, the editor (and a man of uncommon principle), shook his head as he read, for the final time on this notable 3rd of September in 1831, the words he had been compelled to write for the latest edition of the struggling (and uncommonly controversial) newspaper he had begun publishing in January, to advance the cause of immediate emancipation (commonly known as abolition).

He had warned them!

While preaching the peace of Jesus to the slaves, he had appealed to white Christians, philanthropists and patriots to help with "the great work of national redemption through the agency of moral power — of public opinion — of individual duty."

And individually, he had done his best to avert the calamity.

Now, horror-struck but confirmed in the righteousness of his cause, an even more resolved William Lloyd Garrison prepared to call it a day ... a day when the ink from his pen had tried again to warn them, beginning:

> What we have long predicted — at the peril of being stigmatized as an alarmist and declaimer — has commenced its fulfillment. The first step of the earthquake, which is ultimately to shake down the fabric of oppression, leaving not one stone upon the other, has been made. The first drops of blood, which are but the prelude to a deluge from the gathering clouds, have fallen. The first flash of lightning, which is to ignite and consume, has been felt. The first wailings of a bereavement, which is to clothe the earth in sackcloth, have broken upon our ears.

And ending:

> Woe to this guilty land, unless she speedily repents of her evil doings! The blood of millions of her sons cries aloud for redress! IMMEDIATE EMANCIPATION can alone save

her from the vengeance of Heaven, and cancel the debt of ages!

* * * * *

MONDAY
September 5th
In the Courthouse at JERUSALEM

Well enough to attend, Jack went to trial this morning – accused as one of the original conspirators. But the boy Moses, a prisoner belonging to the estate of Joseph Travis, testified that Jack had been tricked by Hark into attending the feast at Cabin Pond, then forced by Hark to accompany the insurgents. Jack was adjudged guilty, but the magistrates voted 3-2 to recommend commutation.

Nathaniel's Dred went to trial, too, the evidence of his guilt manifest to all. The loss of his arm made certain the loss of his life.

Thus, on this day in the Court of Oyer and Terminer, these trials were conducted and concluded:

- DEFENDANT: Jack (Estate of William Reese)
  JUDGEMENT: Guilty – To hang September 12th
              Recommended – Commutation and Transportation
  COMPENSATION TO OWNER: $350

- DEFENDANT: Dred (Property of Nathaniel Francis)
  JUDGEMENT: Guilty – To hang September 12th
  COMPENSATION TO OWNER: $400

At the Usual Place of Execution

At the western edge of town, where the open countryside abruptly began, a large crowd gathered early this afternoon – mostly whites, but also some blacks brought here to witness for themselves the full payment of the wages of sin.

This was a place to which people had rarely come, in the hitherto mostly peaceful history of Southampton.

Beginning today, of course, people would be coming here often – well into the future, the people gathered here today already knew.

Edward Butts, unpracticed at doing this sort of thing, nonetheless did know enough. He tied a tight noose in one end of a strong rope, then slung it over the outstretched limb of a sycamore tree, then secured the other end of the rope to the wagon which conveyed the prisoners from the jail to this place.

Thus, Richard Porter's Daniel and Thomas Barrow's Moses today departed this life – their bodies violently objecting to the passage until finally accepting the blessing of eternal peace – to be buried without ceremony in the pauper's field nearby.

*Tomorrow Jerusalem: The Story of Nat Turner
and the Southampton Slave Insurrection*

And the people of Southampton had yet another extraordinary experience — another indelible memory — to think about and talk about for many years to come.

* * * * *

**TUESDAY
September 6th
In the Courthouse at JERUSALEM**

Much to the regret of the defendant Nathan, the prosecution brought forth as a witness a slave named Daniel, who testified that while in the Greensville County jail with the defendant, Nathan had confided that he was present at some of the killings.

Much to the relief of Nathaniel's boys Nathan and Tom and Davy, Joseph's boy Moses testified that the defendants had gone with the insurgents reluctantly, and had to be watched and threatened by the insurgents, lest they try to slip away.

On this day in the Court of Oyer and Terminer, these trials were conducted and concluded:

- DEFENDANT: Nathan (Estate of Benjamin Blunt)
  JUDGEMENT: Guilty — To hang September 12th
  COMPENSATION TO OWNER: $375

- DEFENDANT: Nathan (Property of Nathaniel Francis)
  JUDGEMENT: Guilty — To hang September 20th
         Recommended — Commutation and Transportation
  COMPENSATION TO OWNER: $300

- DEFENDANT: Tom (Property of Nathaniel Francis)
  JUDGEMENT: Guilty — To hang September 20th
         Recommended — Commutation and Transportation
  COMPENSATION TO OWNER: $300

- DEFENDANT: Davy (Property of Nathaniel Francis)
  JUDGEMENT: Guilty — To hang September 20th
         Recommended — Commutation and Transportation
  COMPENSATION TO OWNER: $300

*

The magistrates instructed clerk James Rochelle to write into the record: "It having been intimated to the Court that the military force assembled at this place will be discharged in a few days, the Court, believing that a strong guard is necessary to the safe keeping of the prisoners now in jail until such as are condemned may be executed, respectfully solicit General Eppes, the Commanding Officer, to retain at this place 50 men as a guard for the jail."

Bill Bryant

* * *

SOMEWHERE in SOUTHAMPTON

Late this afternoon, it began raining, really hard, for the first time since the insurrection, quickly making the cave even more uncomfortable and unbearable.
He hated to think what this same rain might feel like in October.
Every pestering drip added to the sense of urgency he battled constantly, his great willpower struggling with the growing compulsion to begin roaming the countryside within the secrecy of night. Already, he had taken unwise risks.
One night, he ventured near enough to Giles Reese's place to see the white men, waiting ... Another night, he ventured near enough to Elizabeth Turner's place to see the white men, waiting.
Tonight, he resolved, he would go only to the stream — and to the orchard down the road ... He yearned for one of Nancy's apple pies.

* * * * *

WEDNESDAY
September 7th
In the Courthouse at JERUSALEM

On this day in the Court of Oyer and Terminer, these trials were conducted and concluded:

- DEFENDANT: Hardy (Property of Benjamin Edwards)
  JUDGEMENT: Guilty — To hang September 20th
                 Recommended — Commutation and Transportation
  COMPENSATION TO OWNER: $450

- DEFENDANT: Isham (Property of Benjamin Edwards)
  JUDGEMENT: Guilty — To hang September 20th
                 Recommended — Commutation and Transportation
  COMPENSATION TO OWNER: $350

- DEFENDANT: Sam (Property of James Parker)
  JUDGEMENT: Discharged

- DEFENDANT: Jim (Property of William Vaughan)
  JUDGEMENT: Discharged

* * * * *

*Tomorrow Jerusalem: The Story of Nat Turner
and the Southampton Slave Insurrection*

**THURSDAY
September 8th
At the WHITE HOUSE in WASHINGTON**

This morning, the President met with Commodore Jesse Duncan Elliott, to discuss in appropriate detail the recent tragedy in Southampton County, Virginia.

* * * * *

In the Courthouse at JERUSALEM

On this day in the Court of Oyer and Terminer, these trials were conducted and concluded:

- DEFENDANT: Bob (Property of Temperance Parker)
  JUDGEMENT: Discharged

- DEFENDANT: Davy (Property of Joseph Parker)
  JUDGEMENT: Discharged

- DEFENDANT: Daniel (Property of Solomon Parker)
  JUDGEMENT: Discharged

* * * * *

**FRIDAY
September 9th
At the Usual Place of Execution**

Nathaniel's Sam.
Joseph's Hark.
Jacob's Nelson.
Levi's Davy.
Edwin's Nat.
One by one ... hung by the neck 'til dead.

* * * * *

**SATURDAY
September 10th
JAMES ROCHELLE Home**

Feeling better, all things considered, Richard Eppes had happily accepted James Rochelle's invitation to dinner, the General's condition improving during the ample and positively delicious meal served to the people seated around the dining room table – Eppes, his perfect posture and manner accordant with the uniform he proudly wore; Rochelle and his wife Martha, and their son James Henry and daughter Mattie; and the widow Elizabeth Thomas, and her son George Henry and daughters Judy and Lucy.

"Mrs. Rochelle," the General said with his whole heart as he wiped his mouth again with the fine cloth napkin, "my compliments to the cook!"

"You may tell her for yourself, sir, when she brings in the pie – I must say, nobody in the county bakes a more scrumptious apple pie! – Do save yourself some room!"

"Scrumptious, eh?" the General grinned, patting his tummy. "Well, then, I shall conserve what remains of my appetite, and regrettably forego another small serving of those wonderful potatoes."

"A pity," Elizabeth said, "Thomas Gray's father passing away."

"Yes, it is," Rochelle said. "Jeremiah says the magistrates are agreed that Thomas should be permitted a decent mournin' time, without havin' to worry about clients, so they won't be assignin' any new cases to him for a while ... though I'm not sure that's goin' to sit well with Thomas."

"What do you mean?" Martha asked.

"You know how poor the man is – He could use the fees."

"Surely," Elizabeth said, "his share of his father's estate ..."

"Amounts to nothin'," said the clerk of the court.

"But how can that be?" Martha asked.

"Mister Gray," Rochelle began to explain, a trifle uncomfortable at washing even this little piece of the county's dirty linen in the presence of the General and the children, "never could abide his son's feelings about slavery ... So he just left Thomas out o' the will entirely."

"A pity," Elizabeth said.

"Yes, it is," Rochelle said, compelled to add: "Even in view o' all that's happened."

"The hangings," the General observed, finishing off his corn, "have not been a pretty sight. That rebel Will Artist, who shot himself rather than being captured, did himself a favor ... I understand he was a free man?"

"Yes," Rochelle said, "which means that at least five free blacks apparently participated, in one way or another. Hard to imagine why – with nothin' to gain, an' so much to lose!"

Now, the General figured, was as good a time as any to mention it: "I have received several reports that some of the poor whites, hereabouts, have expressed sentiments which might be interpreted as sympathetic to Turner and his bandits – Can you imagine that?!"

"Yes ... I can," Rochelle said, a bit defensively, feeling tested, somehow, but also knowing the reports – and the interpretation – to be accurate.

"May I have another helping of potatoes, please?" James Henry asked.

"Certainly, dear," Martha said.

"General," George Henry said, "do you think 50 men will be sufficient to guard the jail?"

"Well, your uncle Clements seems to think so, and I trust his judgement."

"Our slaves," George Henry noted, "are still talkin' about their night in the jail – They didn't like it much!"

Tomorrow Jerusalem: The Story of Nat Turner and the Southampton Slave Insurrection

"Saved their lives," Elizabeth said. "That was a blood-thirsty mob!"

"Those men had a right to be angry," Rochelle said, sensing Martha's discomfort with the whole mood of this dinner conversation. "Ol' Sam an' the others caused quite a ruckus, arrivin' when they did – 'specially allowin' as how they had just been with the rebels."

"With guns at their backs," Elizabeth reminded everyone.

"George Henry," the General said, "I'm told that you have a particular fondness for botany. Fascinating subject. Difficult, too. But do you have a real career in mind?"

"Not yet, sir. Uncle James wants me to work in his office and study law."

"Well, young man, I have come to respect and admire both of your uncles. Pay close attention to whatever advice either of them gives you – That is a direct order!"

"Yes, sir!" George Henry grinned, saluting the best he knew how.

"Perhaps," the General decided, after considerable debate, even as he smiled and returned the salute, correctly, "another slice of that turkey, please – I am told that Pitt Thomas has been commissioned a major of infantry."

"Well deserved, too," Rochelle said. "He an' the other men – includin' the blacks – who helped to spread the alarm doubtless saved many lives – An' it's virtually certain that Alexander Peete will be confirmed a colonel of cavalry."

"Good to have some legitimate heroes," the General said, "considering the shameful conduct of some other people – I learned today that some of the Hertford militiamen plan to file a formal complaint against Colonel Sharpe!"

"Good for them!" Rochelle said. "People decapitated and disemboweled, an' he wants to be 'paid for his troubles' – Disgusting! When I think o' the poor victims – an' the poor survivors! – Barmer, maimed for life – Harriet Whitehead, havin' to live with those memories – Lavinia Francis – Levi ... "

"Enough of this talk!" Martha finally protested. "Life goes on, people have returned to their homes, the bandits have been crushed, the revolt is over – An' the less said about it, the better, if you ask me!"

"I agree," Elizabeth said. "Where is that apple pie?"

"Life does go on, Mrs. Rochelle," the General said, "but it will never be the same – not here, nor anywhere else in the South, I fear. We have glimpsed the Apocalypse. It is as one of your townsmen wrote to the Enquirer, that this event has made 'a fearful and lasting impression on the minds and imagination of the people' – Are you aware, my dear Mrs. Rochelle, of what is happening out there in the countryside, even beyond Southampton? Folks are buying every sword and gun available, stocking up on ammunition and powder, scouting for places to hide in the woods and swamps, planning escape routes, keeping packages of food and clothing ready – just in case – even though ... "

"But, sir," Martha began, "I ... "

"Even though it is my honest opinion that this region – and particularly Southampton – is now probably the safest in the South, from the threat of insurrection. The impressive show of force we have made, the great parade of state and federal soldiers throughout the region, the promptness of our action – your swift administration of justice and severe punishment, your purging of the worst elements in your slave society – not to mention the dreadful atrocities during the

Bill Bryant

days following the insurrection – All of these facts must convince even the most deluded wretches that an insurrection cannot possibly succeed ... The hope may linger elsewhere, but it ought to be extinguished here ... in my opinion."

"Perhaps," Rochelle said, without conviction, and with a certain barely concealed resentment. The General's oratorical flourish made some sense, but ignored a vital point: The people of Southampton, before the insurrection, considered this probably the safest place in the South – and just look at what happened! Now, the General would have these people believe that they have nothing to fear! The mere suggestion seemed somehow insulting. "A friend o' mine remarked the other day – How did he put it? – 'I fear much that this insurrection is to lead to much more disastrous consequences than are at this time apprehended by anybody' ... Your honest opinion notwithstanding, General, a lot o' people are talkin' about leavin' Southampton."

"Mostly just talk," Elizabeth said, still wondering at the General's words, "though I suspect many of the free blacks would like very much to leave."

"Many of them will be leavin' soon," Rochelle reported, grateful for the new conversational direction. "Upwards o' 200 have already asked to be aboard the ship sailin' for Africa later this year."

"I'll wager," the General said, "Nat Turner wishes he could be boarding that ship!"

"Then, at least," Elizabeth said, "we could sleep more peacefully."

"No," the General said, needing to make a point which needed to be made to everyone in Southampton, and beyond. "No one can sleep peacefully – nor will the insurrection truly be 'over' – until Nat Turner is caught!"

"An' hanged!" Rochelle added.

"Gentlemen!" Martha mildly protested.

"General, sir," James Henry innocently inquired, "where is Nat Turner?"

The General had to hesitate, and shake his head, before answering, with a weak smile: "My boy, your guess is as good as mine – And right now, frankly, I am more interested in the whereabouts of that apple pie!"

"Not to worry, son," Rochelle said, trying to be convincing, knowing that the answer was more important to his son than the General could imagine – more important to everyone in Southampton than the General could imagine, as wise and as perceptive as the General was. "I, for one, very seriously doubt that he is still in Southampton – My guess is he's somewhere deep in the Dismal Swamp – or near Norfolk, hopin' to catch a ship ... Or maybe he's tryin' for the North, though I doubt he could make it without some help – an' nobody's gonna help him – not even the Quakers."

"I would like to meet him," the General said.

"Why?" Rochelle asked.

"To learn what sort of man he is – You know, it's been hard to get a good picture of him. You people don't seem able to find many kind words for him – But he must be an unusual man."

"Not particularly," Rochelle felt obliged to say.

"And yet," the General persisted, "as flawed and doomed as the insurrection was, as untrained and disorderly as his so-called army was, he managed to inspire those men to risk everything in a desperate cause – to traverse more terrain in a day than some of our own soldiers accomplished – to fight, and die, for him – This is not an ordinary man!"

Tomorrow Jerusalem: The Story of Nat Turner and the Southampton Slave Insurrection

"More ordinary than you suppose," Rochelle persisted. "I suspect those men were motivated more by their cause than by their leader." The General was among the best of men, intelligent and wise and compassionate, but he would make no new friends in Southampton with this sort of talk - and he meant to speak to Eppes about it, later, privately, tactfully. To the General, the victims of Nat Turner were statistics, names, brief descriptions - But to the people of Southampton, they were family, friends, neighbors - And the mental images and physical reminders of the insurrection would endure for untold years to come - the blood loss felt more acutely here than any outsider, even the General, could hope to understand. "Pass the gravy, please."

"Even if we do catch him," the General said, "I wonder if he would live long enough to meet the hangman."

"The other day," Rochelle recalled, "I overheard a man sayin' that if he was the one to catch Nat, he would skin him alive - on the spot!"

"That is barbaric!" Martha declared.

"Indeed!" Elizabeth agreed.

"Isn't there a law against something like that?" George Henry asked.

"Actually," Rochelle began, to tell the truth, "there ... "

"In Richmond, a few years ago," the General noted, "I saw a book bound in the skin of a victim of the French guillotine."

"That," Elizabeth said, "is morbid and depraved!"

"Gentlemen!" Martha insisted. "May we please discuss some other subject?"

"Certainly, my dear," Rochelle said. "I saw Hartie Joyner today. That colt o' his has recovered nicely from its wounds - frisky as ever. But you know, it's peculiar - Everywhere a pellet struck the animal, gray hair is growin' - Ah, here comes the pie!"

"My compliments to the cook!" the General exclaimed, as the black servant approached with the freshly baked apple pie. "That was an exquisite meal!"

"Why, thank you, General Eppes, suh," the woman grinned, pleased with herself. "Now jus' you wait 'til you gets a taste o' this!"

* * *

SOMEWHERE in SOUTHAMPTON

Actually standing again in the middle of the Preaching Place, he listened carefully for the whispers and echoes of the past ... but heard nothing.

Then an owl hooted, and he tensed, looking upward through the very gently rustling leaves, to the cratered Moon.

And then he left.

* * * * *

Bill Bryant

MONDAY
September 12th
In the Courthouse at JERUSALEM

On this day in the Court of Oyer and Terminer, the magistrates conducted a hearing regarding the prisoner Thomas Haithcock - a free man of color charged with "conspiracy to rebel and make insurrection."
The prisoner was remanded to the jail.

At the Usual Place of Execution

Five condemned prisoners made one final earthly trip today, by wagon from the jail to the hanging tree, to the usual place of burial for the likes o' them:
Davy, who formerly belonged to the estate of Elizabeth Turner.
Curtis, formerly the property of Thomas Ridley.
Stephen, formerly the property of Thomas Ridley.
Dred, formerly the property of Nathaniel Francis.
Nathan, who formerly belonged to the estate of Benjamin Blunt.
Former slaves, now free, at last.

* * *

SIMON BLUNT Place

Simon Sr. had mixed feelings when he read the message conveyed by a special courier sent by General Eppes.
Simon Jr., thanks to Commodore Elliott's meeting with President Jackson, was being offered a midshipman's warrant in the Navy, plus an invitation to serve under Elliott himself - a splendid and well deserved opportunity, promising the boy an interesting career and life, though it must mean the end of the doctor's dream of his son someday becoming the master of this fine place.
Simon Jr., when he read the message, had mixed feelings, too.

* * * * *

SATURDAY
September 17th
JERUSALEM

Standing near the bridge, Richard Eppes, Clements Rochelle, Edward Butts and Thomas Trezevant stepped well back as the patrol of mounted militiamen passed by, onto the bridge, southward.
"The new proclamation might help," the General hoped. "At least, now we can provide an approximate description of Turner, so folks'll have some idea of who it is they're looking for - Damnation! We

should've done this weeks ago! The Governor wants Turner brought in alive, and this ..."

"Actually," Trezevant began, thinking out loud, "I ... "

"But I swear," the General continued, "it has been like pulling hen's teeth, trying to obtain an accurate description of the man – Considering how many of you Southampton people supposedly knew the man, you'd think at least one of you would remember what he looks like!"

"Nat," the sheriff said, searching for the right word, "was so ordinary – in most ways."

"That information about the scars should help," the deputy sheriff said.

"Actually," Trezevant began again, "I ... "

"Scars!" the General scoffed. "Everybody's got scars! ... Anyway, what we have should serve the purpose – that, and the new reward money. Gentlemen," he chuckled at the thought of it, "just thinking about the $500 state reward and the $500 county reward – plus the other bounties offered by your citizens – I am tempted to join the fox hunt myself!"

"Actually!" Trezevant began, getting their attention, then finishing: "You know, I do believe Nat's complexion was of a somewhat darker hue ... "

* * * * *

MONDAY
September 19th
In the Courthouse at JERUSALEM.

On this day in the Court of Oyer and Terminer, these trials were conducted and concluded:

- DEFENDANT: Joe (Property of John Turner)
  JUDGEMENT: Guilty – To hang September 26th
  COMPENSATION TO OWNER: $450

- DEFENDANT: Lucy (Estate of John Barrow)
  JUDGEMENT: Guilty – To hang September 26th
  COMPENSATION TO OWNER: $275

- DEFENDANT: Matt (Property of Thomas Ridley)
  JUDGEMENT: Discharged

- DEFENDANT: Jim (Property of Richard Porter)
  JUDGEMENT: Discharged

* * *

Bill Bryant

SOMEWHERE in SOUTHAMPTON

His tightly huddled sleeping form here and there illuminated by patches and slivers of sunlight, he instantly widely awoke to the reverberating echo of a shotgun blast ... far away ... then closed his eyes.

* * * * *

TUESDAY
September 20th
In the Courthouse at JERUSALEM

On this day in the Court of Oyer and Terminer, this trial was conducted and concluded:

- DEFENDANT: Jack (Property of Everett Bryant)
  JUDGEMENT: Discharged

Also: Exum Artist, a free man of color, and Berry Newsom, identified for the record neither as a slave nor as a free man of color but as an indentured apprentice to Peter Edwards, were formally remanded for trial in the Superior Court.

* * * * *

WEDNESDAY
September 21st
In the Courthouse at JERUSALEM

On this day in the Court of Oyer and Terminer, this trial was conducted and concluded:

- DEFENDANT: Stephen (Property of James Bell)
  JUDGEMENT: Discharged

* * * * *

THURSDAY
September 22nd
In the Courthouse at JERUSALEM

The girl Becky had kept her coerced promise to Jim and Isaac and Preston — until after the insurrection, when circumstances, and pressures, changed. Even so, her testimony regarding Preston did not damn the man enough to condemn him, in the eyes of the law.

Tomorrow Jerusalem: The Story of Nat Turner and the Southampton Slave Insurrection

On this day in the Court of Oyer and Terminer, these trials were conducted and concluded:

- DEFENDANT: Jim (Property of Samuel Champion)
  JUDGEMENT: Guilty — To hang September 30th
  COMPENSATION TO OWNER: $300

- DEFENDANT: Isaac (Property of Samuel Champion)
  JUDGEMENT: Guilty — To hang September 30th
  COMPENSATION TO OWNER: $400

- DEFENDANT: Preston (Property of Hannah Williamson)
  JUDGEMENT: Discharged

- DEFENDANT: Frank (Property of Solomon Parker)
  JUDGEMENT: Guilty — To hang September 30th
       Recommended — Commutation and Transportation
  COMPENSATION TO OWNER: $600

Solomon's Frank was an especially skilled blacksmith, so highly valued that the magistrates thought it more sensible to sell the man south rather than hang him at such cost to the Commonwealth.

* * * * *

MONDAY
September 26th
At the Usual Place of Execution

Joe met his fate today — Joe, formerly the property of John Clark Turner, the people in the crowd reminded one another.
John Clark Turner ... Nat's friend, not only as a boy, but also as a man.
John Clark Turner ... who reportedly helped the Preacher learn how to read and write and reckon.
John Clark Turner ... whose family really had been much too indulgent of Nat, even by the formerly relaxed standards of Southampton.
John Clark Turner ... a good man, people who knew him had to agree — but tainted forever, all agreed, by his close association to Nat, whom he must have influenced, in some ways.
Joe died well, the crowd observed, as though welcoming his fate.
Then came Lucy, the heroic John Thomas Barrow's Lucy, sitting on top of her coffin in the back of the wagon as she rode from the jail to the sycamore tree.
She seemed proud of herself, not in the slightest repentant.
She, too, died well ... the crowd murmured.

* * * * *

Bill Bryant

WEDNESDAY
September 28th
In the Courthouse at JERUSALEM

On this day in the Court of Oyer and Terminer, this trial was conducted and concluded:

- DEFENDANT: Nelson (Estate of Benjamin Blunt)
  JUDGEMENT: Discharged

* * * * *

FRIDAY
September 30th
At the Usual Place of Execution

Today, Samuel Champion's Jim and Isaac felt the noose, briefly – sharply.

* * * * *

Early October
GILES REESE Place

Between the setting and the rising of the Sun, he had finally begun to roam well away from his field, his hunger for good food exceeded only by his craving for any information.

In rare raids on different kitchen houses – being careful not to take too much and thereby attract attention to the theft – he obtained just enough food to sustain himself.

In repeated attempts to overhear scraps of conversation inside the homes of the white folks and the cabins of the black folks, he heard little, and learned nothing.

The guards at Elizabeth Turner's place had vanished – but so had everybody else, including Nancy.

But the guards who remained at Giles Reese's place did gradually decrease in number and alertness, until finally – soon before dawn with scarcely enough time to reach the safety of his cave – he saw his opportunity, and seized it.

Seeing the lone guard at the slave cabins starting toward the main house, Nat dared to enter Cherry's cabin, paused briefly to stare at the dark corner where his son and daughter were sleeping, then gently but firmly covered Cherry's mouth with his hand to stifle her shock – whispering to her only "It's me" – then led her outside, into the perfect solitude of the nearby woods.

He could not linger long, he told her, as they desperately embraced.

She understood.

But he lingered long enough to assure her that he was all right, all things considered, and for her to assure him that she and the

Tomorrow Jerusalem: The Story of Nat Turner and the Southampton Slave Insurrection

children were well, all things considered — long enough for him to discover and caress the scars across her back, and learn the reason for them — No, he told her, there was nothin' for him to forgive, she had done the right thing, he was the one feelin' guilty, for causin' this — An' besides, those papers wouldn't do the white men any good.

And he lingered long enough to promise her that he would find a way to take all of them, including Nancy, away from here — No, she told him, she did not know where Nancy was — Nobody ever told her nothin', nowadays, certainly not the white folks always starin' at her like they was still lookin' for answers, no an' not from the black folks mostly tryin' to keep a safe distance from her, an' from the guards who until recently had been followin' every move she made.

He lingered long enough for them to love one another, still — long enough, too, to agree on a familiar place here in the woods where she could leave food for him, from time to time — say, every three or four days, jus' a little food.

And then he left, disappearing into the shadows surrendering to the dawn.

He was feelin' better — an' so was she, as she returned to the cabin, unseen, she prayed. Nat's love, she had never doubted, ever. But now she knew as well, again: Nat trusted her!

And there was hope!!

* * * * *

THURSDAY
October 13th
SOMEWHERE in SOUTHAMPTON

Returning to his cave at dawn, he was alarmed when he detected some motion inside the pile of old fence rails.

A dog emerged, with a hambone in its mouth, and scampered away.

Shaken but relieved, he crawled into his cave, discouraged by another night of unproductive roaming — another night without Cherry.

He did not see the two men walking along the far edge of the field.

Nor did they see him.

* * * * *

SATURDAY
October 15th
SOMEWHERE in SOUTHAMPTON

This evening, Nathaniel's Red Nelson (entrusted with a fowling gun) and a friend, and Red's dog, were returning from a possum-hunting trip.

The dog began scampering well ahead of them, into the sunset-lit field from which the animal had emerged a couple of days earlier with a hambone, of all the things to find in a field.

Returning from an early visit to the stream, Nat was planning his night as he approached his cave — and the dog emerged, and began

Bill Bryant

barking, and Nat tried to shoo it away – the insistent barking and the urgent shooing attracting the attention of the two hunters, who warily came closer to the scene of the ruckus.

Then ... Red saw Nat, and Nat saw Red, and the men stared at one another, each wondering what to do.

Nat had to try it: "You got to promise you won't tell the white men where I am ... You got to promise!"

Red immediately fled, followed closely by his friend, the dog dashing ahead of them, barking.

Soon, they were long gone.

* * *

Soon, too, he was elsewhere.

And there, his mind racing to meet the new demands on it, he got down on his knees, and used his sword to carve out a small yet large enough hole inside two adjoining stacks of fodder ... in the middle of a field of fodder stacks, on the property of Nathaniel Francis.

This night, he did not roam.
This night, he thought.
This night, he prayed ... all night.

* * * * *

MONDAY
October 17th
In the Courthouse at JERUSALEM

On this day in the Court of Oyer and Terminer – amid the frenzy of excitement surrounding Red Nelson's sighting of the long lost but not forgotten Nat – these trials were conducted and concluded:

- DEFENDANT: Jack (Property of Nathaniel Simmons)
  JUDGEMENT: Discharged

- DEFENDANT: Shadrach (Property of Nathaniel Simmons)
  JUDGEMENT: Discharged

- DEFENDANT: Sam (Property of Peter Edwards)
  JUDGEMENT: Guilty – To hang November 4th
  COMPENSATION TO OWNER: $450

In Sam's case, the familiar but ever vivid testimony of Levi Waller for the prosecution outweighed the testimony of Peter Edwards for the defense, the master stating for the record that he considered Sam "a Negro of good character."

* * *

*Tomorrow Jerusalem: The Story of Nat Turner
and the Southampton Slave Insurrection*

EVERYWHERE in SOUTHAMPTON

With renewed confidence and zeal, the white men searched for him.
Some now hunted at night as well as during the day.

* * * * *

**TUESDAY
October 18th
In the Courthouse at JERUSALEM**

On this day in the Court of Oyer and Terminer, these trials were conducted and concluded:

- DEFENDANT: Archer (Property of Arthur Reese)
  JUDGEMENT: Discharged

- DEFENDANT: Moses (Estate of Joseph Travis)
  JUDGEMENT: Guilty — To hang November 17th
              Recommended — Commutation and Transportation
  COMPENSATION TO OWNER: $300

Also: The prisoner Isham Turner, a free man of color, was examined by the magistrates, who remanded him to the jail, for trial in the Superior Court.

At the Military Headquarters

Richard Eppes, who in recent weeks had been feeling more unwell than usual, spent this whole day hard at work.
The end of the contest was in sight.

EVERYWHERE in SOUTHAMPTON

Rumors abounded — including, of course, frequent reports that Nat had been seen, or even captured, at this place, at that place ... He was everywhere, at once.

* * *

And the colors of this particular Virginia autumn seemed even more glorious than usual — no consolation to so many folks, white and black, thinking of loved ones not here to see it.

* * * * *

Bill Bryant

WEDNESDAY
October 26th
NATHANIEL FRANCIS Place

Standing not a foot away from the front door of Nathaniel's home, in which the living room lamps were lit, Nat just stood there in the dark, for several painfully long minutes.

More than once during his overbold nightly excursions since the 15th, he had been spotted by white people, and more than once by black people. His cave still was safe, but nowhere else.

The guards at the Reese place had been re-enforced – and, worse, there had been no bundle of food from Cherry in a week, which anguished him in more ways than one.

By degrees, the weather was becoming colder, and he was becoming ever more desperate – desperate enough to begin thinking seriously about surrendering himself, to what seemed to be his inevitable destiny.

Finally, a few nights ago, he did venture toward Jerusalem, coming as close as the intersection of the Barrow Road with the Jerusalem Road – where the moonlit spectacle of the skull upon the post made him stop, disheartened, and reverse his course.

So now he was here, at Nathaniel's, to hand his sword to the one man who – despite all of their personal differences and all that had happened – might be merciful enough to escort him safely to Jerusalem.

Nat's fisted right hand rose upward, hesitated, then knocked softly on the door.

!

Startled – particularly at this hour of the night – to hear someone at the door, Lavinia and her mother-in-law looked up from their knitting and then stared fearfully at one another. Lavinia's right hand reached for the pistol on the table even as her left hand reached protectively toward her baby boy sleeping in the nearby cradle.

*

Again, Nat raised his fisted right hand, again hesitated, again knocked, a bit more loudly.

!

Lavinia, trying frantically to remember if she had locked the door, cocked the pistol, and whispered: "Mother Francis ... Should I go to the door?"
"No!"
"Perhaps we should wake Nathaniel."
"No! ... That is how Salathiel ... No!"

Tomorrow Jerusalem: The Story of Nat Turner and the Southampton Slave Insurrection

Lavinia aimed the pistol at the door.

*

Nat raised his fisted right hand – and in frustration hammered it against the thin air inches from the door, then stepped back ... and vanished.

* * * * *

THURSDAY
October 27th
SOMEWHERE in SOUTHAMPTON

With an autumn sunset strewn across the western horizon, Nat emerged from the fodder stacks in the middle of the field just as Nathaniel emerged from the woods at the near edge of the field.
Each immediately saw the other.
One armed with a sword. One armed with a pistol.
Nat, feeling a surge of relief, quickly shifted his sword to his left hand, then started to raise his right hand in peaceful gesture.
Nathaniel, feeling a surge of duty inseparable from vengeance, cocked and aimed his pistol.
Nat turned to run, stumbling as the pistol spoke, its pellets chewing holes in his hat as it left his head.
Pausing to grab his hat, across the field and into the woods he ran, not thinking of stopping until he was too breathless to go further ... And when he did stop, gasping for air, he knew he had learned two new lessons – not to go anywhere near Nathaniel again, and not to hide again in the middle of a field.

* * * * *

SUNDAY
October 30th
PETER EDWARDS Place

Mounted and ready to ride into the morning countryside, several patrols of militiamen and civilians received their final orders from the officer standing on the top front step of the house.
Off to the side stood the prosperous Peter Edwards and his honest and hardworking but dirt-poor friend Benjamin Phipps, a day-laborer cradling a shotgun in his arms.
The morning was cold, men and horses exhaling brief wispy clouds of frost, but the enthusiasm was warming.
"Remember," the officer declared, "the reward money can be collected only if Nat is brought in alive – An' don' forget the order from Jerusalem: Do not fire your weapon unless you have a damn good

Bill Bryant

reason - Too many folks bein' scared into the woods an' swamps by the least excitement. That's all, men! Good huntin'!"

As the patrols slowly began departing in several directions, to criss-cross yet again the local terrain, Edwards turned to Phipps.

"You jus' passin' through this mornin', Ben, or plannin' to join the hunt?"

"Reckon I'll jus' go about my business, Peter. The thought o' that money is mighty appealin' - but the needle'll have to fall out o' the haystack an' stab me, for me to find it!"

"Well, he's around here somewhere - an' hungry, too, I bet, ever since his woman got caught sneakin' food to him ... Yes, sir, he's hungry!"

"An' cold ... Well, Peter, I'll be on my way now."

Edwards gestured toward the shotgun. "With your constant companion!"

Phipps smiled and patted his gun. "She hasn't left my side these past two months - an' she's well charged with powder - jus' in case!"

* * *

A mile or so from the Edwards place, so cold he feared he could be betrayed by a breath, or a sudden shiver, Nat welcomed the sense if not the reality of the morning sunlight.

He had already resolved himself to endure the day here - here at the side of a pathway snaking through the woodlands of Doctor Musgrave's property - in a crudely dug shallow hole under the top branches of a huge fallen pine tree, his cave well concealed by a shield of carefully arranged pine brush.

* * *

As a patrol noisily passed just in front of him, from the woods on one side of the pathway into the woods on the other side, Benjamin Phipps decided, for no particular reason, to rest for a spell, and sat himself down against the base of an oak tree.

Thereby, he chanced to see ... to his amazement ... the movement of pine brush just across the pathway - and the appearance of a black man's head, poking through, looking around.

Phipps stood, cocked and aimed his shotgun. "Who are you? - Answer!"

Nat did not hesitate to reply, as he emerged from his cave and stood, his sword at his side: "I am Nat Turner ... Please - Don't shoot!"

"Na - ... Toss that sword over here - carefully - unless you've a mind to fight it out, jus' you an' me, an' get it all over with right here an' now!"

Nat hesitated only briefly, then did as he was told.

"On the ground - face down!" Phipps ordered. "An' put your hands behind your back!"

Nat did as he was told.

This man, at least, was not going to kill him.

Phipps took off his belt and bound the prisoner's hands.

*Tomorrow Jerusalem: The Story of Nat Turner
and the Southampton Slave Insurrection*

Then he picked up Nat's sword and gave the pine tree three whacks, to mark the spot of capture.
And then, the white man aimed his gun - at the sky - and fired!
Nat winced.

PETER EDWARDS Place

Like the ripples from a pebble cast into a peaceful pond, expanding in all directions to touch the world, the shotgun blast echoed through the countryside, almost instantly reaching the ears of the mounted patrol which only a few minutes earlier had passed nearby, then paused to rest.
The celebration here began the moment the prisoner arrived at the front gate to the long lane leading up to the main house, Nat walking ahead of the lethal end of Ben Phipps' shotgun, captive and captor flanked by a mounted escort, many of the men firing their weapons skyward, shattering the rule of silence.
Couriers immediately were dispatched to Jerusalem and to Cross Keys, the first of many men who would help to spread the word this day, firing their guns to get people's attention, and to rejoice.
Peter's ol' Jeff and Nathaniel's Red Nelson were sent forth to notify the neighborhood and to invite the local folks to Peter's for a feast.

*

Within an hour of being captured, Nat stood against the front of the house, his wrists and ankles confined by the manacles provided by Peter.
Ben's prisoner was now the focus of the scornful close attention of more than a hundred white men, not to mention dozens of white women and children, and slaves - with more people comin'.
The frequent blusters of gunfire were nerve-rattling.
Amid the steadily increasing commotion, Nat's expression did not change. He was as he seemed - resigned, but not repentant, and thus defiant - captured, but not conquered, and thus a challenge to them, still.
One of Peter's slaves had a mind and a mood of her own, and with or without the master's or anybody else's permission she was determined to let Nat know how she felt about the path down which Nat had led her son, Nathaniel's Sam - So, carrying a small bucket and a ladle, she approached the prisoner, and offered him water.
"Sam my boy," she said to him, holding the ladle to his lips.
Nat sipped the water. "I know." And sipped. "Your boy a brave man."
Then, seeing two militiamen purposefully approaching, the old woman swung the ladle around and began striking at Nat, drawing blood as he tried to block her blows with his chained hands. "You killed my boy!" she shouted, halting only when the militiamen restrained her, disarmed her, and began to lead her away - screaming: "You filled his head with crazy ideas an' got him hanged! You killed my boy!"
Nat now displayed a pained expression ... Sam, hung ... How many others?

Bill Bryant

"Peter!" Ben called out. "Could you come over here, please?"
"Yes, Ben!"
"All right with you if I put him in your cellar, for now?"
"Certainly!"
    Slowly, from the front of the house to the back of the house, the hero of the day marched the prisoner, the excited crowd noisily flowing along with them, Peter leading Nat and Ben down the brick stepway into the cellar.

*

    Alone in this simple prison, the clamoring of the crowd attacking through the barred windows, he sprawled onto the earthen floor.
    Awkwardly, he reached into his pocket and pulled out his Bible.
    Ben had found the Bible, but had respectfully returned it to the pocket.
    Nat would not need to surrender his Bible.

EVERYWHERE in SOUTHAMPTON

    Where the swiftly rippling news did not cause immediate jubilation among the whites, it caused complete panic, many people fleeing from their homes, into the safety of the woods and swamps.
    They fled from the sight of urgently riding horsemen, even if at a distance, even if there was only one rider, even if he was white.
    They fled from the frightening sound of guns being fired, no matter how faint the echoes.
    They fled from the hastily shouted words of breathless passing messengers - "Nat is c- ... comin'? - caught? - comin'?! - Nat is comin'!!!"
    (Not without damn good reason had the firing of weapons been banned. Even in Jerusalem itself, the accidental discharge of a gun had sent the men rushing to arms and the women and children fleeing to the churches.)
    By day's end, the meaning of the message would be clearly understood by most of the people of Southampton, even as the startling news began spreading like a wildfire throughout the region, en route, eventually, to everywhere.

DAVID WESTBROOK Place

    By day's end, Nat was actually further away from Jerusalem than he had been at the day's beginning.
    By all accounts, it was a strange day.
    The unadorned truth is that the journey to Jerusalem became, instead, a slow triumphal parading of the prisoner through the neighborhood toward Cross Keys - Nat aboard the back of a wagon which often stopped where the curious gathered.
    It is true that many whites and some blacks (particularly when the latter were in the presence of the former) heaped verbal abuse upon

Tomorrow Jerusalem: The Story of Nat Turner and the Southampton Slave Insurrection

the prisoner, who did not seem the least bit sorry for all that he had done.

And it is true that some of the militiamen became increasingly intoxicated and thus more disposed to harm Nat than to protect him – which is why, in late afternoon, with Jerusalem still so far away, some of Ben Phipps' friends intervened and helped to convey Nat here, to the farm of Ben's closest neighbor.

* * *

Yes, it was a strange day.

Already, because of Nat's one day of rage and his more than two suspenseful months of hiding, a curious mixture of fact and fiction and fantasy, of legend and myth and pure balderdash attached to his name.

And on this day – The day Nat Turner was caught! – anyone who was remotely near the meandering scene of the great event, and many who were nowhere near it, would form vivid personal memories to be woven into the tapestry of folklore regarding this day, and the next.

What made the day not merely extraordinary, but truly strange, was the fact that it spawned so many wild exaggerations and outright falsehoods.

Some people were willing to claim to have seen or done just about anything, and some people were willing to believe just about anything they heard. And if one believed everything one heard, one would know for a fact that Nat had been persecuted with hairpin-pricks, soundly whipped, rolled downhill in a barrel, burned with hot irons, gashed with knives, and tortured with fiery embers thrust into his mouth.

By day's end, some of these claims had already reached Nat, who scoffed.

In simple truth, no one could have survived the abuses popularly attributed to Nat's tormentors on this day, and the next.

* * * * *

MONDAY
October 31st
DAVID WESTBROOK Place

At daybreak, the wagon was loaded again, one of Ben's friends at the reins, Ben and David Westbrook in the back with Nat – with an impressive contingent of other friends and sober citizens and militiamen mounted and ready to ride.

Westbrook now sported Nat's sword.

One of Nat's manacled hands held his open Bible while the other manacled hand leafed through the book until he found the passage he sought – in the Book of Matthew, Chapter 16, Verse 21.

And in a whisper so soft only he himself could barely hear it, Nat said: "From that time, Jesus began to show unto his disciples that he must go into Jerusalem and suffer many things of the elders and chief priests and scribes ... and be killed."

The wagon jerked forward.

Bill Bryant

* * *

The procession moved slowly but without pause through the countryside, witnessed by the curious and the angry and the unrelievably bereaved, by the morally certain and the morally confused ... white men, women and children, black men, women and children ... standing along the roadways, clustered at the front gates of the farms, congregated at the intersections.
And more memories were created.

* * *

1:15 p.m.
JERUSALEM

From the southern embankment of the Nottoway, the wagon clumbered onto the bridge, across it, onto the northern embankment as the mounted escort opened a path through the awaiting crowd of many hundreds, slowing to a halt at the jail.
In front of the jail, Ben Phipps formally conveyed the prisoner to Clements Rochelle, who handed to Phipps a proper receipt, assuring the reward money.
Rochelle then helped Nat down off the wagon and, surrounded by armed men, led him toward the courthouse, for the preliminary examination to be conducted by magistrates James Trezevant (whose brother had penned the celebrated note to the Governor) and James Parker (in whose field the already fabled battle was so fiercely fought).
The crowd made no effort to disperse, though its mood was more festive than vengeful ... Off to the side stood Richard Eppes, pleased by the rule of law.

*

Among those who observed the transaction were Thomas Gray and a Petersburg man who chanced to be visiting here on this historic day.
"What happens next?" the visitor inquired.
"Two of the magistrates will question him before he goes to the jail," the lawyer said, wondering what the questions would be.
"Then what?"
"Then the trial ... an' the hangin'."
"Of course ... He seemed rather unheroic and spiritless — dejected, emaciated, ragged ... a sad sight."
"Yes ... a very sad sight."
"But I must say: I saw no evidence of the tortures he is alleged to have suffered — Indeed, he does not seem to have been offered the least violence."
"So it would seem," Gray said, wondering what Nat would be thinking now — feeling now.
"I understand that your sheriff has requested extra guards, sufficient to repel any attempt to remove Nat from the jail."

Tomorrow Jerusalem: The Story of Nat Turner and the Southampton Slave Insurrection

"A wise precaution ... yes," Gray said, distracted by the nearby excitement of Ben Phipps describing the capture.

"Why?" the visitor idly asked. "Why did he do it?"

"Why did who do what?" Gray asked, turning to stare at the man.

"Lot o' folks are wonderin'. Your other nigras have all agreed Nat was the instigator — But why? — What motivated him? — What did he really hope to gain by it? — He must've known that he couldn't succeed! ... I remember the question the Enquirer asked back in September: 'Who is this Nat Turner?' — The man who could find the answer to that question would also find a large audience waitin' to hear it!"

"Yes — Yes, he would," Gray told himself aloud.

"People want the mystery unwrapped."

"Yes — Do pardon me, sir. I must attend to some business. Good day!"

Gray did not wait to hear the visitor's response.

* * *

At about 3 o'clock, Clements Rochelle escorted Nat to the jail, where Collin Kitchen inserted the heavy key into the great lock and admitted the prisoner.

Kitchen led his new prisoner along the downstairs corridor — past the cell containing Benjamin Blunt's Ben, awaiting trial, and Joseph Travis' boy Moses, awaiting transportation — past the cell containing Berry Newsom, Isham Turner and Exum Artist, all awaiting trial in the Superior Court ... all of the men forewarned and therefore not surprised, but nonetheless stunned, to see him — Moses and Berry saying his name as he passed by, Nat nodding in reply.

Kitchen then led Nat up the stairs and along the corridor — past the cell containing Thomas Haithcock, awaiting trial in the Superior Court, and Peter Edwards' Sam, awaiting execution — into the cell now reserved for him alone.

So alone, in ways other people could not begin to imagine.

He reached for his Bible.

* * *

Late in the afternoon, at the postal counter near the front of his store, Thomas Trezevant prepared to read to several other men excerpts of a letter he had just finished writing to the editor of the Norfolk Beacon, describing the recent examination of the famous prisoner.

"It's not entirely accurate," Trezevant conceded, "but the readers won't know it ... This'll let people know the crisis is over — an' send a message to the blacks — a clear message!"

"Mister Parker," one of the men said, "told me Nat seemed to be truthful — but unrepenting. That's not your message, I hope!"

Trezevant's finger found what he wanted to read. "Here: 'During all the examination, he evinced great intelligence and much shrewdness of intellect, answering every question clearly and distinctly, and without confusion or prevarication ...'"

"But that sounds ... "

Bill Bryant

"Hold your horses! ... 'He acknowledges himself a coward and says he was actuated to do what he did from the influence of fanaticism' - An' here: 'He acknowledges now that the revelation was misinterpreted by him ... He is now convinced that he has done wrong, and advises all other Negroes not to follow his example' - An' that, gentlemen, is the message!"

The gentlemen unanimously approved, though one did dare to say: "Write what you must ... but he is certainly no coward."

* * *

Late into the evening, at home at his desk upstairs, above the noise of the inn below, Thomas Gray studied the newspapers he had been accumulating, and the personal notes he had been making, since late August.

Tomorrow would be a busy day, if he had his way.

* * * * *

TUESDAY
November 1st
In the Jail at JERUSALEM

Nervous, as any normal man would be on so unusual a mission, Thomas Gray followed Collin Kitchen into the jail, along the corridor, up the stairs.

Like almost everybody else, Kitchen had his own stories to tell, regarding the risin', and told two of them now. "Soon as I heard about it, I high-tailed it out o' Smithfield - But when I got to the bridge over the Blackwater, watch your step here, the guards wouldn't let me across, at first - suspected me o' bein' a common peddler - maybe even a rebel sympathizer! ... An' when I got home, I found one o' my female servants wearin' my wife's clothes, sittin' at my table, entertainin' a friend! ... Here we are. I'll jus' leave you alone with him ... He's harmless enough."

"Thank you," Gray said, hearing the cell door locked behind him.

Nat sat in the corner, waiting.

* * *

A little earlier this morning, before Thomas Gray had an opportunity to approach Jeremiah Cobb, to ask a favor, Jeremiah Cobb approached Thomas Gray, to ask a favor.

The two magistrates who had examined Nat had done their jobs well enough, Cobb explained, but really had not gotten very far toward understanding - or being able to explain - Nat's motivations. The man's rambling references to religion - to signs, portents, omens and such - had proved infinitely more mystifying than meaningful, to James Trezevant and James Parker.

And since yesterday afternoon, Cobb said, Nat had clammed up, declining, politely enough, to answer anybody's questions.

Tomorrow Jerusalem: The Story of Nat Turner and the Southampton Slave Insurrection

Now then, Jeremiah continued, being tactful, Thomas was known to be fairly well acquainted with Nat – known, in fact, to have been on friendly terms with Nat – before the risin', of course.

Therefore, Jeremiah finally got around to asking: "Thomas ... Would you be willing to try to talk to Nat? ... He might trust you."

"Yes ... He might trust me," Gray said, almost convinced of it.

* * *

Thus, Gray was here, now – not as Nat's attorney, but as his ... ?

"Nat," he said, sitting on the stool provided for him.

"Mistuh Gray," Nat replied, with a certain distance and coolness in his tone, concealing the pleasure it truly was, to see Thomas again.

"Sheriff Rochelle tells me he has fully explained to you my ... offer."

"Yes, suh."

"Do you understand it?"

"Yes, suh."

Gray could not ease his nervousness. "Well, I ... I'll need to make some notes as we go along, maybe ask you some questions, to try to get it straight – You understand?"

"Yes, suh."

"Nat ... "

"Suh ... "

Gray resolved himself. Fact o' the matter was, he had known Nat more than fairly well – or thought he knew the man – and had considered Nat to be, well, yes, a friend. And he had always felt that Nat entertained similar sentiments. So there really was no reason for beatin' around the bush, and Gray relaxed, and became self-confidently intense.

"Nat ... I don't need to tell you how I feel about what happened back in August. You know how I feel ... But I do think people deserve to know why you did what you did – an' I suspect you want 'em to know ... Now, I can't an' I won't hide my own feelin's – But I do promise to try my best to be accurate an' fair, in tellin' your story ... I give you my word, Nat – an' my word used to mean somethin' to you."

"It still does," Nat said, taking the promise at face value.

"Good ... So, do you – Do we have an understanding?"

"Yes, suh, Mistuh Gray – Thomas – we do ... I know you. You are a good man ... I trust you."

"An' I sincerely appreciate it," Gray said, more sincerely than Nat could imagine, feeling optimistic about the future for the first time in a long time. Nat's problems would soon be over, and so, too, might be his own. "If you are ready to talk ... I am ready to listen."

* * * * *

Bill Bryant

THURSDAY
November 3rd
In the Jail at JERUSALEM

On the 1st and on the 2nd, Nat had done most of the talking.

Today, the lawyer cross-examined the defendant, clarifying his testimony - testing, for example, his claimed knowledge of the Sun and the Moon, the stars and the planets - testing, too, his claimed familiarity with the right methods of manufacturing paper and gunpowder ... satisfying himself that Nat knew what he was talking about.

And when the civil interrogation was done, Nat asked a favor of Thomas, who thought about it seriously, then granted it. He told Nat, albeit with great brevity and without the gory details, what had been happening in Southampton since the insurrection - including, of course, the trials, and the hangings, and the scope of the search for him, and, yes, the reports in the newspapers.

And Nat, for the first time, truly understood - not only the chaotic effects of the insurrection in Southampton itself, but also its likely impact well beyond Southampton. He had done what Prosser and Vesey could not do. He had made a beginning, to ends unknown.

Their work done, the two men stood facing one another in the middle of the cell.

Nat offered his manacled right hand, and Thomas accepted it, and their handshake was firm.

* * * * *

FRIDAY
November 4th
At the Usual Place of Execution

Sam, the property of Peter Edwards until recently, on this day was hung by the neck 'til dead, then buried.

The crowd observing the execution was larger than at other hangings lately, not because Sam was especially notable, but because people were steadily streaming into town from the countryside, from all directions, eager to be near, if not at, tomorrow's keenly anticipated trial.

Here, soon, it would be Nat's turn.

* * *

THOMAS GRAY Home

Throughout the day, constantly distracted by the noise outside and much too often interrupted by people seeking his attention to this or that problem in the inn, he labored at his desk, trying to complete the task he began soon after he finished with Nat yesterday.

Tomorrow Jerusalem: The Story of Nat Turner and the Southampton Slave Insurrection

Finally, in late evening, he put down his pen and shook his aching wrist. He had done it — not only Nat's confessions, more or less as told to him, but also his own words about the man and the event the man had created.

His eyes burning for rest, straining in the lamplight, randomly he reviewed his manuscript.

> The late insurrection in Southampton has greatly excited the public mind, and led to a thousand idle, exaggerated and mischievous reports. It is the first instance in our history of an open rebellion of the slaves, and attended with such atrocious circumstances of cruelty and destruction, as could not fail to leave a deep impression — not only upon the minds of the community where this fearful tragedy was wrought, but throughout every portion of our country, in which this population is to be found. Public curiosity has been on the stretch to understand the origin and progress of this dreadful conspiracy, and the motives which influenced its diabolical actors.

*

> Every thing connected with this sad affair was wrapt in mystery, until Nat Turner, the leader of this ferocious band, whose name has resounded throughout our widely extended empire, was captured.

*

> I have had ready access to him, and finding that he was willing to make a full and free confession of the origin, progress and consummation of the insurrectionary movements of the slaves of which he was the contriver and head, I determined for the gratification of public curiosity to commit his statements to writing, and publish them, with little or no variation, from his own.

*

> He makes no attempt (as all the other insurgents who were examined did) to exculpate himself, but frankly acknowledges his full participation in all the guilt of the transaction. He was not only the contriver of the conspiracy, but gave the first blow toward its execution.

*

> It will thus appear, that whilst every thing upon the surface of society wore a calm and peaceful aspect, whilst

not one note of preparation was heard to warn the devoted inhabitants of woe and death, a gloomy fanatic was revolving in the recesses of his own dark, bewildered and overwrought mind schemes of indiscriminate massacre to the whites.

*

And it is not the least remarkable feature in this horrid transaction, that a band actuated by such hellish purposes should have resisted so feebly, when met by the whites in arms.

*

Nat has survived all his followers, and the gallows will speedily close his career.

*

It will long be remembered in the annals of our country, and many a mother as she presses her infant darling to her bosom will shudder at the recollection of Nat Turner, and his band of ferocious miscreants.

*

It has been said he was ignorant and cowardly, and that his object was to murder and rob for the purpose of obtaining money to make his escape. It is notorious, that he was never known to have a dollar in his life; to swear an oath, or drink a drop of spirits ... and for natural intelligence and quickness of apprehension, is surpassed by few men I have ever seen.

*

He is a complete fanatic, or plays the part most admirably. On other subjects he possesses an uncommon share of intelligence, with a mind capable of attaining any thing; but warped and perverted by the influence of early impressions.

*

Tomorrow Jerusalem: The Story of Nat Turner and the Southampton Slave Insurrection

> The calm, deliberate composure with which he spoke of his late deeds and intentions, the expression of his fiend-like face when excited by enthusiasm, still bearing the stains of the blood of helpless innocence around him; clothed with rags and covered with chains; yet daring to raise his manacled hands to heaven, with a spirit soaring above the attributes of man; I looked on him, and my blood curdled in my veins.

"Oh, Nat," Gray whispered, focusing his weary eyes on his former friend's words ...

> I am here loaded with chains, and willing to suffer the fate that awaits me.

* * * * *

SATURDAY
November 5th
In the Jail at JERUSALEM

Early in the morning, sitting on a stool, Thomas Gray read aloud his version of Nat's version of the answer to the question: Who is this Nat Turner?
Nat, sitting in the corner, listened with silent yet acute interest.
Likewise listening intently were the eight white men standing against the bars of the cell – James Rochelle, as clerk of the court; Jeremiah Cobb, Thomas Pretlow, James Parker, Carr Bowers, Samuel Hines and Orris Browne, magistrates; and William Parker, as counsel for the defendant ... not to mention Thomas Haithcock, now the lone occupant of the adjacent cell.
When Gray completed the reading, Cobb spoke: "Nat Turner, do you acknowledge the confession just read to you by Mister Gray to be full, free and voluntary?"
Nat, about as satisfied with Gray's account as he could hope to be, under the circumstances, replied: "Yes, suh."
"Very well," Cobb said. "Mister Gray, we shall so certify. Mister Rochelle, please put some people to work making copies, immediately – even if it means working through the whole afternoon and missing the trial – three copies, for now ... Is that agreeable, Thomas?"
"Of course – I would appreciate the return of the original manuscript at the earliest convenience."
"Certainly," Rochelle said.
Quietly, the white men left, Gray lingering long enough to exchange a final nod with Nat – a brief but quite purposeful nod, whose meaning only the two men could possibly interpret.

* * *

Bill Bryant

In the Courthouse at JERUSALEM

Beginning early in the afternoon, the trial began, the chilled crowd outside the courthouse outnumbering the warmed crowd inside the boisterous courtroom.

Not the required and customary five but fully 10 of the magistrates of the Court of Oyer and Terminer of Southampton County, Virginia, sat at tables along the front of the room – Jeremiah Cobb, Thomas Pretlow, James Parker, Carr Bowers, Samuel Hines, Orris Browne, James Trezevant, James Massenburg, Robert Goodwyn and Richard Urquardt.

At separate tables facing the magistrates sat Meriwether Broadnax, attorney for the Commonwealth; the defendant Nat Turner and his attorney, William Parker; and James Rochelle, clerk of the court.

Cobb brought down his gavel, hard, and the courtroom quickly became quiet – the sudden silence from inside the courthouse sending a thrilling chill coursing through the crowd outside, where soon there was almost silence.

"Mister Rochelle," the chief magistrate said.

The clerk of the court stood, to read: "The Commonwealth versus Nat, alias Nat Turner, a Negro man slave late the property of Putnam Moore, deceased ... Charged with making insurrection and plotting to take away the lives of diverse free white persons on the 22nd of August 1831."

Rochelle sat down.

Cobb now asked: "How does the defendant plead?"

Counsel for the defense stood. "The defendant pleads not guilty," Parker said, adding, as Nat had asked him to add: "He says he does not feel guilty."

Amid loud grumbling throughout the courtroom, the lawyer sat down.

Cobb brought down the gavel, hard, several times.

"Mister Broadnax," Cobb said.

Broadnax stood. "The Commonwealth calls Levi Waller to the stand."

The crowd murmured in expectation.

Parker, who in his contacts with his client had formed his own conflicted opinions of the man, on an impulse leaned over and whispered to Nat: "It might interest you to know that you're the only defendant who's been identified, for the record, with a first name and a last name, too."

The faintest hint of pleasure appeared in Nat's eyes, and with the faintest of smiles he nodded in appreciation.

*

Levi's familiar story of what he himself saw at his own place – a story which never ceased to shock and amaze and anger and outrage – seemed even more dramatic today.

The widower declared that he had known the defendant, Nat Turner, for some time prior to the insurrection, and therefore immediately recognized him on the 22nd of August, when Nat finally arrived at the scene of the slaughter.

He saw Nat to be the leader – in command.

*

Tomorrow Jerusalem: The Story of Nat Turner and the Southampton Slave Insurrection

James Trezevant, magistrate, testified next.

He began by assuring the court that prior to the preliminary examination conducted on the 31st of October, no threats were made against the defendant, nor any promises made to him, to obtain his cooperation.

During that examination, Trezevant said, the defendant readily confirmed his leading role in the insurrection, confirmed that he himself had struck the first blow, and confirmed that he himself killed Margaret Whitehead.

Also, Nat had offered various incoherent, confusing statements regarding his relationship with God.

*

The attorney for the defendant could do nothing to oppose the overwhelmingly convincing case presented by the attorney for the Commonwealth, a case supported not only by a host of undisputed facts, but also by the defendant's full, free and voluntary confession — its existence now common knowledge.

Thus, when the time came, Cobb said: "Mister Parker ... The court understands that the defense will introduce no evidence and offer no argument, beyond what we have already heard today."

"That is correct," Parker said.

The chief magistrate looked to his left and to his right, consulting the other magistrates now nodding their heads.

"Very well, then," Cobb said. "Nat Turner ... Stand up."

His chains clanking, Nat stood.

Cobb asked: "Have you anything to say, why sentence of death should not be pronounced against you?"

Calm, deliberate, poised, Nat answered: "No, suh. I have said what I want to say, to Mistuh Thomas Gray, an' I have nothin' more to say."

Cobb pulled from his coat pocket two folded sheets of paper, which he carefully unfolded as the tension in the courtroom increased.

"Attend then," Cobb said, looking at Nat, then staring down at the words he had so thoughtfully composed for this occasion, "to the sentence of the court."

Nat braced himself. So did every other listener, intrigued to know what Cobb had written down, for this extraordinary occasion.

Cobb spoke: "Nat Turner — You have been arraigned and tried before the court, and convicted of one of the highest crimes in our criminal code. You have been convicted of plotting, in cold blood, the indiscriminate destruction of men, of helpless women, and of infant children ... The evidence before us leaves not a shadow of doubt but that your hands were often imbrued in the blood of the innocent, and your own confession tells us that they were stained with the blood of a master, in your own language, 'too indulgent' ... Could I stop here, your crime would be sufficiently aggravated. But the original contriver of a plan deep and deadly, one that can never be effected, you managed so far to put into execution as to deprive us of many of our most valuable citizens — and this was done when they were asleep and defenseless, under circumstances shocking to humanity. And while upon this part of the subject, I cannot but call attention to the poor, misguided wretches who have gone before you. They are not a few in number. They were your bosom associates, and the blood of all cries out aloud and calls upon you as the author of their misfortune – Yes! You forced them unprepared from time to eternity ... Borne down by the load of guilt, your only justification is that you were borne away by fanaticism. If this be true, from my soul I pity you ... And while you have my sympathies, I am nevertheless called upon to pass the sentence of this court. The time between this and your execution will necessarily be short, and your only hope must be in another world. The judgement of this court is that you be taken hence to the jail from whence you came, thence to the place of execution, and on Friday next, between the hours of 10 a.m. and 2 p.m., be hung by the neck until you are dead! dead! dead! ... And may the Lord have mercy on your soul!"

Cobb brought down his gavel – and happy pandemonium erupted inside, and outside, the courtroom.

Cobb, busily accepting congratulations for his eloquence, watched as Clements Rochelle led away the unshaken Nat. The chief magistrate was a much contented man. In the eyes of a nation, a world, observing and scrutinizing Southampton justice during these recent months, Southampton had acquitted itself well, in his eyes: Of the slaves brought to trial, 28 had been convicted – but 11 had been spared the noose – and 15 other defendants had been found not guilty, and discharged – not to mention uncounted other prisoners released without trial – and the people of Southampton, even the hot-tempered men, had accepted the results ... Yes, he was a very much contented man.

And thus, on this unforgettable day in the Court of Oyer and Terminer, this trial was conducted and concluded:

- DEFENDANT: Nat Turner (Estate of Putnam Moore)
  JUDGEMENT: Guilty – To hang November 11th
  COMPENSATION TO OWNER: $375

* * * * *

SUNDAY
November 6th
JERUSALEM

Early this morning, Thomas Gray climbed aboard the westbound stagecoach, scheduled to arrive in Richmond in mid-morning tomorrow, God willin'.

* * *

Nat spent most of the day immersed in his Bible, unbothered by the visitors now permitted to come inside the jail to stand outside his cell, just to see him for themselves.

To some of them, with whom he chatted, he seemed downright friendly – even displaying, with a touch of pride, his hat, with its wounds.

Neither the visitors nor the prisoner posed any threat.

One visitor lingered longer than the others. John Crowley, of Norfolk, was busy doing what he did for a living, and he intended his sketch of the infamous Nat Turner to be as exact a likeness as the artist was capable of capturing.

* * * * *

THURSDAY
November 10th
SOUTHAMPTON

During the excruciatingly slow awakening from the nightmare – whose horrors, all knew, could never be cleansed from the memory of the living – new tensions emerged, new doubts, among the white people.

Many important questions were being asked, and every good question spawned another, and another, and so forth, and so on, until one wished and prayed – and simply wanted to scream – for it all to go away ... knowing that it never would, never could.

It was so easy to blame Nat Turner for what had happened – too easy, and people knew it.

Who else – in addition to his overly indulgent masters, especially those Turners – might be partly to blame? Who made Nat the man, the monster he became? Who helped him form his opinions? Who provoked him?

If, as reported, Nathaniel Francis and his late brother had warned their late sister about Nat, why had they not sounded a more general alarm? Speaking of which: If, as now apparent, so many of the blacks were fully expecting "something" to happen, why had not a single one of them betrayed the conspiracy to the whites? – And why, why, why did Caswell Worrell fail to report Nelson's strange warning? – what if Nelson had been promptly and properly interrogated?

What if the rebels had drunk less brandy and cider? What if more of Nat's sympathizers had managed to join him? – What if the insurgents had broken through to Jerusalem? What if ...

It was easy to curse the killing of innocent whites by the blacks – but damning the obvious didn't help to explain either the causes of the killing or the savagery of it.

Why women?
Why children?
Why babies, for the love of God, why?!
Why were the victims chosen?

And why, pray tell, were some white homesteads bypassed? What made some people so special, or so lucky?

It was natural to want to defend, or at least accept, the killing of so many innocent blacks by the whites. Natural, but uncomfortable.

The rampaging suspicion and vengeful violence of late August were understandable – yes? The blacks needed to be taught a lesson, quickly – right?

But murder is murder ... is it not?

It was not simple to decide, exactly, how to deal with the insurrection and the reaction, and probably never would be.

We must talk about what happened. We must understand, or try to ... No, the less said about it, the better – particularly among strangers, who could not hope to understand what we ourselves may never understand.

People elsewhere surely are sayin' Southampton must have been a hell-hole for the nigras, to make 'em rise, so ferociously ... Well,

Bill Bryant

let other people say what they will – What do they know? We know better.

Every contradiction, every nagging doubt, every unanswered question, every little suspicion strained the solidarity and peace of mind of the white people, who yearned for yesterday, and had to wonder:

Why here?

Why us ... dear God ... why us?

* * *

Slaves who had demonstrated true loyalty to the whites, and sometimes true bravery, had few if any regrets – and new respect from their masters, and other whites, and even some other blacks.

Slaves whose loyalty and bravery had not been tested – meaning most of the slaves in Southampton – tended to count their blessings. Many would forever wonder (as their masters would forever wonder) how they would have responded, with cowardice or courage, if the opportunity to act had come – and on whose side?

In the cabins, the prevailing mood was desperate, more desperate than ever, but resigned, even more resigned.

As among the whites, so among the blacks – slave and free – there was grieving. But the grief was subdued. It was not wise to mourn openly the loss of a loved one or a friend – certainly not if he, or she, was in any way linked to the insurrection.

As among the whites, so among the blacks there was much discussion, much speculation. But it was done in hushed tones, with great care. What once was risky to talk about now could be fatal.

As among many of the whites, so among most of the blacks there was a new unspoken understanding, born of necessity and the sense of survival – to bend over backward to try to assure that it never happened again.

If ever there were any doubts about who was master, and who was slave, in Southampton all doubts vanished.

* * *

CROSS KEYS

From the west and from the east at a leisurely pace, two mounted men came near the intersection, even as from the north at a similar pace another mounted man approached.

They met at the quiet center of Cross Keys – there where so recently so many had closely congregated in terror – very near the doomed oak tree where Charlotte had been made an example.

Each man had reasons to greet the others.

Each man had reasons to avoid the others.

All three just naturally reined to a stop, in the middle of the intersection, to chat. It would have been unpardonably rude not to – and no one could accuse one of these men of ever being unpardonably rude.

Tomorrow Jerusalem: The Story of Nat Turner and the Southampton Slave Insurrection

"Nathaniel," John Clark Turner said to Nathaniel Francis. "George," he said to George Washington Powell.
"Gentlemen," Nathaniel said, nodding.
George merely nodded.
"How's the baby?" John inquired.
"Fine," Nathaniel replied.
"An' Lavinia?"
"Fine ... jus' fine ... thank you."
"Goin' to the hangin'?" John asked.
"Wouldn't miss it," Nathaniel said, grimly.
"Haven't decided," George said. "Where you comin' from, John?"
"Jerusalem ... Been to see Nat."
"How's he holdin' up?" George asked, with a trace of sympathy.
"All right, considerin'," John said, considerin' the man would be hung by the neck tomorrow 'til dead! dead! dead! "We didn't spend much time together ... Too many people there, to allow much of a conversation."
"Still has his Bible, I hope?" said George.
"Yes," said John.
"An' they should take it away from him!" Nathaniel snapped. "He has profaned it!"
"No," George softly disagreed. "He should be permitted to keep it, to the last."
"You forget far too easily," Nathaniel said. "Our blood loss ... "
"I forget nothin'!" George said. "An' jus' 'cause your family's blood loss was greater than anybody else's gives you no right ... "
"Gentlemen!" John intervened, suspecting that Nathaniel's next thrust would be aimed at George's untimely sermon at Barnes, a week before the massacre. "We all have lost people dear to us ... Let 'em rest in peace!"
Nathaniel and George backed off.
"I hear," Nathaniel said, gruffly, "James Parker is gonna sell his Sam - south. Says the court might've found Sam not guilty, but he's not convinced - an' he's not gonna take any chances."
"A wise precaution," George had to agree. "One bad apple ... "
"Look on the bright side," Nathaniel said, without cheer. "We've gotten rid o' a lot o' bad apples - most o' the bad apples in Southampton - damn near all, I hope! We shouldn't be havin' any more trouble - ever!"
"But people will still be worryin'," George said, "because we have seen the worst ... Black folks have, too - Upwards o' 250 or more must've been killed durin' the madness - an' most were 'good' apples," he felt compelled to add. "An' even the guilty ones deserved a trial," he said, thinking of Nathaniel.
"I resent your reference!" Nathaniel declared. "If you, sir, had been in my position ... "
"I might've done the same thing," George said, though doubting it. "I meant no offense, to you ... My apologies."
"Accepted," Nathaniel muttered.
"I wonder," John thought out loud, thinking of Nat in his cell, "if, instead o' hangin' Nat, we should be sendin' him to the Lunatic Asylum in Williamsburg, to be studied. It might permit ... "
"You confuse lunacy with fanaticism!" Nathaniel now angrily argued. "But then, I should expect no better from you, to be Nat's friend to the end - Your family bred that fanatic, an' fanaticism ... "
"Is what made Jesus willin' to be nailed to the cross!" George proclaimed. "An' inspired Joan o' Arc to ... "

237

Bill Bryant

"How dare you compare them!" Nathaniel raged, unsettling his horse.
"I do not compare them," George tried to say. "I ... "
"Mark my words!" Nathaniel sternly instructed both of them ... reining his horse to the left, toward Jerusalem. "You should save your tears an' your pity for Sally an' all the other victims o' that murderer - That nigger friend o' yours is gonna be rottin' in Hell by this time tomorrow!"
And off Nathaniel Francis rode, at a gallop.
John Clark Turner, with a final weary nod to George, headed home.
And the Reverend George Washington Powell dismounted, and headed for the tavern.

* * *

SOUTHAMPTON

Evening came, and night, and sleep, for most of the people.
Southampton was peaceful.
Tomorrow would bring to an end the life which had caused so many deaths, so much suffering.
And perhaps tomorrow's act of justice - or vengeance or martyrdom - would prove to be an act of healing.
Suspiciously, yet steadily, some of the old trust was returning.
It had to.

In the Jail at JERUSALEM

He did not sleep, nor did he care to.
Soon enough, he would begin sleeping forever ... finally at peace.
His cell was cold, but not too cold. In the adjacent cell, Thomas Haithcock was in a restless slumber.
Since the trial, Thomas had become bolder, or less afraid, or both, and had in whispered bits and pieces answered a few of Nat's many mostly unasked questions - including questions Thomas Gray had avoided. As Nat needed to know, so he grieved to learn, the barest of the gory details.
Since the trial, too, a parade of occasional visitors had been permitted to venture up the stairs to see for themselves the celebrated prisoner - some come just to gawk and create a memory to talk about for the rest of their lives, some with a real purpose.
John Clark Turner had come, to inquire if he was being treated all right, and getting enough to eat ... to say farewell to a good friend, formerly ... to say he would not forget the better times - though he could not forget, or forgive, what had happened, of course ... Of course, Nat understood.
An imposing man in a fine military uniform had come several times, to stare - to study him, it seemed - each time departing without a word, or any change of the serious expression on his face.
An artist had traveled all of the way from Norfolk to sketch his portrait - an excellent likeness, several observers agreed.
Now, the white folks would have his image as well as his words - and deeds - to help them remember Nat Turner!

*Tomorrow Jerusalem: The Story of Nat Turner
and the Southampton Slave Insurrection*

He had been here!
He had done something!
He had gotten their attention!
Tomorrow, they would hang him - but only his body. His memory, they could never kill.
He would haunt them forever!
He could have lived no other life, just this one. He had gone in the direction where the circumstances and logic of his life compelled him to go. He had done what the Spirit commanded him to do.
He could mourn the fallen. But he could not regret the rising, the trying.
Thinking of Cherry, he reached into his pocket for his Bible.
His task had come more rough than smooth, but surely he had borne it, and would do so to the end.
So let the Sun rise, let tomorrow come, and let them do what they will to his body.
Despite them, soon, yes, praise God, he would finally be at peace.

* * * * *

Late Morning
November 11th, 1831
In the Courthouse at JERUSALEM

Sitting at a table in the empty courtroom - now perhaps the only quiet place in town - Richard Eppes struggled to apply himself to the chore at hand.
Trying not to think about the chore to come, the General tried to concentrate on the aggravating paperwork spread across the table.
Again, he consulted the pocketwatch on the table.
It was not time.
When, back in August, he had ridden with such dispatch toward Jerusalem, to take command of the situation, he had no idea of the situation into which he was riding - except that it required him, to command. The experience since then had been, to say the least, not what he had expected, or wanted, or could have dreamed in a thousand years.
Now, his staff of officers having dwindled to one, himself, the General frowned at the very thought of being forced to serve as his own paymaster - a bookkeeper's job, a thankless mathematical drudgery for which he had less than little enthusiasm.
He had been away from home too long, doing his duty, missing his family and his friends, neglecting his business affairs. Yet here he was in this strangely silent courtroom in faraway Jerusalem, the commanding general, toiling as a paymaster!
No ... Not yet time.
The insurrection was doomed before it began. The slaves at their best could not have prevailed against the whites at their worst - though not, he had concluded, for lack of courage. In due time, the superior firepower, organization, training and experience of the whites would have crushed even a sustained rebellion here. The "war" had no chance of success.

Bill Bryant

The danger now was elsewhere — especially in the deeper South, where at least at first the slaves would be far more numerous, and far more desperate.

This much was certain: The cost of the next eruption would be far greater than the dear price paid here.

The General began gathering his paperwork. The paymaster was quitting, for now.

As for the Preacher, well, his chores were almost done. Only one remained ... Then, good Christian Richard Eppes reasoned, it would be for God and history to try to judge Nat Turner — as villain or hero, murderer or warrior.

It made the General uncomfortable to think that in death Nat probably would not be buried, but, according to the current plan, would become a skeleton on display in a doctor's home. Some of the more intensely religious men, worried by the Preacher's supernatural claims, were arguing for severing the head from the body, to discourage any possible resurrection! ... An inglorious end, at best.

Whatever the final judgement of Nat Turner, Richard Eppes had been obliged to recognize, this must be said: The man was no coward!

He reached for his pocketwatch.

It was time.

Noon
At the Usual Place of Execution

Not since the panic of the insurrection had so many people come into Jerusalem, come from near and far and wide on this cool but clear and brightly sunny day — to witness the public conclusion of the private passion of Nat Turner.

For the journey of a few hundred yards from the jail, Nat rode aboard the wagon so often recently employed for this purpose, sitting between Clements Rochelle and Edward Butts. Nat's manacled hands held his Bible, close.

More than 50 special guards, mounted and afoot, escorted the wagon during its slow progress through the crowd ... to this place.

Nat's poise and sense of dignity impressed even his intended victims, who today seemed more somber than celebratory, more reserved than rowdy, more simply thankful to be alive than on previous such occasions.

Beneath the solid limb of the sycamore tree, just beneath the waiting noose, the man at the reins halted the wagon.

Rochelle and Butts stood, the sheriff getting down from the wagon, the deputy sheriff routinely pulling the business end of the rope, hard, several times, to test it — just to be sure.

Two people had early on positioned themselves very near the tree, ready to seize the opportunity to approach the prisoner.

The first to reach him was Giles Reese. "Nat!"

Nat turned around. "Mastuh Giles ... suh."

"Nat ... I need to know ... Why not me? — Why did you let me live, Nat?"

Nat smiled. "Mastuh Giles, you were too powerful a man to begin with. An' besides, we were afraid o' your two fierce bulldogs — But we were gonna return to you, after we had collected a sufficient force."

Reese seemed satisfied with the answer, even seemed to appreciate the honor and humor of it, nodded, and began backing away.

Tomorrow Jerusalem: The Story of Nat Turner and the Southampton Slave Insurrection

"Mastuh Giles!"
"Yes, Nat?" Reese reluctantly replied, dreading this moment.
"Cherry be all right?"
Reese hesitated. "Yes ... She's jus' fine."
"An' the children?"
"Fine ... jus' fine."
"I be mighty obliged to you if you take good care o' my family — Please, suh," he asked without begging.
"Yes, o' course," Reese muttered, then abruptly turned, and walked away — his place at the side of the wagon quickly occupied by a woman.
"Nat — I am Harriet Drummond, sister to Sally Francis — I live over in Brunswick County now."
"Yes'm. I remember you, Miss Harriet."
"Nat ... The family wants to know why you didn't kill little Joe?"
Nat softly sighed, and softly smiled. "When I lifted that baby boy up in my arms an' held him, an' he jus' smiled at me, so sweet ... I couldn't do it ... I jus' couldn't do it."
"Thank you ... Nat."
"Yes'm."
"Nat!" Butts said.
Nat stood — and stretched one final time — and stared up at the sky, and said, to no one in particular but within the hearing of many: "When I am dead, the Sun will refuse to shine, an' there will be other signs o' disapproval in the heavens, an' it will rain ... for the last time."
Some of the people near the wagon exchanged expressions of puzzlement. Others shared in nervous laughter.
"We shall see," Butts said, to Nat and to himself.
Nat closed his eyes as Rochelle began reading aloud the official order of execution, opening his eyes to the sunlight again as Rochelle ended the reading "on this 11th day of November 1831, by order of the Southampton County Court of Oyer and Terminer!"
Focusing on his beloved Bible one final time, Nat extended it to Butts, who with respect accepted it and put it in his own coat pocket.
Butts then reached for the noose.
Rochelle turned and looked upward at the prisoner. "Nat ... If you would like to say somethin', you may."
"No, suh — Mistuh Butts, I would appreciate it if you would get on with what we came here to do."
"As you wish," Butts said.
The crowd became deathly still and silent as Butts encircled Nat's neck with the noose, then stepped down off the wagon, paused ... and raised his hand, to signal the man at the reins.
Nat took a deep breath, and closed his eyes and began to smile yes sweet Jesus yes finally at

Bill Bryant

The Aftermath

Bill Bryant

*Tomorrow Jerusalem: The Story of Nat Turner
and the Southampton Slave Insurrection*

1831 ...
SOUTHAMPTON COUNTY and Elsewhere

All who in somber silence observed the hanging saw – and would never forget – Nat seemed to pass over to the other side the instant his body began to fall toward the earth it could not reach. Not a muscle murmured in protest.

Then unexpectedly – as Nat had predicted – the noontime sky darkened, and great storm clouds gathered, and the cold wind-swept rain came heavily down, lashing at the countryside.

And then ... as Nat had predicted ... it did not rain again in Southampton for an unusually long time, an uncomfortably long time, an ominously long time, which frightened many people, white and black alike, and inspired much fervent praying. Just as the seemingly endless search for Nat had painfully prolonged the suspense and deepened the impact of the tragedy in August, so the seemingly endless drought painfully sustained the obsessive wondering and worrying about the meaning of it all.

When, finally – thank God! – the drought ended, throughout Southampton County the sigh of relief was as profound as it had been on the day Nat was hung, months ago.

And life went on.

* * *

And the future changed.
The dam had been weakened.

* * *

• Thomas Gray had gone to Richmond, where on the 7th of November he discovered that all of the printing presses in the city were busily engaged.

• On the 10th, in Washington, he obtained a copyright for his manuscript, and then immediately started for Baltimore.

• On the 22nd, copies of **The Confessions of Nat Turner** printed in Baltimore became available in Washington for 25 cents per copy.

On the 25th, the Richmond Enquirer quoted from the pamphlet, and cited only one defect, its style. To be specific: "The confession of the culprit is given, as it were, from his own lips ... but the language is far superior to even what Nat Turner could have employed. Portions of it are eloquently and classically expressed. This is calculated to cast some shade of doubt over the authenticity of the narrative, and to give the Bandit a character for intelligence which he does not deserve, and ought not to have received" ... The Enquirer's doubts would echo widely – but not subtract an ounce of the weight of Nat's real or imagined words upon the reader.

And there would be many readers. More than 50,000 copies were printed during the lingering sensation of the insurrection.

Nat Turner and Thomas Gray thus entered history together, with intense effect.

- During November, in a letter to the Governor of South Carolina, the Governor of Virginia declared that according to the reports he had received from Southampton regarding the insurgents: "All died bravely."

- On the 3rd of December, with the General Assembly soon to convene for what promised to be a dramatic session perhaps deciding the future of slavery in Virginia, Governor Floyd began entertaining a special guest — John Calhoun of South Carolina, the Vice President of the United States, en route to Washington.

The guest counseled his host that a move by Virginia toward emancipation at that time would be, well, untimely. Later would be better.

On the 5th, Calhoun left Richmond.

On the 6th, Floyd in his opening message to the members of the Virginia Senate and House of Delegates (including Jeremiah Cobb) made appropriate sad reference to the recent tragedy in Southampton, but did not mention emancipation.

- While the Vice President was somewhere along the road to Washington, the merchant ship James Perkins was sailing out of Norfolk, for Liberia. On board were some 240 free blacks from Southampton, including James and Peggy Ben and others from among the ablest, most talented and least idle of the county's blacks.

- The prisoner Moses was transported south. The estate of his late owner was compensated $300 ... The prisoner Ben was convicted, and on the 20th of December was hung. His owner was compensated $400.

* * *

January 14th, 1832
Approaching JERUSALEM

In the afterglow of sunset, the romance of the American Revolution seemed very far away as the laboring horses and untiring wheels of the stage-coach advanced along the cold dry road through the lonely countryside.

The quick winds of early evening, like slivers of broken glass, sharply pierced the barely tolerable chill of the passenger compartment where the young Frenchman was marveling, again, at his traveling companion's ability to sleep like a baby amid such awful conditions.

Of minor nobility, the Frenchman and his friend were nearing the end of a long journey through these remarkable United States, a mission to study the prison systems of the new democracy — but also an opportunity to try to understand the Americans, to watch their revolution at work.

The journey had been fascinating, yet fatiguing.

The Frenchman yearned to be home.

He is an intense but gentle, shy little man, a gentleman of great intellect and dignity, and painstaking curiosity.

*Tomorrow Jerusalem: The Story of Nat Turner
and the Southampton Slave Insurrection*

Braving the wind again, he lifted the window flap, to stare at the slowly passing fields and forests. Everything he saw was so gray, so ... dry, of life.

And yet - as the grisly signpost at the last crossroads had forcefully reminded him (as it purposefully reminded everyone who saw it) - here is where it happened.

Somewhere around here.

He was in Canada when it happened, but the news reached him soon after he returned to the United States, where the news always traveled fast, thanks to the insatiable appetite of the Americans for gossip and newspapers and correspondence. The stage-coaches on which he had been a passenger also carried the mail, so he had seen the volume of it and the eagerness with which it was received, especially in the more remote places, where many of the Americans were to be found, making new paths through the wilderness, breaking new ground.

The Americans fed on the news - any news - like starving dogs feasting on the scraps from the dinner table.

And what happened here wasn't just any news.

What happened here was truly extraordinary, a monumental event, meaningful, in one way or another, to all of these people; perhaps, to the whole world.

The Americans were peculiar, a unique people, a restless, seething, politically turbulent democracy pushing hard against so many varied frontiers simultaneously - a people obsessed with their self-expectations and unbridled hopes, constantly engaged in self-evaluation and self-improvement. They were relentlessly enterprising, working hard in clearing the land, making useful new products, building communities. Everywhere, committees of volunteers abounded, to do this thing or that thing to make the community better - preferably without the involvement of the government.

The whole scene was even more remarkable because of the great diversity of the Americans. A Massachusetts man, for example, could not be confused - ever - with a South Carolina man. Much more than accent made them very different.

And as for the Virginia man, well!

The Frenchman and his friend had first encountered the Virginians in the forests of Kentucky and Tennessee, discovering a people apart from the other Americans, rough and energetic folk branching out from the Virginia family - a family pre-eminent in American history, and properly proud of it. The Virginians seemed to possess, to a degree much greater than the other Americans the Frenchmen had met, an intuitive love of country, a love mingled with prideful exaggeration and prejudices.

And here the visitors were in Virginia, briefly.

Tomorrow, God willing and the weather permitting, they would be in Norfolk, soon to be comfortably aboard a steamboat heading up the Chesapeake Bay toward Washington.

The visitor now staring at the darkening countryside would be glad to leave the South.

Here, nowhere could one escape the presence of slavery, that dangerous contradiction in the bold American experiment, that cancer growing even as the democratic spirit of the times was growing.

Wherever he had been, North and South, he had sought out and closely listened to the conflicting opinions of the Americans regarding slavery. Someday, he was told, an emancipation would be accomplished, but no time soon - too costly. And even with an emancipation, he was told, the problem of blacks and whites in America

Bill Bryant

would not go away unless the blacks went away, back to Africa. Otherwise, one race must eventually exterminate the other. So he was told, by many.

As for the overshadowing thought of insurrection, a slave revolt could not hope to succeed, he was assured several days ago in South Carolina, by Mister Poinsett. If the slaves ever became enlightened enough to pool their resources and create a truly formidable league, surely they would also be enlightened enough to see, given their situation, that no ultimate success could be hoped for. According to Mister Poinsett.

But what was to stop the slaves, in ignorance and desperation, from trying it again?

A sudden rumbling of wooden planks announced that the stage-coach was now on a bridge, no doubt the bridge into Jerusalem, at last.

"Gustave," the Frenchman said, gently poking at his companion ... poking harder. "Gustave, mon ami - Arrete!"

"Ou sommes nous?" Gustave mumbled.

"Nous sommes en Gerusalemme ... finalement."

"Ah ... Gerusalemme!"

"Ici ... c'est la tragedie," the Frenchman whispered, looking up and down the dark street as he alit from the stage-coach in front of the seven-gabled inn, knowing that before the dawning of tomorrow he must leave this place, unseen and unexplored. "Gustave ... s'il vous plait ... Attendez les bagages. J'arrange aux chambres."

"Naturalement ... massuh!"

He smiled, thinly, then walked quickly to the inn.

In the welcome warmth, he asked the first man he met where he might locate the proprietor of the establishment - and, incidentally, who here might be able to tell him about ... about what happened here.

The man almost glared at the stranger, briefly, before replying: "That would be one an' the same man - over there - the fellow sittin' at the table in the corner. You jus' come in on the stage from Fayetteville?"

"Yes. I ... "

"See any signs o' rain the last day or so?"

"No. Not since... "

"Oh ... Well, there's your man over there."

"Thank you."

"You are mos' welcome."

The Frenchman approached the man at the table in the corner, slowing warily as he perceived the man's troubled expression and somewhat intoxicated condition, which discouraged curiosity. "Pardon mois - Pardon me," the stranger said, hesitating until he was sure he had the man's attention. "I was told... "

"Wha'? ... What were you told?"

"That you are the proprietor of this ... "

"You on the Fayetteville stage?"

"Yes. I ... "

"Seen any signs o' rain since you crossed into Virginia?"

"No ... No, I ... "

"Oh ... Please do pardon my poor manners," the man said with a sudden if slowly rising surge of energy, and obvious sincerity, standing now with a little difficulty but wholeheartedly determined to be civil and hospitable, especially to this stranger. "Permit me to introduce myself. I am Thomas Gray - the proprietor o' this establishment, an' occasional lawyer ... at your service, sir!

Tomorrow Jerusalem: The Story of Nat Turner and the Southampton Slave Insurrection

"And I," the stranger said, standing as tall as he could and offering his hand, "am Alexis, Comte de Tocqueville – My friends call me Alex!"

* * *

- In January of 1832, with the General Assembly session proving to be even more dramatic than expected, John Hampden Pleasants and the Constitutional Whig endorsed the concept of gradual compensated emancipation. Pleasants and the Whig were publishing the transcribed text of the wide-open debates in the legislature, a decision condemned by many, including rival editor Thomas Richie and the Enquirer, charging that the publication of such candid opinions, on such sensitive issues, was a disservice to Virginia and to the South – a traitorous deed.

- In February of '32, the Enquirer deplored the consequences of the statewide horror excited by the Southampton bleeding – the raising of the "floodgates of discussion," the mass meetings of citizenry, the public petitions to the legislature, the breaking of 50 years of silence by the newspapers regarding the "delicate" subject of the colored population – while in the General Assembly "we now see the whole subject ripped up and discussed with open doors, and in the presence of a crowded gallery and lobby" – all experiences "indeed new in our history. And nothing else could have prompted them, but the bloody massacre in the month of August."

- The 1831-32 session of the General Assembly produced the first – and last – free and full legislative consideration of gradual compensated emancipation ever conducted in the South.

Among the voices of conscience appealing for emancipation, with transportation to Africa, Delegate William Broadnax of Dinwiddie County perhaps expressed it best: "Let us translate them to those realms from which, in evil times, under inauspicious influences, their fathers were unfortunately abducted."

But the senators and delegates finally concluded that nothing could be done at that particular time – or should be attempted until the strong support of popular opinion could be obtained – and not until some complicated and expensive plan could be contrived to accomplish the awesome task.

In response to immediate needs, the representatives of the people did decide to strengthen the state's militia with adequate weapons and monthly drills, expand the system of local patrols, and create troops of special public guards. The legislature also called for stricter enforcement of existing laws governing the blacks, and specified new crimes and punishments designed to discourage slave preachers and slave religious meetings and slaves learning how to read and write. Similar new legislation limited the religious activities and schooling of free blacks.

- In April of '32, amid the continuing public and political turmoil, Governor Floyd asked Thomas Dew, eminent young professor of political economy at the College of William and Mary, in Williamsburg, to review the recent debates in the legislature and offer his own conclusions and recommendations.

Bill Bryant

Dew did so, authoring a powerful report which greatly changed the landscape of public and political thinking in the United States, especially in the South.

With compelling statistics and reasoning, Dew argued strongly against emancipation, with or without transportation, contending it would be ruinous to the economy and peace of Virginia - particularly if the freed slaves remained, idle and worthless and vengeful.

Consider! "But one limited massacre is recorded in Virginia history; let her liberate her slaves, and every year you would hear of insurrections and plots, and every day would perhaps record a murder; the melancholy tale of Southampton would not alone blacken the page of our history, and make the tender mother shed the tear of horror over her babe as she clasped it to her bosom; others of a deeper dye would thicken upon us; those regions where the brightness of polished life has dawned and brightened into full day, would relapse into darkness, thick and full of horrors."

Persuasively, in light of such a grim alternative, the professor maintained that slavery was an institution morally good and economically sensible, a benefit to all, including the slave - freedom being "something which he cannot comprehend."

Logically, he concluded that "the time for emancipation has not yet arrived, and perhaps it never will."

Copies of the report circulated widely, of course. Throughout the South, white people respected its commanding statistics and reasoning.

Gradually, Dew's opinion became the prevailing opinion of the South.

* * *

- Thomas Haithcock, Isham Turner, Exum Artist and Berry Newsom were tried in the Superior Court. Newsom was convicted, and hung on the 11th of May 1832. The historical record indicates that two of the other three men were convicted, and hung, the acquitted defendant probably Haithcock. However, according to one account, all three men were acquitted.

- Royalties from **The Confessions of Nat Turner** did not sustain Thomas Gray very long. In July of '32, by order of the Court of Oyer and Terminer, little Ellen Gray was made a ward of the county and entrusted to the home of the family of the lawyer William Parker.

- Nat's wife Cherry and their daughter were sold away from Southampton, disappearing into time. Their son Redic, much like his father in ability, remained in Southampton, becoming a hard-working and obedient slave, with a wife and children.

- In all contemporary and subsequent historical accounts, baby Joe Travis was the fifth victim of the insurrection. However, according to the tradition of the old Travis family of Brunswick County, some kinsmen of Joseph Travis, hearing of the insurrection, hastened to the Travis place, found the baby alive, and brought him back to Brunswick, where he lived the rest of his life.

- Where the Barrow Road met the Jerusalem Road, the skull of the insurgent remained on its pike so long that the intersection became known as the Blackhead Signpost. When the skull weathered away, the signpost was painted black.

*Tomorrow Jerusalem: The Story of Nat Turner
and the Southampton Slave Insurrection*

- Throughout the region, camp meetings became infrequent.

- In August of '32, the tension throughout Southampton was acute, among whites and blacks alike, sharing the terrible vivid memories of '31.

Hoping to limit the opportunity for plotting, some masters worked their slaves harder than during previous months of jubilee. Preparing for the worst, many white families kept emergency provisions at hand and knew where to go, to hide, deep in the woodlands or in the swamps. Rumors began easily during the month, false reports spreading like wildfires, making many whites flee to their secret places.

Thus began the August Fever – the August Madness – which would afflict the people of Southampton, especially the whites, every year for more than a century.

* * *

- In 1833, to provide an attractive alternative to Andrew Jackson, the men of the Rockbridge Conspiracy arranged the publication of an anonymously authored biography: **Sketches and Eccentricities of Col. David Crockett of West Tennessee.** The book, which became extremely popular, and other efforts by the conspirators made a legend of Davy Crockett and posed a serious political threat to Andy Jackson. Actually written by the clerk of the United States House of Representatives, the book was initially attributed to the person who filed its copyright, an unknown country lawyer in Virginia named James Strange French, of Jerusalem.

- In January of 1835, Alexis de Tocqueville published the first volume of his **Democracy in America**, an instant classic, brilliantly describing the dynamics of the American democracy and the character of the American people. Regarding the "calamity" of slavery, the Frenchman offered a bleak view of the future, noting: "The danger of a conflict between the white and black inhabitants of the Southern states of the Union (a danger which, however remote it may be, is inevitable) perpetually haunts the imagination of the Americans like a painful dream."

- In 1836, the pro-Crockett plot abruptly ended. The conspirators had made Davy a legend. The Alamo made him a martyr.

- Also in '36, James Strange French published a book of his own, the not well written novel **Elkswatawa: or, Prophet of the West.** The book's main character – based on Tecumseh's brother Tenskatawa, who led a Shawnee uprising in 1811 – had a certain resemblance to the character of Nat Turner.

* * *

- Several years after the insurrection, James Parker read a newspaper story regarding a slave who had been hung in Mississippi for attempted insurrection. On the scaffold, the slave acknowledged that he had once belonged to Mister James Parker of Jerusalem, Virginia, and had been sold south for a similar offense.

- The coming of the railroad in the 1830s sent the riverport town of Monroe into fatal decline, so Fielding Mahone became a tavern-keeper in Jerusalem, where his son little Billy soon made quite a reputation for himself. Reportedly, Billy "smoked and chewed and cussed like a pirate, and gambled like a Mississippi gambler." He was "the leader in all deviltry" - "a bad little wretch," in the opinion of some mothers who tried to warn their sons away from him.

- In 1837, the congregation of Turner's Meeting House, which had burned (or had been burned) down, built a new church not far away: Clarksbury Methodist.

- On the 8th of December 1837, at the family home in Jerusalem, Mattie Rochelle married John Tyler Jr., son of the United States Senator.

- In 1838, midshipman Simon Blunt Jr. and his crewmates began a voyage of exploration which during the next four years became the first circumnavigation of the globe by a ship of the United States Navy.

- In 1841, Mattie Rochelle Tyler's father-in-law became the President of the United States upon the death of William Henry Harrison - Tippecanoe and Tyler, too, having been elected partly because of the pro-Whig feelings aroused by the Rockbridge conspirators, who thus belatedly succeeded.

- In 1845, an impoverished Thomas Gray died in Portsmouth, Virginia.

- In 1846, Thomas Richie publicly accused rival John Hampden Pleasants of harboring abolitionist sentiments. Defending his sacred honor, the editor of the Whig challenged the editor of the Enquirer to a duel. Richie shot Pleasants, dead.

* * *

- In youth, George Henry Thomas clerked in his uncle James Rochelle's office before receiving an appointment to the United States Military Academy at West Point. During the Mexican War, his gallantry was conspicuous. To honor the local hero, the citizens of Southampton purchased in Philadelphia a fine ceremonial sword, engraved with the names of his Mexican battles. The ceremony embarrassed the modest officer, who so esteemed the sword that he would wear it only once, at his marriage to a girl from New York. (During one of his visits home, George Henry reportedly got into some trouble for teaching some of the Thomas slaves, but was not prosecuted.)

- In youth, George's cousin James Henry Rochelle received an appointment as an acting midshipman in the Navy. Subsequently, the Southampton lad served ably under Commodore Matthew Perry during the Mexican War, received an appointment to the new United States Naval Academy at Annapolis, became one of the school's first graduates, then began cruising the Mediterranean.

- Graduated in 1847 from the new Virginia Military Institute at Lexington, the feisty little Billy Mahone (in manhood shorter than 5-6 and lighter than 100 pounds) was attracted to the idea of a military

*Tomorrow Jerusalem: The Story of Nat Turner
and the Southampton Slave Insurrection*

career, but instead became a civil engineer, working for a railroad company.

* * *

- Nathaniel and Lavinia Francis prospered, and had six children. Nathaniel died of pneumonia in 1849 on a business trip to Mississippi. Lavinia would die at home, in 1885.

- Harriet Whitehead continued to live at the family place, quite alone among her slaves and variously regarded with compassion or pity or curiosity. She died in 1852, and was buried near the others, finally.

- Slaves who during the insurrection had proved their loyalty – particularly those who had intimately shared the danger and hardship – were rewarded in many ways for the rest of their lives in slavery. Some became widely respected among the white people of Southampton, honored most by those who would not let anyone forget who had saved them from Nat Turner. Red Nelson went wherever he pleased, hospitably received everywhere. Red was seen drinking with the white men.

* * *

- Southampton-born slave boy Fed Moore went eventually to the Deep South. Sold several times while growing up to manhood and given a new name, he witnessed, and he suffered, the worst horrors of slavery. Escaping to the North, he made his way ultimately to England. In 1856, British abolitionists sponsored publication of the book telling his painful story: **John Brown – Slave Life in Georgia**, which helped to fan the flames of abolitionism not only in Britain, but also in America.

- Some years after Peter Blow and his family left Virginia and settled finally in Alabama, the Southampton-born slave Sam had to be sold, and was given a new name. In 1857, as the plaintiff Dred Scott, he was denied his freedom by the United States Supreme Court in an earthquaking decision shattering the Missouri Compromise and increasing sharply the tensions between North and South ... Soon after the decision, the children of Peter Blow purchased Dred and gave him his freedom. And when the free man died in 1858, in St. Louis, the children paid for their Sam's funeral.

- Like his father, John Buchanan Floyd served as Governor of Virginia. Subsequently, in August of 1859, serving as the Secretary of War under President Buchanan, Floyd received information regarding an alleged plot to seize the federal arsenal at Harper's Ferry, Virginia, to incite a slave rebellion. But Floyd took no action, explaining later: "I was satisfied in my own mind that a scheme of such wickedness and outrage could not be entertained by any citizen of the United States" ... In fact, of course, men led by John Brown (himself partly inspired by Nat Turner) did seize the arsenal, but were relatively soon surrounded by federal troops under the command of

Bill Bryant

Colonel Robert E. Lee. Brown was captured, tried for treason, convicted, and hung.

* * *

- After 20 years in the Navy, Lieutenant Simon Blunt Jr. retired. He died in 1854, in Baltimore. His mourners included his wife Ellen, daughter of Francis Scott Key, author of the popular poem "The Star-Spangled Banner."
- In 1856, James Henry Rochelle ably served aboard the USS Southampton during Commodore Matthew Perry's historic door-opening mission to Japan.

* * *

- In black tradition, the First War, Nat's War, was followed by the Second War, Abe's War ... To the North, it was the War of Southern Rebellion. To the South, it was the War of Northern Aggression ... To all, it was the Civil War - the worst of wars.
- In February of 1861, Virginians voted in a fateful referendum to decide their course of action. The free white men of upper Southampton cast a strong majority of their votes for the Union. The free white men of lower Southampton voted overwhelmingly for secession. When Virginia did formally secede, the white people of upper as well as lower Southampton rallied to the cause, many of the menfolk volunteering to fight. Most sons of Southampton serving in the federal military - with one particularly conspicuous exception - shifted their allegiance to the new Confederate States of America ... Ardent secessionist Billy Mahone, the president of the Norfolk and Petersburg Railroad, became an officer in the Confederate Army.
- In March of 1862, serving as the executive officer on the CSS Patrick Henry, Captain James Henry Rochelle witnessed the extraordinary engagement in Hampton Roads between the Confederate ironclad Virginia and the Union ironclad Monitor. In a letter soon after the battle, Rochelle described the Monitor as "a craft as the eyes of a seaman never saw before - an immense shingle floating on the water, with a gigantic cheese box rising from its center." The description became widely popular, North and South ... Rochelle would later command several ships of the James River squadron, then serve as the final commanding officer of the Confederate States Naval Academy.
- On the 3rd of July 1863, at Gettysburg, men of Southampton moved forward with Kemper's Brigade, Pickett's Division, in the epic doomed charge from which General Robert E. Lee's Army of Northern Virginia, and the South, would never recover ... After the battle, Lee offered his resignation to President Jefferson Davis. Reportedly, Lee favored as his successor General Billy Mahone.
- The leading Union generals in the Civil War were Ulysses S. Grant, William Tecumseh Sherman and the latter's roommate at West Point - George Henry Thomas of Southampton - the Rock of Chickamauga, whose stubborn resistance and orderly withdrawal at the Battle of

Tomorrow Jerusalem: The Story of Nat Turner and the Southampton Slave Insurrection

Chickamauga in September of 1863 saved Grant's army from a disaster. That action, and several later decisive victories by the soldiers of the fatherly General Thomas, helped to propel Grant to success in the western campaign and command of all Union forces, including those directly facing Lee.

- In July of 1864, at Petersburg, Billy Mahone became the Hero of the Crater. His quick reaction closed the breakthrough gap explosively created in the Confederate defense line — thereby prolonging the terrible bleeding another year, until Grant and Lee could settle the matter once and for all, honorably, at Appomattox ... At the surrender in April of 1865, almost half of the men remaining in the battered Army of Northern Virginia were in brigades commanded by Billy Mahone.

- By the end of the war, upwards of 100 black men from Southampton, most of them escaped slaves, had enlisted in the Army of the United States.

* * *

- George Henry Thomas died in 1869, in New York, mourned and honored throughout the North ... During and for decades following the Civil War, the spinster sisters of the heroic Rock of Chickamauga uniquely expressed the conflicted sentiments and self-divided opinion of many of the white people in Southampton, with a gesture: Dear brother George's portrait continued to hang on the wall at Thomaston ... facing the wall.

- James Henry Rochelle came back to Jerusalem following the war, then went away again for several years to help make hydrographic surveys of the largely unexplored Amazon River in South America, then came home again, to stay. He died in 1889, a much beloved and greatly honored local hero.

- Following the war, Billy Mahone became the most powerful man in Virginia — a railroad tycoon, a millionaire, the king-maker of Virginia politics, a member of the United States Senate.

Because he changed from Democrat to Republican, and because he was a populist who appealed to black voters (notably with programs of public education), many white people in Virginia intensely disliked him.

Among the folks back home in Southampton, the Hero of the Crater, like the Rock of Chickamauga, aroused very mixed emotions.

When he died in 1895, Mahone left a testament which included this observation: "I never learned my wretched error, the awful blunder of the South, the curse of her institution of slavery and her traditions until I sat in the United States Senate, and day by day had borne in upon me the amazing significance of our form of government, what it meant, on what basis it was founded, how great and grand it was above any previous human effort, what it meant for humanity."

* * *

Bill Bryant

- Southhampton-born Anthony B. Gardner died in 1886, in Africa – honored as a delegate to the Liberian Constitutional Convention and three-term President of the Republic of Liberia. At his death he was the last surviving Signer of the Liberian Declaration of Independence.

- In 1888, reportedly at the urging of postmistress Mattie Rochelle Tyler, the name of Jerusalem was changed – to Courtland.

Tomorrow Jerusalem: The Story of Nat Turner and the Southampton Slave Insurrection

"That Thicket"

Bill Bryant

*Tomorrow Jerusalem: The Story of Nat Turner
and the Southampton Slave Insurrection*

August 2000
BRYANT Home
WILLIAMSBURG, VIRGINIA

Beginning to try to write these closing words, I am momentarily overwhelmed by a sudden surge of memories and anecdotes, observations and opinions I wish to share with you regarding why and how I have written this book and what I have learned in the process.

But I remain focused on a particular scene, that especially pleasant day several years ago down in Southampton County when I met historian Dan Crofts, whose excellent work in Southampton has dealt mostly with the years following the uprising. He and I were among a busload of folks being guided through the countryside by Gil Francis and Kitty Futrell, and the tour paused at old Clarksbury Methodist Church, for a visit inside and boxed lunches outside.

Dan approached me, introduced himself, and said he understood I was working on a book about Nat Turner, which I confirmed.

Then with a knowing smile he said: "I'm glad you're the one in that thicket, not I."

Instantly, I adopted forever "that thicket" as the right way to describe my very real experience – not only as someone seeking the historical truth about Nat Turner, but also as someone whose search for the personal meaning of Nat Turner began when I was a child.

I've been thankful to Dan ever since, for simplifying a complexity quite familiar to all who have seriously tried to understand what happened in 1831, and the man who made it happen.

*

That thicket began to grow before the uprising ended, the natural result of so extraordinary and violent an event, at that time, at that place.

And it grew fast.

Thus, returning to the Constitutional Whig and reviewing the other newspapers, John Hampden Pleasants noted on the 3rd of September 1831: "We have been astonished ... to see the number of false, absurd, and idle rumors, circulated by the Press."

Thus, too, in November of 1831, Thomas Gray began his own account: "The late insurrection in Southampton has greatly excited the public mind, and led to a thousand idle, exaggerated and mischievous reports."

And in 1900, William Sidney Drewry's classic book candidly began: "This attempt to separate truth from fiction has been exceedingly difficult, owing to the numerous misrepresentations and exaggerations which have grown up about the subject."

Now, in 2000, I also testify to the unique challenge of exploring and explaining the life of Nat Turner – a task I made harder by going deeper into some parts of the thicket than other historians have gone, and by going into some parts where no other historian has gone.

Bill Bryant

*

Fatefully but not knowing it, I wandered into the thicket while I was a little boy, during the 1940s.

My father was a Navy man, so we moved from place to place, along the Atlantic. But my father's family were Southampton people, and throughout childhood I visited my grandparents' home near Courtland, on a narrow dirt road meandering down to the Nottoway River, to where the old bridge once crossed.

Out on the main highway was an historical marker, briefly mentioning Nat Turner, the slave insurrection, near here, the loss of white lives. As soon as I could read, I memorized that sign.

Otherwise, although the name of Nat Turner did occasionally arise during conversations among the older folks, I learned very little about him. As a boy, I imagined that his lingering spirit was somewhere out there in the woods, hiding, lurking ... Through the mist of many years, I can still dimly remember my beloved grandma Bessie's pleasant way of warning us misbehaving youngsters that unless we started behaving ourselves better Nat Turner would come out of the woods and get us – and then we'd be sorry! I remember her saying it with a gentle smile, but we got the message.

I became a serious student of history early in my life. But not until the 1970s did I become a serious student of the story of Nat Turner. I began by reading, and rereading, the existing historical literature, and I began visiting Southampton again, venturing into the countryside with a purpose.

In August of 1981, for the 150th anniversary of the insurrection, I prepared an essay published in the Richmond Times-Dispatch, expressing a view of Nat Turner and the insurrection more moderate than the prevailing view.

Finally, in June of 1990, frustrated at how much I did not know and would never know unless I tried much harder and went much deeper, I decided to commit myself to the work which has become **Tomorrow Jerusalem**.

I made that commitment because I believe that the story of Nat Turner belongs to the American people, white and black alike, and is important; that it should be told as accurately and as responsibly as possible; and that such a telling may help advance the cause of human understanding and reconciliation – the highest priority of the continuing American Revolution, in my opinion.

Meaningful reconciliation is based upon the truth, and I have made a sincere effort to find it.

*

Now, it's time to thank some of the many people who have assisted me with this task.

Let's begin with the people who have written the books I have read, and reread.

At the top of the list:

- William Sidney Drewry – **The Southampton Slave Insurrection**. Published in 1900, this was the first and for many years thereafter the only attempt to write a history of the uprising.

An imperfect work, it is nonetheless a remarkable accomplishment for its time, a bible to students of the story.

- Henry Irving Tragle – **The Southampton Slave Revolt of 1831.** Published in 1971, this is a magnificent compilation of material – contemporary newspaper accounts, trial records, correspondence and other documents, including Thomas Gray's **The Confessions of Nat Turner** ... Drewry and Tragle together are the basis of any serious study – and both were on the desk next to my typewriter during the past year of completing this work, and were frequently consulted.

The following historians have contributed significantly to our understanding of various aspects of the story neglected by others:

- Herbert Aptheker – **Nat Turner's Slave Rebellion.**
- F. Roy Johnson – **The Nat Turner Slave Insurrection.**
  The Nat Turner Story.
- Eric Foner – **Nat Turner.**
- Stephen Oates – **Fires of Jubilee.**

And these historians have well described Southampton during the years following the uprising, shedding light on the local and national consequences of the event:

- Thomas Parramore – **Southampton County, Virginia.**
- Daniel Crofts – **Old Southampton.**

Beyond these sources, most others are unreliable. As a rule, public references to Nat Turner – in general history books, magazines and newspapers – are riddled with errors of fact and interpretation, sometimes amazingly so. (One recent book devoted only three pages to Nat Turner yet contained more than 30 errors. And even the Library of Congress specifies his lifetime as 1800?-1831. Why the question mark?!)

I'm also indebted to the historian whose 1938 work, combined with other circumstantial evidence, persuaded me that Alexis de Tocqueville probably traveled through Southampton:

- G.W. Pierson – **Tocqueville and Beaumont in America.**

*

During the 1970s and 1980s, I studied the existing historical literature, noting the common knowledge and identifying the unanswered questions and unexplored paths of inquiry; and I became familiar with the actual historical sites in Southampton.

Beginning in 1990, I created a synthesis of the previously published accounts, and I initiated my own process of original research, moving in many directions, fully expecting, and more than

Bill Bryant

fully experiencing, the twists and turns, surprises and disappointments appropriate to the thicket.

That process has been much more productive, and enjoyable, than I ever hoped it would be – because so many people have been so helpful in so many ways!

To the story of Nat Turner I have managed to add many new details, some minor, some major, all of them together greatly strengthening my ability to present a better explanation of what happened in Southampton in 1831, enabling me to offer a truer image of Nat Turner, and of the other folks involved in his story. But most of the credit for this new information belongs to the hundreds of people who have assisted me.

The following don't fit into any other category of assistance, but merit special mention:

- Maurice Person, who went out of his way one day to visit my home and enable me to examine Nat Turner's Bible, which no historian had seen since Drewry, who merely noted its existence.

- John McKnight, my physics professor more than four decades ago, now my consultant in celestial mechanics, the source of my information regarding the Sun and the Moon at certain critical moments.

- Dick Woodward, an extraordinarily gifted teacher of the meaning of the Bible, the man to whom I logically turned for early guidance in understanding the scriptural passages related to Nat Turner.

- Kimberly Cumber, an archivist with the North Carolina Department of Cultural Resources who helped me trace Tocqueville's path.

- Various personnel at the splendid Library of Virginia, particularly Marianne McKee, Mark Fagerburg and Paige Buchbinder, who helped in the selection and preparation of the maps of the United States, Virginia and Southampton; and archivist Henry Grunder. Nolan Yelich, the librarian of Virginia, has been an encouraging friend.

- The always helpful staff of the Walter Cecil Rawls Library in Courtland, with its biographies of George Henry Thomas and Billy Mahone.

- Dennis Mroczkowski, director of the Casemate Museum at Fort Monroe, and Michael Crawford, head of the early history branch at the Naval Historical Center, who clarified aspects of the federal involvement in Southhampton.

- Dennis Blanton, the Center for Archaeological Research staffer who teamed up with some Arkansas tree scientists several years ago to prove that the Jamestown settlers arrived during an acute drought, helping to explain the early struggle there. My

*Tomorrow Jerusalem: The Story of Nat Turner
and the Southampton Slave Insurrection*

conversation with Dennis helped me figure out how to deal with the drought following the hanging of Nat Turner.

- Kirk Flynn, the Williamsburg artist who not only applied the finishing touches to the maps provided by the Library of Virginia, but also enhanced the earlier work of some Southampton folks in mapping the town of Jerusalem and the path of the insurrection. (No map of Jerusalem has been published until now, and previous maps of the insurrectionary path have tended to confuse as much as clarify.)

- The more than 40 friends who, in addition to believing in this enterprise and wishing me well, have actually invested in its success, with financial assistance and important services. I knew when I began this work in 1990 that such support would be imperative, as it proved to be. Without these friends, this work would have been impossible.

- My son Michael Bryant and my friend Leslie Revilock, whose computer talents have brought my typewritten manuscript to its present form.

- Dylan Pritchett, whose fan club I joined when he was a senior in high school, is now a nationally known black story-teller associated with the Kennedy Center's Partnership in Education program, and a wonderful friend and advisor to me.

- Nancy Lawrence ... Almost a decade ago, following a tour of the Southampton countryside, my special friends Richard and Nancy Lawrence and their family and I lunched outside along the river in Courtland. Nancy said she wanted to help, by personally paying the fee with the copyright office of the Library of Congress and by personally handling the paperwork — and she said that to discourage piracy I could let it be known that she was doing it. And now for the fifth time she has done it. So I thank you, Nancy Lawrence, director of the copyright office of the Library of Congress.

My thanks to my family — not only my ever patient, tolerant and supportive wife Dorothy, but also four cousins to whom I am notably indebted:

- Pete Joyner, whose genealogical research has enlightened my sense and appreciation of family relationships. (Thanks to Pete, I learned that one of our long-ago uncles was Captain James Bryant, and another was Collin Kitchen, whose photograph as an old man is in Drewry. It intrigues me to think that as a little boy I sat upon the lap of a woman who as little Bessie Kitchen may well have sat upon the lap of Nat Turner's jailer.)

- Billy Joyner, a minister who provided much of my early insight regarding the spiritual aspect of Nat Turner, and has been a constant inspiration.

Bill Bryant

- Frank Bryant, a history teacher who very ably introduced me to the historical sites in Southampton and has very ably accompanied me every step of the way since the 1970s. No one has been more supportive.

- Kenneth Dobyns, who, although of my mother's family rather than my father's, took upon himself the challenge of explaining the strange Sun on the 13th of August 1831 – and did so, brilliantly. (Incidentally, the island created in the Mediterranean had disappeared by the time Nat Turner was hung.)

Generally, I must say that I consider myself blessed to have been born into the families of my father and mother, a collection of diverse and good people who strongly influenced my mind and attitude in the direction necessary to the task I am now completing.

*

Finally, we come to that category of very special people whose cooperation and courtesy have enriched not only my research, but also my life.
The people of Southampton!
Before I start naming some of them, I share with you another scene vivid in my memory, to make an important point:
On the 150th anniversary of the insurrection, an especially hot and humid Sunday in August of 1981, my cousin Frank and I purposefully got together in Courtland and went to Cabin Pond, to talk. And we talked at length and in depth about the story of Nat Turner – about the attempts to tell it, the shortcomings of those attempts, the many questions posed but not answered, the many questions not even asked – and about the great historical significance and current relevance of the story, the reasons it should be better known – until, in puzzlement and frustration, I declared: "Why has no one written <u>the</u> book?"
Immediately, Frank replied: "Because no one from Southampton has written it."
I didn't really understand what he meant.
Now I do.
I am not a native son of Southampton, but I am surely a grandson of Southampton. If I were not, I would not have become so interested in Nat Turner. Nor would I have commenced this work. Nor would I have spent so much time down there during this past decade, getting to know better not only the place but also its people, particularly the people who could answer some of those questions. (One published teller of the story spent half a day in Southampton. Another spent a day and a half. Enough said.)
This additional caring, this extra cause for commitment, has made a difference, a great difference, in the results of my effort.
Some of the people of Southampton:

- Gilbert Francis ... Gil passed away a few years ago. I miss him. We all do. The great-great-grandson of Nathaniel, Gil was the leading local authority on Nat Turner, the source of much new information and insight, a truly wonderful friend. The first

Tomorrow Jerusalem: The Story of Nat Turner and the Southampton Slave Insurrection

time I met him (having earlier conveyed to him a copy of my first manuscript), I was uneasy, concerned that a negative reaction from him might doom my project in its infancy. Gil quickly put me at ease, approving my work and pledging his wholehearted cooperation, and saying: "I am not yet ready to accept Nat Turner as a hero, but I do reject him as a criminal. And I wonder: If I had been in his place, would I have had his courage? Slavery was evil!" From that day on, my project had no better friend in Southampton. Nor did I ... I must mention that through coincidence, or causality, young Gil Francis married a girl named Betty Lincoln, now perhaps Abraham Lincoln's closest living kin in Virginia – a remarkable historical and personal linkage. I should note, too, that their middle son Rick has taken on much of his father's responsibility as a local custodian of the story, and is doing very well at it indeed.

- Kitty Futrell ... The first time I met Kitty, she asked me which Bryants I belonged to. I said I was the grandson of Willie and Bessie Bryant, who had lived along the Old Cypress Bridge Road. That was good enough for her, and she invited me into her home, and into her trust. Several hours later, as I was leaving, she instructed me to go by Mister Willie's grave and thank him. Which I did. Being Mister Willie's grandson made a difference ... From the beginning, Kitty has helped me graciously and generously, not only as a source of good information and insight, but also as a champion of accuracy – vital services, which she and Gil (and now Rick) have performed countless times for local and visiting teachers and students, researchers and reporters, and other folks. Being a local custodian of the story is a significant responsibility, and no one now takes it more seriously than Kitty, whom I professionally and personally admire, deeply.

- The Southampton County Historical Society and its truly outstanding president, Lynda Updike ... Considering the abundance of local history and the need to pay attention to a lot of other things besides the story of Nat Turner, the society has demonstrated exemplary diligence and objectivity in documenting him and the insurrection – most notably through its series of four videotapes featuring Gil and Kitty, and a fifth featuring Rick; its help with occasional tours of the countryside; and its efforts to preserve important artifacts, including Nat Turner's sword and the key to the lock of the old jail. (The lock is at the Library of Virginia, for now.) I am pleased to note that the society in October of 1998 formally endorsed my work – not for its literary quality, which is a matter of individual judgement, but for its historical integrity, which has always been my highest priority ... As a friend and as a critic, Lynda has been a constant encouragement, another good reason to try harder. And she is a great president of the society, overseeing a diverse and active program as well as editing one of the finest newsletters I've ever seen.

- Nat Turner's family ... The late Herbert Turner, Nat's great-great-grandson, escorted my cousin Frank and me to the site of the "cave" where Nat was captured, then to the site of the Preaching Place (which until then was known to only a few local

Bill Bryant

black folks). Herbert's son Alvin has since become my friend, and I've enjoyed my several encounters with Herbert's brother Asphy ... Soon after a newspaper recently reported that Rick Francis and Alvin Turner never had met, Rick picked up the telephone. And a week or so later, they met, and shook hands. I know both men well enough to know they'll be good friends and partners in telling better the story.

- S. V. Camp, the talented surveyor who worked closely with Kitty to prepare the map of the path of the insurrection and the map of Jerusalem.

- Jim Magee, a man with a powerful mind and a corresponding artistic talent, and the leading local black interpreter of the story of Nat Turner.

- Bob and Patsy Marks, the fine folks whose lovely home was once the Simon Blunt place – and Jim and Marla Hummings, who are determined to rescue the ruin of the Peter Edwards place.

- Keith Francis, who does not now live in Southampton but fits best into this category, as the source of new information regarding Etheldred Brantley and George Washington Powell.

- Billy Cole, a Southhampton native whose local knowledge has been helpful in various ways.

*

Writing these closing words has been difficult, because I – and you – do owe so much to so many. It is a debt beyond measure.

The story of Nat Turner, the search for his obviously important but elusive meaning, continues to this day – challenging us to appreciate not only the complex reality which confronted our ancestors, but also the complex reality which confronts us, the big difference between the two realities being that we now know what we're capable of accomplishing together, if we try harder. I happen to believe there is no limit to our potential. I share Mister Lincoln's view: "The struggle of today is not altogether for today. It is for a vast future, also."

I pray that **Tomorrow Jerusalem** makes our task easier.

Sincerely ... William T. Bryant*

---

* I finish in this more formal manner to distinguish myself from other Bill Bryants. At one family reunion, there were four of us ... My parents gave me the first names of my grandfathers. My Southampton grandpa Bryant's name was Willie, of course. And my western Virginia grandpa Mason's name was Turner.

*Tomorrow Jerusalem: The Story of Nat Turner
and the Southampton Slave Insurrection*

P.S.: Soon after I completed the writing of **Tomorrow Jerusalem**, Rick Francis and I made a new acquaintance: Nat's great-great-great-grandson Bruce Turner. Late in October at First Baptist Church in Courtland and early in November at Chowan College in Murfreesboro, Rick and Bruce and I participated in panel discussions noting the bicentennial of Nat's birth.

The day after the program in Courtland, the Norfolk Virginian-Pilot published an article with a photograph showing Rick and Bruce chatting amiably on the church steps.

Following the program at Chowan, I wrote a letter to some friends: "As opening speaker, I stressed the theme of reconciliation. Early in my presentation, I displayed the Virginian-Pilot photo. Then, pointing at Bruce, I told the audience to keep in mind that my uncle was his granddaddy's jailer. Then, pointing at Bruce and Rick, I noted that Bruce's grandaddy and associates killed 36 members of Rick's family. Then I basically said that if these two men could get along well, the rest of us should be able to get along better."

I treasure my friendship with both.

Bill Bryant

*Tomorrow Jerusalem: The Story of Nat Turner
and the Southampton Slave Insurrection*

As we would have our descendants judge us, so we should judge our fathers. In order to form a correct estimate of their merits, we ought to place ourselves in their situation, to put out of our minds, for a time, all that knowledge which they could not have and we could not help having ... It is too much that the benefactors of mankind, after having been reviled by the dunces of their generation for going too far, should be reviled by the dunces of the next generation for not going far enough.

Thomas B. Macaulay
Historian

About the Author

    A native of Virginia now living in Williamsburg, Bill Bryant is a former newspaper journalist who has devoted the past three decades to civic activism and writing, seeking to contribute to the progress of the continuing American Revolution.
    Because his father's family is from Southampton, where the insurrection happened, Bryant has been interested since childhood in the story of Nat Turner, and became a serious student of the story during the 1970s.
    He began work on **Tomorrow Jerusalem** in 1990.